Visualizing Research

Visualizing Research

A Guide to the Research Process in Art and Design

Carole Gray and Julian Malins

ASHGATE

Published by
Ashgate Publishing Limited
Gower House
Croft Road
Aldershot
Hants GU11 3HR
England

Ashgate Publishing Company
Suite 420
101 Cherry Street
Burlington, VT 05401-4405
USA

Ashgate website: http://www.ashgate.com

British Library Cataloguing in Publication Data
Gray, Carole
Visualizing research : a guide to the research process in art and design
1.Art – Research 2.Design – Research 3.Universities and colleges – Graduate work
I.Title II.Malins, Julian
707.2

Library of Congress Cataloging-in-Publication Data
Gray, Carole, 1957-
Visualizing research : a guide to the research process in art and design / by Carole Gray and Julian Malins.
p. cm.
Includes index.
ISBN 0-7546-3577-5
1. Design--Research--Methodology--Handbooks, manuals, etc. 2. Art--Research--Methodology--Handbooks, manuals, etc. 3. Research--Methodology--Handbooks, manuals, etc. I. Malins, Julian. II. Title.

NK1170.G68 2004
707'.2--dc22 2004004900

ISBN 0 7546 3577 5

Typeset by Wileman Design
Printed and bound in Great Britain by MPG Books Ltd, Bodmin, Cornwall

Contents

List of figures

💻 see website www.visualisingresearch.info
and p. 5

Authors' biographies

Carole Gray and Julian Malins currently hold research posts at Gray's School of Art, The Robert Gordon University, Aberdeen, Scotland. Carole is a Research Professor and Julian is a Reader in Design. Both have PhDs and extensive experience of supervising and examining research degrees in art and design and related areas. Both are practitioners with a belief in the creative relationship between practice, teaching and research. A visual artist, Carole makes context-specific artwork using new materials and technologies. As a designer and maker Julian maintains a long-term interest in ceramics research, in particular how new technologies can support new models of craft practice.

After completing 'the wrong PhD' in 1988 – an investigation of art college teaching styles – Carole has since focused on understanding experiential, constructive learning styles, especially visual learning styles, and increasingly within higher degree frameworks. Much of this research has been done with Julian.

Carole is currently the co-ordinator of *On the Edge* – a major AHRB funded research project with Ann Douglas as principal researcher. This work investigates the value of art in remote rural locations (www.ontheedgeresearch.org). It presents a unique opportunity to develop and evaluate co-operative and discursive methodologies in visual arts research, including creative visual methods, and appropriate 'artistic' strategies of evaluation and dissemination. Carole is particularly interested in how this particular research can inform curriculum development in terms of cultural and contextual responsiveness and responsibility, and its role in developing the School's contribution to the culture in which it is located, through strategic partnerships and co-operations.

Julian's PhD focused on methods for firing studio ceramics. One of the most significant challenges arising from the research was to resolve the tensions between the established research methodology in applied sciences and those emerging alternative approaches in Art and Design. This led to an ongoing exploration of appropriate research methods for artists and designers.

He is currently involved in a number of projects concerned with exploiting web-based technologies for teaching and learning. These include the development of innovative managed learning environments, reflection and assessment systems designed to encourage a constructivist approach to learning, and interfaces designed to support students with disabilities.

As committed practitioners, educators and researchers, Carole and Julian continue to be excited by the challenges posed by research, and they continue to learn.

By way of a foreword: 'Alice is in wonderland'. Discuss

DOWN THE RABBIT HOLE

> Alice was beginning to get very tired of sitting by her sister on the bank, and of having nothing to do: once or twice she had peeped into the book her sister was reading, but it had no pictures or conversations in it, 'and what is the use of a book,' thought Alice 'without pictures or conversation?'
>
> So she was considering in her own mind whether the pleasure of making a daisy-chain would be worth the trouble of getting up and picking the daisies, when suddenly a White Rabbit with pink eyes ran close by her.
>
> There was nothing so VERY remarkable in that; nor did Alice think it so VERY much out of the way to hear the Rabbit say to itself, 'Oh dear! Oh dear! I shall be late!' (when she thought it over afterwards, it occurred to her that she ought to have wondered at this, but at the time it all seemed quite natural); but when the Rabbit actually TOOK A WATCH OUT OF ITS WAISTCOAT-POCKET, and looked at it, and then hurried on, Alice started to her feet, for it flashed across her mind that she had never before seen a rabbit with either a waistcoat-pocket, or a watch to take out of it, and burning with curiosity, she ran across the field after it, and fortunately was just in time to see it pop down a large rabbit-hole under the hedge.
>
> In another moment down went Alice after it, never once considering how in the world she was to get out again.
>
> *Alice in Wonderland* by Lewis Carroll

This is both an exciting and a highly challenging time to be a research student in art and design. Exciting because, to an extent, we are able to invent and explore new methods and approaches to research that are directly relevant to our disciplines. Methodologies that locate reflective practice at the heart of our inquiries quite literally enable us to create books with pictures and conversations. Often, those conversations enable us to reach out from our core disciplines to other specialisms, thereby providing opportunities for multidisciplinary research. Challenging, because much of this research territory is relatively uncharted. It is easy to get lost down a rabbit hole.

To confront the challenges successfully, to exploit the opportunities and to enjoy the excitement – the very real excitement – that pursuing a research degree presents you with, requires three things: passion, self-confidence and method.

You – the student – bring the passion. Without passion, without a very real hunger for knowledge and discovery, research cannot happen. We are driven by our sense of wonder, to ask questions and seek their answers, and the research degree provides us with our wonderland. If we lose that sense of wonder – that relentless search for truth and beauty – then the whole enterprise becomes pointless. So the critical thing is to nurture your creative vision, self-critical thinking and passion for your research.

However, every wonderland of research presents us with the odd Mad Hatter and potions of criticism that can make us feel very small indeed. Which is where self-confidence and belief in the integrity of our inquiry becomes essential. This is perhaps especially the case in art and design when at times we cross over into other disciplines. 'Pretty work', I heard a social scientist say to a PhD student in jewellery, 'but I fail to see how this extends our knowledge of human communication'.

If art and design research is to demonstrate its unique contribution, then it is incumbent on all of us who practise it to argue, clearly and patiently its virtues and value. We should not do this defensively, but assertively from a position of self-belief and confidence. The priority of your research supervisors is to strengthen your confidence and to work with you supportively through those times when it can become severely tested.

So, you bring the passion, your supervisors build your confidence – and this book provides an essential and unique guide to the methods.

Carole Gray and Julian Malins are experienced research degree supervisors in art and design at Gray's School of Art in Aberdeen. For over a decade they have been pioneering new methodologies that place creative practice at the centre of the research process. Their distinctive contribution has been to refine ways in which creative art and design practices become research methodologies themselves, exploring and mapping research territories and providing sources for knowledge that can only ever be gained through such practice. Furthermore, they have worked with their students in developing visual tools and techniques that both define research questions and communicate outcomes. The use of multimedia as a research tool and the means of rendering transparent the dynamic processes of creative practice that drive the research agenda, have also been championed by students and staff at Gray's.

The 'Gray's Approach' to research in art and design has inspired and informed many others, including myself. Most importantly it has resulted in real examples of practice-centred research across diverse areas of inquiry, which have led a cultural and methodological shift in art and design research. This shift has not been without its critics, some of whom have argued – rightly – that the lack of methodological guidance and rigour in practice-centred research can, at times, lead to inquiries of questionable merit.

You have fallen down a rabbit hole of wonder. To journey through it with any sense of purpose and direction what you really need is some sort of map. There are a number of excellent books that can guide you in terms of methodologies in the social and natural sciences, and some that are of great value in analysing visual material, but to date there has been no text to guide students through those methodologies most directly relevant to research in art and design.

Visualizing Research provides such a guide, drawing on the experience of a world class supervisory team, and some pioneering examples of doctoral research. The book takes you on a journey through the research process, helping you to draw your own map, negotiate the challenges of your studies and reach a meaningful, fulfilling destination. This book is certainly not the only one you will need in supporting your research, but my expectation is that it will be a constant companion in the challenging journey ahead of you; providing advice, posing questions and presenting possibilities.

In particular, this book will help you make sense of your broad area of interest and frame a question that can focus your work and thinking. Ultimately, it will help you to make that 'original contribution to knowledge' expected of research students in any discipline.

At the very outset of a research degree, this objective can feel somewhat daunting. But as you will discover, being original is easy. Making a difference to the world with art and design – that is the real challenge and, I would argue, should be your overriding mission. Here's a short story for you.

> Once upon a time there was a man who owned only three jackets and two ties. According to one account: 'he is an unlikely looking hero, with bottle-lensed spectacles straight from the "boffin" drawer in central casting and the ruddy complexion of a moderately unsuccessful pig-farmer'.[1] He went everywhere on a bicycle, and was a Labour district councillor in Cambridge, gaining a reputation for battling on behalf of tenants who were under threat of eviction – usually from property owned by Cambridge colleges. He was also a Cambridge academic himself. Devoted to his students, he would wait until the end of the teaching term before decamping to Silicon Valley.

Every time you type in a computer password you are making use of research that Roger Needham did in 1966. This genius in computer security, the design of operating systems, memory management systems and networking, and the founding director of Microsoft's Cambridge laboratory, died in 2003. When the history of the digital revolution is one day written, there is a very good chance that this modest man – this good citizen with an acute sense of wonder – will be given a place in history above that of even Bill Gates. Let us hope so, especially because of his vision of research. Needham once wrote these words:

> It's very easy to do research if you think research is just finding out what nobody knows. Well, that's not good enough; if you want to do research, you want to do research that would have some influence. A lot of research is done which sure adds to our knowledge, but it adds to our knowledge in ways that we didn't find very useful. The best research is done with a shovel, not tweezers.

Fundamentally, art and design is about making our world a more usable, beautiful and meaningful place. This diverse family of creative disciplines has the potential to explore questions of great significance and value to our dangerous, damaged and uncertain world. To realize that potential we must bring focus to our vision, values and talents in new, highly relevant and socially responsible ways. We must visualize research differently.

So, read this book, pick up your shovel, and get digging.

Mike Press

NOTE

1. Naughton, J. (2003) *Lay it on in shovels for Roger.* The Observer, 16 February 2003.

Acknowledgements

This book would certainly not be in existence but for the amazing generosity and inspiration of our colleagues and students, past and present, at Gray's School of Art. These good people have shared their ideas, real experiences and valuable expertise, helping to shape, challenge and develop our thinking, and in this respect a very special thanks goes to Anne Douglas.

In many cases their work has directly contributed to the content of this book, so thank you Allan Watson, Eleanor Wheeler, Jon Pengelly, Heather Delday, Katie Bunnell, Karen Scopa, Susannah Silver, Iain Burt, Kirsty Cull, Stefanie Bourne, Gordon Burnett, Ian Pirie, Richard Dyce, Ian Cargill, Iain Morrison, and Seaton Baxter. Thanks to all those other researchers who have completed higher degrees that are cited in the book: Julie Ross, Ray Flavell, Jane Prophet, Gavin Renwick, Roz Hall, Anna Miszewska, Lily Diaz-Kommonen.

For keeping our feet on the ground as well as providing secretarial support, thanks to Simmone Davidson and Linda Graham for their calm efficiency and good humour. And of course we thank the Robert Gordon University for allowing us the necessary time and resources to develop the book.

Special thanks go to Mike Press, who not only has provided us with encouragement and sound advice, but who has also contributed such an inspirational foreword to the book.

We would also like to thank colleagues from other institutions and organizations who have provided critical insights and made vital contributions to the ongoing development of the debate about research in Art and Design: Malcolm LeGrice, Rachel Cooper, Ken Friedman, David Durling, Richard Buchanan, Chris Rust, Michael Biggs, Beryl Graham, Pekka Korvenmaa, Stuart Evans, Darren Newbury, Pam Schenk, John Swift, Judith Mottram, Brian Thompson, Bob Jerrard, Norm Sheehan, John Wakeford, Andrew Stonyer, Susan Tebby, Martin Woolley, Ray McAleese. The late Brian Allison was a consistent supporter of our work – we hope he would have approved of this book.

We also acknowledge the role of various networks/organizations and their associated international conferences and publications in developing the research debate: *European Academy of Design, Doctoral Education in Design, Research into Practice and Computers in Art and Design Education.*

We would also like to acknowledge a number of creative thinkers who have been particularly inspirational: Edward Tufte, Donald Schön, Colin Robson, Egon Guba, David Kolb.

We are indebted to Suzie Duke and her colleagues at Ashgate for the patient way they encouraged and guided us through the process of bringing this book to publication.

Thanks and love to our respective partners and families, for without their unstinting support this book would not have been possible. And finally, this book is dedicated to the memory of our respective parents:

Harriet and Harry Gray

Margery and Fredrick Malins.

Introduction

WHAT DOES THE BOOK AIM TO DO?

This book aims to guide postgraduate students in Art and Design[1] through the research process. It may be used in conjunction with a formal programme of study – from masters to doctoral level – in the development and implementation of a research project. The book describes and evaluates appropriate strategies for undertaking research in Art and Design, and it may help to embed research experience into contemporary practices, in order to maintain and develop professional 'fitness' and competitiveness.

This book is primarily for use by:

- **Research students** beginning a research degree[2] in Art and Design and related visual/creative disciplines, for example performing arts, architecture, media studies. It may also be useful to research students in other experiential learning contexts as it acknowledges the generic structure of the research process.
- **Masters students** in Art and Design and related visual/creative disciplines thinking about doing a research degree and/or whose study involves developing and implementing a small-scale research project.

Although written primarily as a learning guide for postgraduate students, **research supervisors** and **research managers** could also use this book (and adapt/extend material in it) to support their postgraduate students.

In addition, the book may be helpful to **academic staff** in Art and Design and related visual/creative disciplines wishing to undertake a structured research project, or as part of preparation for staff development in the supervision of research students.

WHAT IS THE PEDAGOGIC APPROACH?

This book is about learning – learning to do research. It is generally accepted that learning in Art and Design is **experiential.**[3] We learn most effectively by doing – by active experience, and reflection on that experience. We learn through practice, through research, and through reflection on both. This active and reflective learning makes a dynamic relationship between practice and research. Practice raises questions that can be investigated through research, which in turn impacts on practice. The framework for this learning is the academic framework of postgraduate degrees involving student-centred learning strategies and project-based work. This framework provides an explicit structure and criteria for learning.

Experiential learning relates directly to the theory of **constructive** learning. Constructivism is based on three key principles; the first being that learning is constructed as a response to each individual's experiences and prior knowledge; the second is that learning occurs through active exploration; and the third principle is that learning occurs within a social context – interaction between learners. So this book encourages students to engage in active exploration of the research process in relation to practice and the context of research.

The use of **metaphor** has long been acknowledged as being a powerful means of enhancing our understanding through imaginative strategies (Lakoff and Johnson, 1983; Ortony, 1993). Valuable work has been carried out on the use of metaphor, especially spatial and social metaphors, as a way of encouraging greater 'naturalness and intuitiveness' in Human Computer Interface design (Stanford University[4]). We have used the metaphor of 'journey of exploration' to describe the research process. In the context of this book metaphor is used as a way of helping students to **engage imaginatively** with the research process and visualize themselves as explorers of unknown terrain. This kind of engagement helps to develop 'deep' learning – meaningful learning of intrinsic value.

The book is called 'Visualizing Research'. This title highlights the importance of **visual thinking** and visualization in the learning process in Art and Design education. We tend to have visual/experiential learning styles (Riding and Rayner, 1998; Mortimore, 2003) and you are encouraged to use your visual skills to make sense of your research experience whenever possible. As the body of formal research develops and matures, we may be able to see a research methodology characterized by the visual. In developing material for this book we have literally tried to visualize research processes and methods wherever relevant. The book has a related website – www.visualising research.info – that includes colour versions – and in some cases multimedia versions – of visuals used in the book, extending what is possible in the paper-based format.

The sequence and structure of 'journey' reflects the generic **research process**, which would be familiar to most disciplines

- planning and preparation for research,
- surveying the research context,
- locating your research questions in relation to the context,
- generating and gathering data through the use of research methods,
- evaluating, analysing and interpreting your research outcomes,
- communicating your research findings.

However, we have tried to relate this generic process to Art and Design learning styles – introducing wherever possible visual approaches – and in developing the use of metaphor, hence the chapter headings:

Chapter 1. *Planning the Journey*: an introduction to research in Art and Design.

Chapter 2. *Mapping the Terrain*: methods of contextualizing research.
Chapter 3. *Locating Your Position*: methods of orienting and situating research.
Chapter 4. *Crossing the Terrain*: establishing appropriate research methodologies.
Chapter 5. *Interpreting the Map*: methods of evaluation and analysis.
Chapter 6. *Recounting the Journey*: recognizing new knowledge and communicating research findings.

WHY HAS THIS BOOK BEEN WRITTEN?

During the 1990s, extensive debate occurred about the nature of 'research' in Art and Design.[5] Various positions were taken: 'practice is research', 'practice is research equivalent', 'no way is practice research'. Confusion reigned and we were struggling in the swamp! Defining 'research' became an obsession. It seemed important to claim part of the territory of research for the creative and performing arts and design (CPAD) and to give identity to it by naming our research 'practice-led' or 'practice-based' research.[6] This was an attempt to characterize a research approach that still adhered to the widely agreed generic definition of research as 'accessible systematic inquiry' but that championed the development of a 'space' in which practice – making art work and reflecting on it – could become a central part of the research process. Although the terms irritate some (Payne, 2000) they have served some purpose, not least in securing funding for 'practice-based' postgraduate research in CPAD, for example the UK's Arts and Humanities Research Board[7] postgraduate funding schemes. Throughout this difficult period, research students were bravely taking risks with research methodologies and alternative thesis formats and a tentative methodological confidence emerged. By the end of the 20th century, some important clarifications about the research/practice debate appeared. In the wake of massive confusion after the UK's 1996 Research Assessment Exercise the following appeared:

> Professional practice qualifies as research when it can be shown to be firmly located within a research context, to be subject to interrogation and critical review and to impact on or influence the work of peers, policy and practice ...[8]

Following this, the AHRB provided a helpful definition of research as a process involving three key features:

- clearly-articulated research questions to be addressed through the research, and a related series of objectives which will enable the questions to be explored and answered
- the specification of a research context for the questions, and a rationale for why it is important that these particular questions should be answered or explored; this description of context should make clear what other research is being or has been conducted in this area; and what particular contribution this particular project will make to the advancement of creativity, insights, knowledge and understanding in this area
- the specification of appropriate research methods for addressing and answering the research questions, and a rationale for the use of particular methods.

So what has emerged is the framing of research involving practice understood as a process, with explicit questions to be asked in relation to a context, a clear methodological approach, the outcomes and outputs of which are open to critical review, and that the research has some benefit and impact beyond the individual practitioner-researcher.

At last a sense of direction – time to move on, drop the labels and get on with some good quality research. Yet the debate must continue in a mature way, acknowledging the pluralism and diversity of practices and research approaches, taking new risks and embracing promising developments.

There is a drive to improve the **quality** of research in the Art and Design sector, not least the learning experience of our research students and completion rates for higher degrees. The report from a UK Council for Graduate Education (UKCGE) working group on research training in CPAD (2001) recommended that **explicit standards for research training** should be established and that more research resources, materials and tools should be developed and made as accessible as possible (section 6 of the report). This book draws on the QAA standards and criteria for higher degrees (www.qaa.ac.uk/public/COP/cop/contents.htm – accessed July 2003) and research by Shaw and Green (1996, 2002) on assessment domains for higher degrees.

In the AHRB's review of provision for postgraduate study and training (January 2002) two important recommendations concern developing a framework of research training requirements (para 82) and, related to this, the provision of funding for such training (para 84). This book is a response to these recommendations.

At present, most Higher Education institutions lack the expertise and resources to deliver specific research methods training in Art and Design, therefore training is usually generic and limited (UKGE *Working Group Report on Research Training in the Creative & Performing Arts and Design* – UK Council for Graduate Education, 2001). There is, however, considerable demand for specific art and design related research training materials in an accessible form. We believe this demand will continue to increase as **postgraduate funding opportunities** develop through bodies such as the AHRB. A strategic priority of AHRB is the **development of innovative and creative research methods**. This book aims to encourage research and masters students to consider exactly this priority, whilst demanding a rigorous and reflective approach.

The content of this book is derived from the **creative relationship between research, practice and teaching in Art and Design**, and the authors' combined experiential knowledge of all three areas, and their related research expertise. Since 1993, the authors (in collaboration with colleagues and students) have published consistently on a variety of research issues – from speculations on research philosophy and methodology in Art and Design to more pragmatic responses to developing research training resources.[9] These publications/developments reflect over ten years' experience of carefully developing, supervising and examining research degree programmes and actively carrying out and managing research projects in Art and Design. Working in collaboration with colleagues and research students, we have been instrumental in helping to shape formal research in our sector and have pioneered the exploration of alternative submission formats for PhD, including theses in digital formats and theses that present a range of coherent evidence in different media.

This book offers our hard-won learning about research to others who may extend and re-shape it, or indeed challenge it vigorously, offering in its place a completely different perspective.

HOW TO USE THIS BOOK

This is intended primarily as a **guide** for new postgraduate researchers in Art and Design. Although it has been written specifically for students, the research journey can be shared and shaped by supervisors, and the book can be used to supplement programmes of postgraduate training. To get the most out of this book, it will be necessary to relate its content to your particular research project, relevant theoretical frameworks and study situation. In the spirit of creative research, you may need to extend and adapt the material for your own purposes.

The chapters contain **sections** of content relevant to each particular stage of the research process. The **topics** within these sections are not exhaustive and you should follow up at least some of the references suggested, and in particular source information of direct relevance to your own subject area. The book's **website** – www.visualisingresearch.info – includes:

- extended visual materials and updated information related to each chapter,
- reflection and action suggestions – example tasks,
- links to other research resources,
- related papers by the authors and colleagues,
- a link to the publisher's site – Ashgate.

Where you see this symbol – – in a chapter, please refer to the website for colour and/or multimedia versions of visuals.

In addition, the information contained in this book will not always appear in an order that suits your circumstances. For example, the topic entitled 'A Reflective Journal' is in Chapter 2. For many researchers the information contained in this section may be particularly useful at the beginning of the research programme. Similarly, topics relating to 'making a new contribution to knowledge' are in Chapter 6, but it may be helpful to read this material as you plan your research project. The **overview map** of this book (Figure 1) and the chapter descriptions can be used to help plot your own route through its contents.

We have included suggestions for **reflection** and **action** at the end of each section. You are prompted to stop and think and also try out some ideas outlined in the section in your own research situation. Your supervisors may find the suggestions helpful in structuring specific learning tasks and supplementing your research training.

Key terms in this book are **highlighted** when they first appear. These are brought together at the end of the book to form a **glossary** of research in Art and

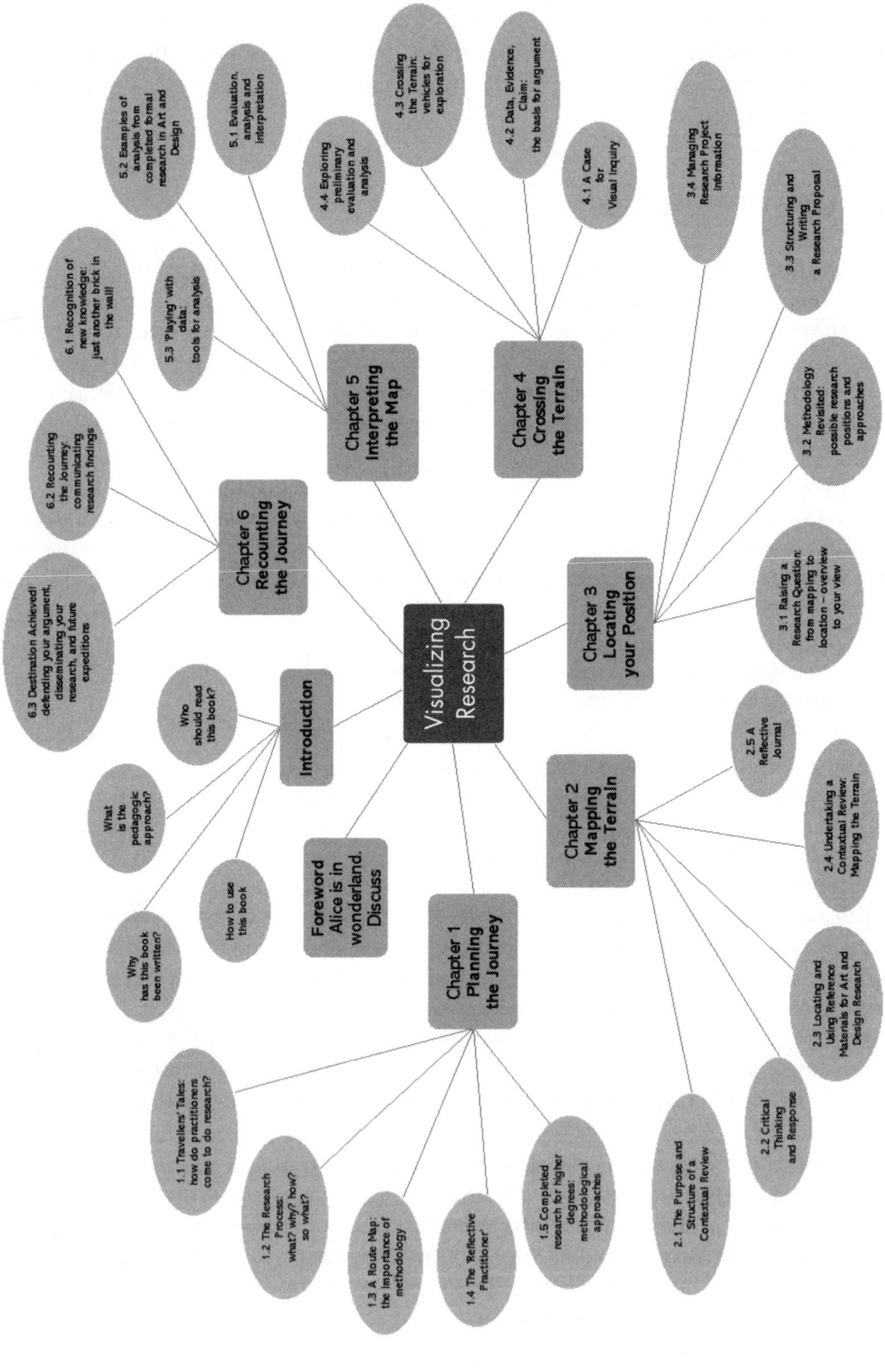

Figure 1 Overview of the book's content

Design. The book also contains an **index** that can be used to locate specific topics and themes.

At the end of each chapter we have included a list of useful references for further study. These are not exhaustive and should be extended by sourcing specific materials relevant to your research area.

We hope that you find the book a useful companion on your journey of discovery and in stimulating your own attempts at Visualizing Research.

REFERENCES

Arts and Humanities Research Board (January 2002) Review of the AHRB Postgraduate Programme and Proposals for changes to AHRB provision of postgraduate study and training.

Gray, C. and Malins, J. (1993) Research procedures/methodology for artists & designers. In: *Principles and Definitions: Five Papers by the European Postgraduate Art & Design Group* (Winchester School of Art).

Kolb, D. A. (1984) *Experimental Learning: Experience as the Source of Learning and Development* (New Jersey: Prentice Hall).

Lakoff, G. and Johnson, M. (1983) *Metaphors we Live by* (University of Chicago Press).

Malins, J. and Gray. C. (2000) Educating the practice-based researcher: developing new environments for collaborative and constructive learning. In D. Durling and K. Friedman, (Eds) *Doctoral Education in Design: Foundations for the Future* (Staffordshire University Press).

Malins, J. and Gray, C. (1999) The digital thesis: recent developments in practice-based PhD research in Art and Design. *Digital Creativity*, 10(1), pp. 18–28.

Mortimore, T. (2003) *Dyslexia and Learning Styles* (London: Whurr Publishers).

Ortony, A. (1993) *Metaphor and Thought*, 2nd edn (Cambridge University Press).

Payne, A. (Ed.) (2000) *Research and the Artist: Considering the Role of the Art School* (Oxford University Press).

Quality Assurance Agency, Codes of Practice – Quality and Standards in Higher Education, Postgraduate Research Programmes. www.qaa.ac.uk/public/COP/cop/contents.htm (accessed July 2003).

Riding, R. and Rayner, S. (1998) *Cognitive Styles and Learning Strategies* (London: David Fulton).

Shaw, M. and Green, H. (1996) Standards in research awards: length, weight or quality? Developing an approach for resolving the dilemma. *Innovation & Learning in Education: The International Journal for the Reflective Practitioner*, 2(3), pp. 4–10.

Shaw, M. and Green. D. H. (2002). Benchmarking the PhD – a tentative beginning. *Quality Assurance in Education*, 10(2), 116–124.

UK Council for Graduate Education (2001) *Working Group Report on Research Training in the Creative & Performing Arts and Design*, November.

NOTES

1. We are using 'Art and Design' to denote our particular educational sector as it is the term commonly used in the UK by the Research Assessment Exercise, Quality Assurance Audit, UK Council for Graduate Education, and so on. We acknowledge that there is a spectrum of subject areas with distinct differences between them. However, this book offers an introduction to postgraduate research where subjects are connected through generic learning level criteria and standards. The materials in the book would need to be interpreted, and if necessary adapted, to each student's particular research project and learning context.
2. We acknowledge that there are different types of research degrees, for example professional doctorates. However, the book concentrates on Masters, MPhil and PhD, as this is where our experience is located.
3. Kolb's (1984) *Experiential Learning Cycle* has four stages: the learner's immersion in a concrete experience, followed by reflection on that experience, followed by conceptualization (making meaning), and finally a stage of planning new actions/experiences.
4. http://hci.stanford.edu/hcils/concepts/metaphor.html (accessed June 2003).
5. The debate sparked off in 1989 by the UK CNAA (Council for National Academic Awards) declaring that practice, and not just reflection on practice, could be a legitimate component of a research degree. Various conferences since have documented this debate, for example Matrix, RADical, European Academy of Design, Doctoral Education in Design, Research into Practice.
6. For an extensive set of descriptions see the Symposium on Practice-based Doctorates in Design and the Creative and Performing Arts (moderated by Ken Friedman, July 2001), archived at www.jiscmail.ac.uk
7. The Arts and Humanities Research Board (AHRB) – www.ahrb.ac.uk
8. 'This is a research assessment exercise. Those submitting practice as research should be prepared to make ... a succinct statement of the research content of the practice.' Guidance Note 4 Panel Secretaries: Sample Comments on 1996 Panel Criteria.
9. For example, papers by Gray and Malins (1993) and Malins and Gray (1999, 2000). In 1997/98 the authors developed a unique part-time web-based distance learning research masters degree aimed at embedding research strategies and skills in professional working contexts – the *Research Masters in Art and Design* (MRes).

1 Planning the journey: introduction to research in Art and Design

CHAPTER OVERVIEW

1.1 TRAVELLERS' TALES: HOW DO PRACTITIONERS COME TO DO RESEARCH?

Socrates asked questions, Aesop told stories. In learning contexts, the use of Socratic dialogue involves the teacher asking questions that the student tries to answer. In Aesopic dialogue (Ferguson *et al.*, 1992) the student asks questions and the teacher answers with stories. Stories are a powerful and memorable means of making sense of the world and engaging imaginatively in learning. Our question then – 'How do practitioners come to do research?' – will be addressed by a number of stories from practitioners who have been through the process of research for higher degrees.

The Artist's tale

'After graduating from a traditional, studio-based BA Honours degree, I maintained an individual studio-based model of visual art practice. I undertook a collaborative Public Art commission with a fellow artist and found the experience enabled us to work on a larger scale, in a non-art context, and to produce work that we would not have conceived individually, and which combined both our ideas and skills. I continued learning about Public Art by contributing to project administration, fundraising, and manufacturing work through a Public Art organization. These experiences helped to focus my questions about the roles and functions of art and artists contributing to social and cultural development.

I undertook postgraduate study in Exhibition Interpretation, this experience of education contrasted with my art college experience, as it was more interdisciplinary and collaborative. I began to recognize the particular strengths and weaknesses of the existing educational model for visual artists and began a personal quest to find new routes for visual artists and new models of practice.

These questions provided an opportunity to re-think the nature of art practice both pragmatically and philosophically. I developed a proposal for an alternative arts venue with the aim of encouraging, supporting and facilitating experimental interdisciplinary projects between artists and other professionals. To investigate further the practicalities of developing an interdisciplinary and collaborative model of art practice, and to address the implications of this challenge to individual "authorship", I undertook a practice-based PhD.'

The Designer-maker's tale

'After finishing my degree at art school I set up my own business making and selling ceramics in a rural studio/workshop. After several years I returned to full-time education to complete a Masters degree. My particular interest was in using firing techniques that, whilst producing what I hoped was visually exciting glazes, had a tendency to be environmentally unfriendly. Wishing to continue to produce interesting work without falling out with my neighbours or damaging my health in the process, led me on a quest for alternative techniques that would not be harmful to the environment or people. When an opportunity arose to undertake a PhD project that had similar objectives to my own I applied immediately. As the research progressed, the study became increasingly focused and I began to realize that my original aims had been overambitious. Coming from a non-scientific background led to some significant challenges, especially when it came to thinking about methodology. The research provided some contributions to knowledge in the field of ceramics but for me the real significance of the PhD lay in the questions it raised regarding what might be appropriate research methodologies for artists and designers.'

The Undergraduate's tale

'On completion of the third year of my undergraduate degree in product design, I was presented with a Vacation Award that provided the finance for me to investigate environmentally friendly design for three weeks in Oslo, Norway. Unaware of what constituted research, I dived right in and began planning my trip. I organized a series of interviews and visits with individuals and institutions in the hope that they would hold the answer to my questions: what is environmentally friendly design? How can it be achieved? The experience of exploring and discussing these questions was both exciting and nerve wracking. It took me out of my comfort zone of designing and I realized I had an interest in research. On completion of my undergraduate degree I looked around for an opportunity that would allow me to explore my interest in both research and environmentally friendly design. The PhD was that opportunity. It has been a great learning experience – I find I am able to do things I never thought I would do, for example present a paper at an international conference. There have been many high and low points throughout the study. I've had to put a lot into it, but feel I have got a lot in return. The PhD has certainly been a challenge!'

The Lecturer's tale

'I'd been teaching in art college for a couple of years – working mainly from intuition based on my experience as a young practising artist about what students needed to learn and how. Having had no formal teaching education, I began to wonder if I was doing this right – nobody else seemed to know – were there things I needed to learn? Out of curiosity I became involved in a series of seminars at the local university about higher education, involving a range of lecturers from other disciplines. As we discussed approaches to teaching and learning it became pretty obvious that I was a different kind of beast! At almost every point I had to declare 'we don't do it like that in Art and Design!'. In the end they got so fed up with me saying this that they challenged me to explain more clearly what exactly we did do. Of course I didn't know enough about teaching and learning in art and design to answer them properly, but the gauntlet was thrown down and I had to do some serious research. But I didn't know what that was either! The whole thing was a mystery, but I decided there was no way back. I embarked on a PhD armed only with my experience of practice and determined to bring to the research a creative and visual approach, even though I was doing "educational research". In the end, the PhD research turned out to be a difficult but life changing experience. By the way, what I discovered about teaching and learning was much less significant than the experience of doing the research, and since then I've never stopped being a researcher.'

From these stories we can see that, typically, the experience of being a practitioner, or teaching and learning about practice, raises important questions, and in some cases, provokes challenges to the actual survival of the practitioner. In reflecting critically on practice we 'begin to wonder', to sense that things could be different, better – 'new routes', 'new models', 'alternative technologies'. We are challenged by others to 'explain more clearly' or to be more environmentally friendly.

Where most angels fear to tread, we embark upon a 'quest', seize opportunities to 'explore', leap into the unknown and 'dive right in'. We find ourselves engaged in in-depth study where we must revisit our assumptions and focus our questions. The experience is simultaneously 'exciting and nerve wracking' presenting 'significant challenges' that take us out of our 'comfort zone'. If we are tenacious and persevere we reach another level – 'able to do things I thought I never would do', as one of our contributors says. Research can be a 'life changing experience' – hopefully a positive one – through which we can become more critical, reflective and creative practitioners.

Reflection and action: suggestions

- How have you come to the decision to do research? What are your motives? Write a short story about it.
- What do you hope to gain by undertaking research? Include this at the end of your story.

1.2 THE RESEARCH PROCESS – WHAT? WHY? HOW? SO WHAT?

Research is a process of accessible disciplined inquiry. The process described here is essentially generic but should be framed and customized by your particular discipline and subject area. The process is usually shaped by three apparently simple questions:

- 'what?' – the identification of a 'hunch' or tentative research proposition, leading eventually to a defined and viable research question
- 'why?' – the need for your research in relation to the wider context, in order to test out the value of your proposition, locate your research position, and explore a range of research strategies
- 'how?' – the importance of developing an appropriate methodology and specific methods for gathering and generating information relevant to your research question, and evaluating, analysing and interpreting research evidence.

A fourth question – the provocative 'so what?' – challenges you to think about the significance and value of your research contribution, not only to your practice but to the wider research context, and how this is best communicated and disseminated.

Although the stages are presented here in a numbered sequence for clarity's sake (Figure 1.1), in reality they are part of a continuous iterative cycle, or helix, of experience (consistent with Kolb's 1984, 'experiential learning cycle'). Stages can be revisited several times, and usually some are concurrent with others, for example, reflection, evaluation and analysis are ongoing activities at every stage (see Orna and Stevens, 1995, chapter 1, pp. 9–12). Be prepared to be flexible and responsive to your research situation. Each stage in this overview is expanded upon in subsequent chapters.

Key stages of the process

What might you research?

Stage 1. We have seen from the 'travellers' tales' that ideas for research can emerge from a vague but nagging hunch, a personal dissatisfaction, or some other issue within creative practices identified by the practitioner. Alternatively, there may be a professional stimulus to which the practitioner must respond creatively in order to survive and thrive, for example new approaches to practice in response to cultural, social economic, or environmental challenges. Whatever the initial impetus, the 'what' should come from a genuine desire to find something out, or else it is unlikely that the study or the enthusiasm for it will be sustained.

Why is your research needed?

Stage 2. You should consider whether your idea really could be developed into a viable research topic that needs researching. Usually there is a good personal reason for undertaking the research – especially issues relating to practice – but is there a wider need and can this be confirmed?

Stage 3. You will need to make an initial search for information that supports your hunch (research proposition) and ideally suggests that research is required. It is important to get some feedback on this from your peers and others in professional and research contexts. Gather some background information on your research proposition and its ethical implications.

Stage 4. If there is no apparent external rationale for the research then it could be considered too much of an indulgent and idiosyncratic idea for a research project. You could stop now!

Stage 5. More positively, you could refocus your initial proposal in response to what you have so far discovered. You may have identified research that is similar, or even identical, to what you are proposing. In this case there is no point in reinventing the wheel! The chances are that this completed research has raised new questions to be answered. This gives you a real opportunity and a firm basis from which to develop your own particular research proposal.

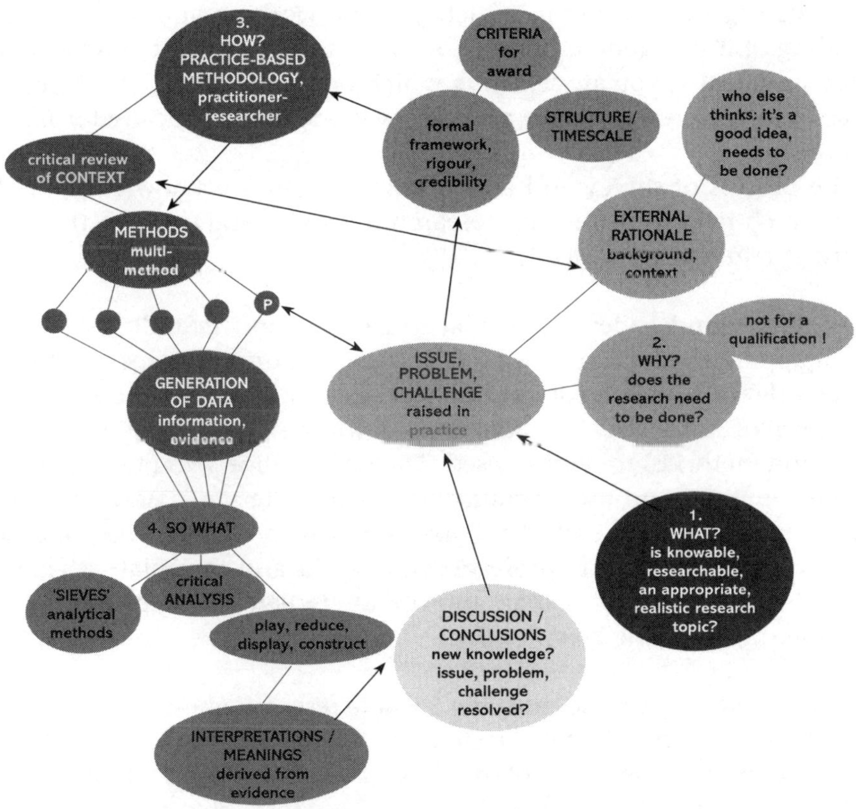

Figure 1.1 The Research Process – important issues to be considered at the start of the research

These preliminary stages are extremely important in 'planning your journey' and beginning to identify and formulate a research question and a suitable research strategy (this is covered in detail in Chapter 3 – Locating Your Position). In 'planning the journey' it is crucial to have some idea of where you want to go and why. Also, you should take advantage of the knowledge of explorers who have visited similar areas. Research is a journey of exploration through which individuals can make small but significant contributions to understanding the landscape of research in Art and Design.

The next stages in the research process usually involve finding already completed research in the public domain, and using this knowledge to help situate yourself as a researcher and focus your research question. In traditional research terms, this kind of survey and evaluation would be called a 'literature review'. Increasingly, information exists in a wide range of media, for example in digital formats on the web, as documented events/exhibitions, and not simply in paper-based 'literature'. Therefore, the term *'contextual review'* is used to encompass all kinds of information in different media in the public domain (this is covered in detail in Chapter 2 – *Mapping The Terrain*).

Stage 6. The contextual survey and review is an essential process for several reasons:
(a) by surveying the context in which you are working you increase your understanding of it in a general sense, both historically and in contemporary terms;
(b) more specifically, you are selecting which particular pieces of information relate directly to your research area and can evaluate them critically for relevance and significance;
(c) in the process of survey and critical review, 'gaps' in knowledge can be identified, which help to focus your research question, and confirm that you are not likely to reinvent the wheel!

This stage of survey and review helps you to gain an understanding of your research context by 'mapping the terrain' in which you are working. It helps to situate you as a researcher, and develop a focus for your project. In 'mapping the terrain', it is crucial to have some idea of who else has contributed to the 'map' and what 'projections' (perspectives and methods) they have used. The review allows you to acknowledge their different contributions, but also encourages you to state your views critically – both positive and negative! At the end of this process you should be in a good position to 'locate your position' within the professional context and formulate a viable research question in 'uncharted terrain' and an appropriate research strategy (this is covered in detail in Chapter 3 – *Locating Your Position*).

Stage 7. This stage concerns identifying a viable research question in relation to what you have discovered through the Contextual Review. The research question can then be used to develop a realistic plan of work with an aim, objectives, rationale, methodology, projected outcomes and outputs. Most research questions will raise some ethical issues. These should be considered in relation to the design of the research project (more on this in Chapter 3).

How might you do research?

The next phase of the research process is very much an active one! So far you have 'planned the journey', 'mapped the terrain' and 'located your position' in it. Now you will set off across that landscape on a journey of discovery – 'crossing the terrain' (this is covered in detail in Chapter 4).

Stage 8. First of all you need to consider which modes of transport – that is, methodology and methods – you will use. This depends on the terrain. It is important to consider initially a wide range of options, to examine some useful examples, and perhaps try a few out (as pilot studies). You might adopt a methodology in which your practice, or aspects of it, may play a role in the investigation. You might need to use several methods – a multi-method strategy – in which two or more methods are used to address your research question. This is a kind of 'triangulation' of methods. Your research methods must be used rigorously in order to yield good quality evidence. This stage might require you to test out the ground before venturing onto it, to retrace your steps, to use more than one vehicle, to go off in different directions, to explore many kinds of terrain, to collect a range of data in order to begin to provide enough evidence to be in a position to address your research question. It is important to document your whole journey – you might keep a reflective journal to record your progress. It is important to carefully organize and manage the information you amass so none is lost on the way.

Having actively explored the terrain, the next stage concerns evaluation and analysis – 'interpreting the map' (this is covered in detail in Chapter 5).

Stage 9. The material you have gathered in crossing the terrain provides evidence for questioning and, hopefully, substantiating your research proposition. Keeping an open mind, you need to reflect on your experiences and the collected information. You need to evaluate and select – what's valuable, relevant, significant, and what isn't? You need to 'sieve' the material using criteria derived from your research objectives. You need to 'play with the data', visualizing possibilities, making creative connections. You sometimes need to take things apart to understand them and then put them back together, perhaps in a different way, in order to make sense and develop meaning. From this analysis you should arrive at an interpretation of your research evidence.

So what?

The final stage of the research process concerns the critical synthesis of the whole experience, demonstrating its value and significance through effective communication and dissemination – 'recounting the journey' (this is covered in detail in Chapter 6).

Stage 10. By this stage you should be in a position to make a conclusion about what you have discovered and its value and significance to the wider research context. At PhD level this should be a new contribution to knowledge. At Masters levels you should be able to demonstrate a critical evaluation of your research context and show that you have an understanding of methodological issues. Your research findings need to be made 'accessible' and presented in a variety of imaginative ways. The thesis – your argument – may comprise several complementary but coherent elements – a body of work, a written text, other supporting material in various formats. It will be necessary to 'defend' your argument – especially for a research degree – in an examination viva. An important part of any thesis is the identification of future research leading on from your work. This brings the research process full cycle – the identification of new research questions and new territory to be explored.

We might therefore conclude that research in Art and Design should:

- be required and relevant – have clear external, professional and personal rationales for the need for the research;
- be intentional – it is envisioned, proposed, prepared for, strategically planned and focused;
- be disciplined – be rigorous, critical and ordered (but not necessarily systematic in the scientific sense) – it is a structured investigation;
- develop a research approach which acknowledges practice as:
  - an initiator of the research questions, which are usually complex and 'messy',
  - providing the context for the research,
  - playing a part in the research methodology and in developing innovative and creative, but nonetheless rigorous, research methods,
  - imaginatively making visible/tangible the research findings,
- be revelatory – contributing alternative and/or new perspectives and insights
- be public – the whole process and its outcomes are open to scrutiny and possible future use by others.

Having an initial strategic view of the whole process helps to you to imagine and visualize the development of your own research project and to start to plan your journey.

Reflection and action: suggestions

- The research process is described as 'iterative'. Make your own visualizations of the key stages using cyclical/helical structures, or some other structures relevant to your preferred learning style.
- We have used the metaphor of 'journey of exploration' to visualize the research process. What other metaphors might be relevant for your research?

1.3 A ROUTE MAP: THE IMPORTANCE OF METHODOLOGY

This section describes the importance of knowing how to research. It provides some definitions of 'methodology' and 'method', and describes different philosophical positions in research – research paradigms. It proposes what might be the developing characteristics of a more 'artistic' research methodology.

Fishing

If research is a process, then learning about research is about learning *how* to research. We could almost say that the process is more important than the product – the journey is more interesting than the destination. Knowing how to research is perhaps much more valuable than finding out a particular thing, gaining a particular piece of knowledge, particularly as 'Knowledge keeps as well as fish!' (anon.). All knowledge is tentative. Today's knowledge is tomorrow's joke – the earth is the centre of the universe and is flat! If knowledge has a sell-by date, then the most important thing is meta-knowledge – knowing about knowledge, knowing how to acquire, manage, analyse, synthesize and communicate knowledge. Research is about searching for alternatives. Being sceptical and critical are crucial research characteristics in progressing from one piece of knowledge to a better, more 'fit' version. If we accept the 'fish' argument then 'fishing' – knowing *how* to do research, knowing about methodology – is perhaps the most important part of the research process.

> 'Use your methodology to discipline your passion, not to deaden it.' (Rose, 2001, p. 4)

The terms '**methodology**' and '**method**' are often abused and sometimes used interchangeably, but there is a distinct difference.

> *Method*:
> 1. 'a way of proceeding or doing something, especially a systematic or regular one';
> 2. 'orderliness of thought, action, etc';
> 3. '(often plural) the techniques or arrangement of work for a particular field or subject'. (New Collins Concise Dictionary, 1986)

Methods are specific techniques and tools for exploring, gathering and analysing information, for example observation, drawing, concept mapping, photography, video, audio, case study, visual diary, models, interviews, surveys, and so on.

Methodology is the study of 'the system of methods and principles used in a particular discipline' (New Collins Concise Dictionary, 1986).

> The comparative study of method presumes that some methods exist, but methodology implies no choice among existing methods. The situation is quite the contrary. Methodological sophistication leads to appropriate choices among methods. It can also lead researchers to develop and apply new methods. (Friedman, 2002)

Only through investigating and comparing different research approaches and the various methods used are we enabled to make an informed decision about how to proceed. The aim of methodology is to help us understand, in the broadest possible terms, not the products of inquiry, but the process itself:

> to describe and analyse . . . methods, throwing light on their limitations and resources, clarifying their presuppositions and consequences, relating their potentialities to the twilight zone at the frontiers of knowledge. It is to venture generalisations from the success of particular techniques, suggesting new applications . . . suggesting new formulations. (Kaplan, 1964 p. 23)

This suggests that methodology, as well as being a way of explicitly structuring thinking and action through questioning and evaluation, can be creative and transformative (Jayaratna, 1994). This kind of methodological innovation has been demonstrated in various examples of completed research in Art and Design – if no established methodologies exist then invent them!

Back to basics

As formal research in Art and Design has grown, one of the most urgent debates has been about methodology. How can we carry out rigorous and respectable inquiry using methodologies and methods appropriate to practice – research without wearing a lab coat and safety goggles? It was clear, and still is, that there are no simple answers! The most fruitful way to identify appropriate methodologies has been through an analysis of completed research, and through evaluations of research in progress. The growth in completed research degrees in our sector has begun to give us some methodological confidence. This process of validation is necessarily slow, and such is the diversity and creativity of the sector that many different kinds of 'route maps' are likely to emerge. Indeed, methodology in its scientific sense implies a common or shared research approach that is transferable. This is not likely to be effective for creative practitioners! What might be more useful is the notion of '**protocols**' (Langlois, 2003) – explicit 'rules of conduct' specifically related to an individual's research project, allowing a clear understanding of procedure (transparency), but acknowledging that complete transferability is not achievable, nor perhaps desirable.

So how should you start to consider your research approach? A common misconception is first to try to identify specific methods – rather like looking down the wrong end of a telescope when we should be looking out into the methodological universe. This might be appropriate if we had a whole raft of methods from which to choose – as in science and social science, having over 300 years and 150 years (respectively) of research experience. Academic research in Art and Design is in its infancy relative to these more established research models. We must start from first principles and examine our assumptions about research. We must consider basic questions such as:

- *What could* research in Art and Design be?
- *Why might* artists and designers do research?

before we ask

- *How might* artists and designers do research?

These are essentially philosophical questions, to which there will be only individual personal answers. The first one – 'What could research in Art and Design be?' – relates to what is 'knowable' in our discipline – what is capable of being researched? It is an ontological question about the nature of reality. What is the 'real world' for us? The second one – 'Why might artists and designers do research?' – is not simply a question about motivation, but also an epistemological question about the nature of the relationship between the knower and the known. Schön says 'a practitioner's stance toward inquiry is his attitude toward the reality with which he deals' (Schön, 1983, p. 163). What position or role should the researcher (as practitioner) adopt in carrying out the research? The third question – 'How might artists and designers do research?' – is clearly a question about methodology.

Paradigms of inquiry

This fundamental questioning of our assumptions about research is an important process. The answers to these questions are the 'starting points or givens that determine what inquiry is and how it is to be practiced' (Guba, 1990, p. 18). They form the basis of different 'paradigms of inquiry'. The methodology of science basically remained unchallenged for 300 years as the most reliable way of generating knowledge and explaining natural phenomena. It represents the positivist paradigm of inquiry. Most 20th century inquiries might be characterized by adherence to a **post-positivist** paradigm, in that many of the classical tenets of inquiry have been (and are being) challenged, in all disciplines. This is not only evident in science, for example chaos and complexity theory, but also in social science – especially in 'new paradigm research' (Guba, 1990) – where critical theory and constructivist paradigms currently hold sway. Figure 1.2, 'Paradigms of Inquiry', attempts to summarize these paradigms in relation to ontology, epistemology and methodology.

According to Guba (1990), the choice of methodology should be a consequence of ontology and epistemology – that is, methodology is evolved in awareness of what the researcher considers 'knowable' (what can be researched, what is an appropriate research question), and in an awareness of the nature of knowledge and the relationship between the researcher and the 'knowable'. For instance, the positivist paradigm of inquiry is characterized by a 'realist' ontology (reality exists 'out there'), and an objectivist epistemology (the researcher is detached); methodology is therefore experimental and manipulative. In contrast, the constructivist paradigm is characterized by a 'relativist' ontology (multiple realities exist as personal and social constructions) and the epistemology is subjectivist (the researcher is involved); as a consequence, methodologies are hermeneutic (interpretative) and dialectic (discursive).

What might characterize an 'artistic' or 'designerly' paradigm of inquiry? It is our collective task to develop this, and will require contributions from many practitioner-researchers over the coming years. Guba's analysis of both positivist and post-positivist paradigms provides us with a framework to help describe and contextualize in philosophical terms, the research we do, and reveal our belief and motives for this research.

	Positivism	Post-positivism	Critical Theory	Constructivism	Artistic ?
ONTOLOGY (The nature of reality, the 'knowable')	**Realist** – reality exists 'out there' and is driven by immutable natural laws and mechanisms. Knowledge of these entities, laws and mechanisms is conventionally summarized in the form of time- and context-free generalizations. Some of these latter generalizations take the form of cause-effect laws.	**Critical realist** – reality exists but can never be fully apprehended. It is driven by natural laws that can only be incompletely understood.	**Critical realist** – reality exists but can never be fully apprehended. It is driven by natural laws that can only be incompletely understood.	**Relativist** – realities exist in the form of multiple mental constructions, socially and experientially based, local and specific, dependent for their form and content on the persons who hold them.	
EPISTEMOLOGY Nature of relationship between inquirer and the 'knowable'	**Dualist / objectivist** – it is both possible and essential for the inquirer to adopt a distant, non-interactive posture. Values and other biasing and confounding factors are thereby automatically excluded from influencing the outcomes.	**Modified objectivist** – objectivity remains a regulatory ideal, but it can only be approximated, with special emphasis placed on external guardians such as the critical tradition and the critical community.	**Subjectivist** – in the sense that values mediate inquiry.	**Subjectivist** – inquirer and inquired are fused into a single (monistic) entity. Findings are literally the creation of the process of interaction between the two.	
METHODOLOGY How should the inquirer go about finding out knowledge?	**Experimental / manipulative** – questions and/or hypotheses are stated in advance in propositional form and subjected to empirical tests (falsification) under carefully controlled conditions.	**Modified experimental / manipulative** – emphasize critical multiplism. Redress imbalances by doing inquiry in more natural settings, using more qualitative methods, depending more on grounded theory, and reintroducing discovery into the enquiry process.	**Dialogic, transformative** – eliminate false consciousness and energize and facilitate transformation.	**Hermeneutic, dialectic** – individual constructions are elicited and refined hermeneutically, and compared and contrasted dialectically, with the aim of generating one (or a few) constructions on which there is substantial consensus.	

Figure 1.2 Paradigms of inquiry (adapted from Guba, 1990)

Research positions in Art and Design

From an analysis of previous and ongoing research degrees in Art and Design a series of characteristics emerge which help to define research, in terms of ontology, epistemology and methodology.

With regard to the 'knowable', the kinds of projects that have been tackled seem to embrace both positivist and constructivist research ontologies. Exploring 'what's out there' in an external 'realist' sense – especially in relation to technological issues. Andrew Stonyer's PhD research 'The Development of Kinetic Sculpture by the Utilisation of Solar Energy' (Stonyer, 1978) can be seen to take this position. In contrast, almost ten years later, Anna Miszewska's MPhil research on 'The Intelligible Practice of Sculpture' (Miszewska, 1987) provides an example of an investigation of practice as a personal creative construction, one of many diverse relative interpretations of practice in the visual arts. (For further details of these projects and others see the ARIAD Index – www.ariad.co.uk)

With regard to epistemological issues, the practitioner *is* the researcher; from this informed perspective, the practitioner identifies researchable problems raised in practice, and respond through aspects of practice. The role is multifaceted, sometimes it is:

- a generator of the research material – art/design works, and participant in the creative process,
- a self-observer through reflection on action and in action, and through discussion with others,
- an observer of others for placing the research in context, and gaining other perspectives,
- a co-researcher, facilitator and research manager, especially of a collaborative project.

In the role of 'practitioner-researcher', subjectivity, involvement, reflexivity is acknowledged; the interaction of the researcher with the research material is recognized. Knowledge is negotiated – inter-subjective, context bound, and is a result of personal construction. Research material may not necessarily be replicated, but can be made accessible, communicated and understood. This requires the methodology to be explicit and transparent (documentation is essential) and transferable in principle (if not specifics).

From these basic philosophical positions, it is clear that researchers have been characteristically eclectic, diverse and creative in the methodologies they have adopted. When necessary, they have drawn on positivist experimental methodologies, constructivist interpretation and reflection, and invented hybrid methodologies involving a synthesis of many diverse research methods and techniques. So a characteristic of 'artistic' methodology is a pluralist approach using a multi-method technique, tailored to the individual project. Increasingly, this has involved the use of multiple media to integrate visual, tactile, kinaesthetic, experiential data into 'rich' information.

Many projects have been collaborative and inter-disciplinary, either by design or necessity; this may be as a result of the complexity of Art and Design research issues. It also demonstrates a willingness to examine other fields and make sensible connections. It requires an outward-looking attitude and an awareness of other research cultures and paradigms.

Methodology is responsive, driven by the requirements of practice and its creative dynamic. It is essentially qualitative and naturalistic. It acknowledges complexity and real experience – it is 'real world research', and all 'mistakes' are revealed and acknowledged for the sake of methodological transparency. If 'knowledge keeps as well as fish', today's fact is tomorrow's stinking absurdity. What is important, is knowing *how* to research. Research skills may be the only ones worth having in the future!

Reflection and action: suggestions

- *What could* research in Art and Design be?
- *Why might* artists and designers do research?
- *How might* artists and designers do research?

1.4 THE 'REFLECTIVE PRACTITIONER'

Reflective practice

The 'reflective practitioner', 'reflective practice' and 'reflection in action', are important concepts for artists and designers engaging in research. The concepts derive from Donald Schön (1983) and are the focus of his book, *The Reflective Practitioner: How Professionals Think in Action*. The subtitle is telling. The book is an exploration of how professional practitioners in a range of disciplines (design, planning, management, psychotherapy) think and act – how they set problems and solve them in real world professional contexts. Schön proposes that much of this activity is personal knowledge, not usually articulated, sometimes indescribable, and that it relies on improvisation learned in practice. In fact he likens it to an intuitive 'art' – 'knowing-in-action, the characteristic mode of ordinary practical knowledge'. This kind of 'knowing' is dynamic – knowing *how* rather than knowing what. Schön identifies that the professional's inability or unwillingness to articulate this kind of knowledge has led to a separation of academic and professional practice. This sounds familiar – much of the debate about research in our sector has focused on the fear of losing creativity by speaking about it, and even worse, by writing about it!

One of the consequences of this separation has been that research *about* (into) practice has tended to be carried out by other academic researchers (historians, educationalists, sociologists, psychologists, and so on) from an external perspective. These approaches reflect more the classic scientific method, where the researchable is objectified, and the researcher remains detached. A reliance on others to carry out research could undermine the development of a research base within our sector. Schön points the way forward:

> . . . when we reject the traditional view of professional knowledge, recognising that practitioners may become reflective researchers in situations of uncertainty, instability, uniqueness, and conflict, we have recast the relationship between research and practice. For on this perspective, research is an activity of practitioners. It is triggered by features of the practice situation, undertaken on the spot, and immediately linked to action . . . the exchange between research and practice is immediate, and reflection-in-action is its own implementation. (Schön, 1983, pp. 308–309)

Reflective practice therefore attempts to unite research and practice, thought and action into a framework for inquiry which involves practice, and which acknowledges the particular and special knowledge of the practitioner. It is a framework that encourages reflection in different ways. Retrospective reflection – 'reflection-on-action' – is a critical research skill and part of the generic research processes of review, evaluation and analysis. 'Reflection-in-action' is a particular activity of professional practitioners and involves thinking about what we are doing and reshaping action while we are doing it. In this sense it is improvisational and relies on feeling, response and adjustment. Schön likens it to conversation, especially in relation to design. He suggests that designing is a 'reflective conversation with the materials of a situation' (Schön, 1983, chapter 3, p. 78).

This dynamic process – reflexivity – is an important concept in the development of post-positivistic research methodologies, especially constructivist ones – '. . . we understand and become aware of our research activities as telling ourselves a story about ourselves . . .' (Steier, 1992, p. 3).

Let us return briefly to the idea of 'professionalism'. McKernan (1998, p. 46) suggests that 'the most outstanding feature' of the professional is the 'capacity for self-evaluation and self-improvement through rigorous and systematic research and study of his or her practice' where '. . . the problems of practice are open to reflection and inquiry.' Our book aims to encourage this kind of critical approach through the exploration and application of appropriate research strategies in Art and Design. The 'extended professional', then, is a reflective practitioner-researcher.

The practitioner-researcher

The 'practitioner-researcher' is a particular role, defined as: 'someone who holds down a job in some particular area and at the same time carries out . . . inquiry which is of relevance to the job' (Robson, 1993, chapter 15, p. 446). Robson discusses the advantages and disadvantages of this role (albeit from a social science perspective) most of which ring true for practitioner-researchers in Art and Design. For most of us, problems can arise in terms of time available and other commitments, and possible lack of research experience and confidence. Robson points out a major disadvantage as that of 'insider' problems – the difficulty in adopting an open-minded approach and not allowing preconceptions to cloud the issues. Given that absolute objectivity is impossible, this is a challenge for all researchers – positivists and post-positivists! It can be addressed to some extent by always exposing ideas and practices to other professionals for feedback, support and advice. In seeking the views of others, which will inevitably be subjective, we can develop inter-subjective views, which are less likely to be one-sided. Of course, keeping a critical view of your research at all times is essential.

However, the advantages of the practitioner-researcher role are compelling: your 'insider' knowledge, experience and status usually lends your research credibility and trustworthiness in the eyes of your peers, that is, you are not an 'external' researcher. Most importantly, you are inquiring as a reflective practitioner, acknowledging the complexity, dynamism and unpredictability of the real world.

> One of the essential characteristics of practitioner research is that it is one's own practice that is reflected upon. . . . To look at one's own creative practice means taking on both a creative and a reflective role, in a sense creating a new research model which may use other models but will inevitably have its own distinct identity. (Douglas, 1994, p. 45)

Reflection and action: suggestions

- Consider what characterizes your professional context. How do the best 'professionals' operate in that context?
- In what ways are you already, or could be in future, a reflective practitioner?

- What problems do you think you might encounter being a reflective practitioner-researcher?

1.5 COMPLETED RESEARCH FOR HIGHER DEGREES: METHODOLOGICAL APPROACHES

This section describes the development of 'practice-based' research degrees in Art and Design. It starts with a challenge for the sector to shape up – research has a role in developing this 'fitness'. It outlines first some 'pioneer' research projects, and then a selected range of completed formal practice-based research projects with research methods highlighted. The section concludes by proposing the emerging characteristics of higher degree research in Art and Design.

'. . . loosest thinking and worst writing known to history . . .'

In a dramatic speech at the 1995 UK Turner Prize ceremony, Brian Eno offered a challenge to art education:

> The Turner prize is justly celebrated for raising all sorts of questions in the public mind about art and its place in our lives. Unfortunately, however, the intellectual climate surrounding the fine arts is so vaporous and self-satisfied that few of these questions are ever actually addressed, let alone answered . . . the arts routinely produce some of the loosest thinking and worst writing known to history . . . Why has the art world been unable to articulate any kind of useful paradigm for what it is doing now? (Eno, 1996, pp. 258–259)

Eno went on to talk about how contemporary science has been able to engage the public and broaden social dialogue about complex issues, and bemoans the fact that no equivalent dialogue has happened in the arts. He said:

> The making of new culture . . . is just about our only growth industry aside from heritage cream teas and land-mines, but the lack of a clear connection between all that creative activity and the intellectual life of the society leaves the whole project poorly understood, poorly supported and poorly exploited. (Eno, 1996, pp. 258–259)

Practice-based research is uniquely placed to respond to these criticisms, through asking questions of ourselves about the place and value of Art and Design in society and encouraging an intellectual social dialogue; through clear and critical thinking and expression; through the articulation of a paradigm, in order to make 'new culture' and gain the understanding and support of society for this.

We consider research for higher degrees to be the best mechanism to raise awareness of critical and contextual issues of practice, to analyse and interpret ideas, and to develop new creative and cultural strategies based on rigorous evidence and research experience.

Describing the elephant

Practice-based research is like an elephant – a large, complex thing, with many different and intriguing parts, textures, structures, and movements (Figure 1.3). In a Hindu story, several blind men attempt to describe a mysterious creature they have come upon (see the poem by John Saxe, in Gray, 1998); because the elephant was so large each could only have a partial experience of it through incomplete sets of senses, and any one individual could not fully comprehend the complete beast. Only by making analogies and sharing each other's perceptions of the mysterious creature could the totality of the beast be appreciated. Similarly in the case of describing and developing research in Art and Design; the experiences of many researchers are required to define the parts in order to form the whole picture.

However, attempts have been made to describe 'practice-based' research, proposing key characteristics and methodologies. These have been formulated by studying the evidence provided by the 'pioneers' and recently completed higher degrees. These characteristics have taken time to emerge, have been partial, and have developed in response to contextual changes in the last 30 years – postmodern concepts, for example pluralism; developments in social science methodology, for example **naturalistic inquiry**, which places the researcher firmly within the research process, often as 'participant'; contemporary science, for example chaos and complexity theory acknowledging unpredictable and messy realities; culture, for example mass media, visuality, bricolage; philosophy, for example difference, 'the other'; contemporary technological advances, for example interactivity, collaborative networks. Research approaches now can be much more pro-active, involving practitioners researching through creative 'action', and 'reflecting in and on action' (Schön, 1983).

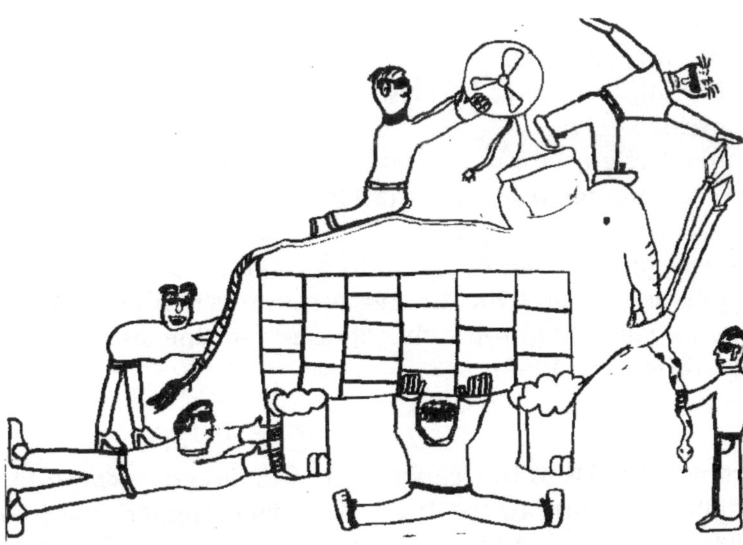

Figure 1.3 Practice-based research is like an elephant (drawing by Thomas Pattison, age 11)

Some examples of completed PhD projects: pioneers and settlers

From the research undertaken so far, it is possible to characterize (and speculate further) the emerging characteristics of practice-based research. Let us examine a number of completed examples, whose methodologies and methods have been examined and validated by external examination for MPhil and PhD.

Pioneers

It is possible to identify examples of 'pioneers' who used their own practice as a vehicle for inquiry. Andrew Stonyer's PhD completed in 1978 – 'The development of kinetic sculpture by the utilization of solar energy' – demonstrates the beginnings of inquiry through practice. The project was concerned with the development of a kinetic sculpture in which movement is a response to light and heat from the sun. The investigation resulted in the construction of maquettes, control mechanisms and a temperature sensitive kinetic sound sculpture, in which 'patterns of kinetic movement express the existence of states of wholeness between the sun and the technology'. A written text explored the theoretical and methodological framework of the research, reflecting on practice, bringing the thesis to resolution.

In the following ten years at least a dozen more PhDs and MPhils were completed, all involving the development of some 'experimental', creative practice. Some examples are as follows.

1980 Raz, Fashion & Textiles; Connor, Newling (both MPhil), Fine Art.
1981 Saleh, Graphic Design.
1982 Cooper, Graphic Design; Scrivener, Computer-aided Graphic Design; Goodwin, Painting; Newton (MPhil) Fine Art/Computing.
1983 Tebby, Sculpture.
1984 Greenhill (MPhil), Sculpture.
1985 Onyeneke (MPhil), Fashion & Textiles.
1986 Jerrard, Industrial Design.
1987 Rivlin, Graphic Design; Miszewska (MPhil), Sculpture.
1988 Pepper, Fine Art /Holography; Power (MPhil), Sculpture.

Details of these pioneer projects can be found in ARIAD (http://www.ariad.co.uk). For an excellent critical review of early UK Art and Design research policy and completed research in Fine Art, see Chris Brighton's PhD 'Research in fine art: an epistemological and empirical study' (Brighton, 1992).

Settlers

The number of completed PhDs in the 'creative arts and design' is currently increasing annually. For example, according to the UK's HESA data (Higher Education Statistics Agency, October 2002) there were 180 completions in 2000/2001 (90 full-time and 90 part-time), compared with 60 completions in 1994/1995 (17 full-time and 43 part-time). There is an expanding pool of examples to evaluate.

The following box provides a 'snap shot' of some completed practice-based PhDs since 1992, in terms of the methods used and the format of the thesis. This selection is by no means exhaustive – they have been chosen because we have either first-hand knowledge of them or a reasonable amount of information.

The examples are presented here in chronological order of completion so as to demonstrate the shift from what could be seen as 'positivist' methodologies to more naturalistic and 'artistic/designerly' forms of inquiry. There is evidence of innovation in the methods used and, in some cases, in the format for final submission of the thesis as a coherent argument, generally comprising a number of related kinds of evidence. All this illustrates a growing confidence in how artists and designers do research, and provides ideas for the design of new research projects.

Methods and thesis format: a selection of completed research degrees in Art and Design

Researcher and date completed	*Subject area/ research proposition*	*Methods/tools used*	*Format of thesis*
Watson 1992	Sculpture/role of chance as a creative stimulus	• experimental object making • reflection in action (audio and video recording) • public participation in making chance/choice making projects	• illustrated written text • flow charts tracking decision making • interactive multimedia database • exhibition of sculpture and drawings
Douglas 1992	Sculpture/structure and improvisation in making	• observation and reflection on own practice • experiments with new materials and scale • metaphor i.e. improvisation	• illustrated written text • multimedia/animations as visual analysis of process (Laserdisc) • site specific exhibition of sculpture • related exhibition of documentation
Malins 1993	Ceramics/ environmentally safe firing systems	• experimental kiln design • glaze tests • laboratory methods, e.g. scanning electron microscopy • visual evaluation using semantic differential methods	• illustrated written text • video of firing processes and capture of reflective glaze surfaces • presentation of fired ceramics
Wheeler 1996	Architectural ceramics/ use of glazed brick/ tile as features integral to buildings	• four commissioned site-specific artworks as case studies • interviews with residents, architects, clients • clay and glaze experiments	• site specific architectural ceramics • illustrated written text • exhibition – documentation of sites and related work

Pengelly 1996	Printmaking/ environmentally sensitive framework	• experiments with non-hazardous processes and materials • reflective narrative • participatory studio workshops • morphological matrices • interviews with practitioners (audio and visual documentation)	• exhibition of environmentally safe prints • illustrated written text • interactive multimedia risk assessment database
Graham 1997	Interactive computer-based artworks/ audience/artwork relationship in gallery settings	• interactive artwork • curation of nationally touring exhibition and development of related catalogue • observation • questionnaire	• interactive artwork • illustrated written text (both paper-based and CD-ROM Acrobat format to include video clips) • exhibition catalogue
Bunnell 1998	Designer maker practice/integration of new technology	• CAD/CAM, 2D/3D modelling techniques to develop an experimental range of objects • databases for storage and management of multimedia data • peer review through invited national/ international exhibitions	• thesis in digital format (on CD Rom using a series of linked FileMaker databases)
Silver 1999	Art in public contexts/ roles of artists	• urban art projects (involving three artists) and related publications • generative metaphor • collaboration with local communities, policy makers • video 'sweatbox' reflection and analysis method	• written text
Burt 2000	Multimedia/use in Art and Design practices	• surveys e.g. audio interviews presented through a multimedia interface • investigations of own practice resulting in multimedia artworks • collaborations with practitioners through case studies	• thesis in digital format (Director software, 2 CD Roms)
Hall 2000	New media/inclusivity, democratic cultural participation	• action research • workshops with youth group • communication (use of informal meeting spaces, phone calls, emails, text messages)	• written text

		• digital imaging projects • research diary as a reflective space • website	
Flavell 2001	Applied art/glass as a means of drawing and expression	• 'reflective risk' methodology • material experimentation • visual documentation of making processes (including video clips)	• thesis as an Acrobat document on DVD which includes video clips
Ross 2001	Participatory art practice/inclusive strategies for environmental change	• participatory action research • conversational interviews • SAM – signifier, allegory and metaphor	• written text including illustrated project descriptions
Diaz-Kommonen 2002	Design/ multidisciplinary collaboration (art, design, new media, archaeology)	• collaborative design of a digital archaeological archive • activity theory	• published book
Renwick 2003	Visual arts/ spatial determinism in post-colonial situations	• 'decolonizing methodologies' • field work • community development tools • collaborative sketchbook • visual journal • exhibitions	• a boxed set of documents, some almost entirely visual ('parallel readings', not linear)
Scopa 2003	Visual arts/ interdisciplinary collaborative strategies	• five different collaborative visual art projects • HEI student projects and student evaluations • interviews with practitioners using collaborative practices	• written text including illustrated project descriptions

(For details of these examples and to extend the range of relevant projects please follow up through, for example, Index to Theses, ARIAD, the Research Training Initiative Case Studies http://www.biad.uce.ac.uk/research/rti/, HEI websites.)

Emerging key characteristics of research methodologies in Art and Design

From these examples (and others) the starting points for research are issues arising from practice, usually the researcher's own practice (providing a personal rationale), but also issues that can be recognized as valid in the wider professional context (providing an external rationale). This practice-based approach to research naturally prompts us critically to consider and evaluate methods used in practice as to their appropriateness as robust and rigorous methods for accessible and disciplined inquiry, for:

- experiencing/exploring, gathering, documenting information and generating data/evidence,
- reflecting on and evaluating information, selecting the most relevant information,
- analysing, interpreting and making sense of information,
- synthesizing and communicating research findings, planning new research.

What methods of practice can be effectively used in this process of inquiry? From the completed formal research to date, the following specific methods can be identified:

- making art/design/creative work through specific project frameworks or as a body of work exploring the research questions, which might include, or be supplemented by, any of the following:
  - observation and related notation/use of symbols,
  - visualization – drawing (in all forms), diagrams,
  - concept mapping, mind mapping,
  - brainstorming/lateral thinking,
  - sketchbook/notebook,
  - photography, video, audio,
  - 3D models/maquettes,
  - experimentation with materials and processes,
  - modelling/simulations,
  - multimedia/hypermedia applications,
  - digital databases, visual and textual glossaries and archives,
  - reflection-in-action/'stream of consciousness'/personal narrative,
  - visual diary/reflective journal/research diary,
  - collaboration/participation/feedback, for example workshops,
  - use of metaphor and analogy,
  - organizational and analytical matrices,
  - decision-making flow charts,
  - story boards, visual narratives,
  - curation,
  - critical writing, publications,
  - exposition and peer feedback/review.

These have been augmented with useful social science methods, usually adapted and/or re-contextualized in some way e.g.:

- interviews, questionnaires, surveys (seeking the opinions of others),
- case study – in-depth study of relevant examples,
- participant-observation – researcher as participant/collaborator in the research,
- personal construct methods – making sense of ourselves in our world(s),
- evaluative techniques, for example semantic differential, multiple sorting,
- soft systems methods.

An expanding battery of appropriate specific methods has now been rigorously used and validated or is currently being tested. We shall explore these methods further in subsequent chapters, especially Chapter 4 – *Crossing the Terrain.*

The use of multiple methods

Characteristic of the completed research is the use of a range of methods, mostly visual and mostly derived from practice, or adapted from other research paradigms to the practice-based research context. The use of two or more methods of gathering information on an issue is called 'triangulation'. In the physical/geographical sense triangulation was a measuring technique used by navigators and surveyors for pinpointing a location from two or more different positions. Using our metaphor of exploration, triangulation is particularly useful in helping us to map the terrain and locate our position, and travel to another place. Triangulation (Figure 1.4) helps us to get a 'fix' on something in order to understand more fully the complexity of issues by examining them from different perspectives, and by generating data in different ways by different methods. The more information we have from varying perspectives, the more able we are to test our ideas. The different views either corroborate or refute our original proposition or hunch, thus making our research more rigorous and robust. Using several complementary methods is more likely to yield a more significant, critical and holistic view than any single method alone. Naturally, there are disadvantages to this approach (for example more time and resources required, possibility of conflicting/confusing data) however, the exploration of the uncharted, complex, dynamic terrain of practice requires many different kinds of vehicles to 'boldly go' where no-one has gone before!

The multi-method concept also suggests the use of multiple media, not only in its information technology sense (multimedia/hypermedia), but its value in using and integrating different kinds of media that provide different kinds of complementary

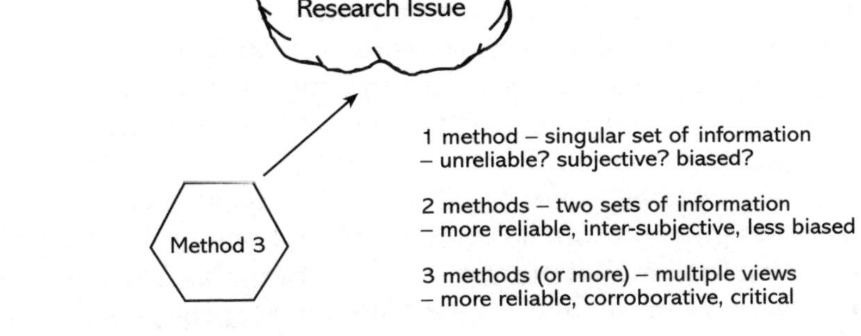

Figure 1.4 Triangulation

sensory information. The involvement of practically all our human senses, as well as other independent sensory instruments, is more likely to give us a comprehensive and 'rich' perspective on the research issue being explored.

What researchers in Art and Design now have are the beginnings of a dynamic and evolving procedure for inquiry, which places practice and the practitioner at the very heart of research.

Reflection and action: suggestions

- What methods do you use in practice that could be appropriate research methods for your own research project?
- What other metaphors and analogies can be used to describe practice-based research?
- Find three different completed higher degree projects. What methodologies and methods have they used?

Looking back on Chapter 1: Planning the Journey

Embarking upon postgraduate research we usually set off in hope and expectation, perhaps not really that clear about exactly why. In presenting various personal experiences of research from 'travellers' who have completed the journey of research for higher degrees, we hope we have stimulated you to think about your motives for doing your research project and what you wish to achieve.

In posing four apparently simple questions – what? why? how? so what? – we have familiarized you with the likely process of research, its critical stages and related actions in anticipation of embarking on research. Having an initial strategic view of the whole process helps you to imagine and visualize the development of your own research project and to start to plan your journey.

Before setting off on any journey of discovery it is invariably sensible to check out available maps – taking advantage of the different continents and countries already charted (various paradigms and strategies of inquiry – old and new). Even if these are not particularly useful in helping you get to where you want to go, they may suggest an alternative sense of direction, and provide some orientation for your own particular route map (research methodology). In uncharted terrain you may have to take on the role of cartographer.

When practitioners engage in research they attempt to bring together creative action and critical reflection in the same creative space – a kind of yin-yang dynamic. Practitioners learn by doing, we 'know' by doing, by experiencing. The research journey obliges us to make tacit knowledge explicit through reflective practice so that others may see our progress through the landscape.

New research terrain is charted every day. Thanks to early pioneers and brave settlers research in Art and Design can claim some territory and draw some boundaries. The diverse and eclectic characteristics of our particular landscape are becoming clearer and more confident – we now have new routes, alternative perspectives and creative constructions.

REFERENCES AND FURTHER READING FOR CHAPTER 1

References

Allison Research Index of Art and Design (ARIAD) http://www.ariad.co.uk.

Brighton, C. (1992) Research in fine art: an epistemological and empirical study. PhD thesis, University of Surrey.

British Library Index to Theses, www.theses.com (requires subscription).

Douglas, A. (1994) *The Creative Process as Material for Research Degrees, Matrix 2: A Conference on Postgraduate Research Degrees in Design and the Visual Arts* (Central Saint Martins College of Art, The London Institute).

Eno, B. (1996) *A Year With Swollen Appendices.* (London: Faber & Faber).

Ferguson, W., Bareiss, R., Birnbaum, L. and Osgood, R. (1992) *ASK Systems: An Approach to the Realization of Story-Based Teachers* (Evanston, Illinois: Northwestern University, The Institute for the Learning Sciences).

Friedman, K. (2002) RTI Discussion List (rti@jiscmail.ac.uk), 25 January 2002 Subject: method and methodology.

Gray, C. (1998) Inquiry Through Practice: developing appropriate strategies. in: *No Guru, No Method? Discussions on Art and Design Research* (University of Art & Design Helsinki).

Guba, E. G. (ed.) (1990) *The Paradigm Dialog* (Thousand Oaks, CA: Sage).

HESA (2002) Higher Education Statistics Agency data (www.hesa.ac.uk).

Jayaratna, N. (1994) *Understanding and Evaluating Methodologies* (London: McGraw Hill).

Kaplan, A. (1964) *The Conduct of Inquiry* (San Francisco: Chandler).

Kolb, D. (1984) Experiential Learning: Experience as the Source of Learning and Development (Englewood Cliffs, NJ: Prentice Hall).

Langlois, A. (2003) L'art par immersion ou l'immersion de l'art, chapter 3 L'art et la vie ou l'immersion de l'art, 2.1 Des protocols (French DEA thesis).

McKernan, J. (1998) *Curriculum Action Research: a Handbook of Methods and Resources for the Reflective Practitioner*, chapter 1 (London: Kogan Page).

Miszewska, A. (1987) *The Intelligible Practice of Sculpture.* MPhil thesis, Nottingham Trent University (formerly Nottingham Polytechnic) collaborating establishments East Midlands Arts Association, Royal College of Art, Camberwell School of Art.

New Collins Concise Dictionary of the English Language (1986) Managing editor W. T. McLeod (London & Glasgow: Collins).

Orna, E. and Stevens, G. (1995) *Managing Information for Research*, chapter 1 pp. 9–12 (Maidenhead, Berkshire: Open University Press).

Research Training Initiative http://www.biad.uce.ac.uk/research/index.html – case studies of completed research for higher degrees.

Robson, C. (1993) *Real World Research*, chapters 1 and 15 (Oxford: Blackwell).

Rose, G. (2001) *Visual Methodologies* (London: Sage).

Schön, D. (1983) *The Reflective Practitioner: How Professionals Think in Action* (New York: Basic Books).

Steier, F. (1992) *Research and Reflexivity* (Thousand Oaks, CA: Sage).

Stonyer, A. (1978) *The Development of Kinetic Sculpture by the Utilisation of Solar Energy*. PhD thesis, De Montfort University Leicester (formerly Leicester Polytechnic), collaborating establishment The Slade School of Fine Art, University College, London.

Suggested further reading

Allison, B. (1996) *Research Skills for Students* (London: Kogan Page).

Cohen, l. and Manion, L. (1994) *Research Methods in Education*, chapter 11 Triangulation (London: Routledge).

Cooper, R. (1996) Assessment issues in design research. In: *RADical International Research Conference Proceedings*, Robert Gordon University, Aberdeen.

Denzin, N. K. and Lincoln, Y. S. (1994) *Handbook of Qualitative Research* (Thousand Oaks, CA: Sage).

Denzin, N. K. and Lincoln, Y. S. (Eds) (1998) *The Landscape of Qualitative Research: Theories and Issues*, chapter 1 (Thousand Oaks, CA: Sage).

Douglas, A. (1996) Relationship between practice and research: the crafting of a metaphor. In: *RADical International Conference Proceedings*, The Robert Gordon University, Aberdeen.

Feyerabend, P. (1988) *Against Method* (London: Verso).

Gray, C. and Pirie, I. (1995) 'Artistic' research procedure: research at the edge of chaos? In: *Design Interfaces, European Academy of Design Conference Proceedings* (European Academy of Design, University of Salford).

Gray, C. and Malins, J. (1993) Research methodologies/procedures for artists and designers. In: *Principles and Definitions* (Winchester School of Art).

Lincoln, Y. S. and Guba, E. (1985) *Naturalistic Inquiry* (Thousand Oaks, CA: Sage).

Orna, L. and Stevens, G. (1995) *Managing Information for Research*, chapter 4 (Maidenhead, Berkshire: Open University Press).

Press, M. (1995) It's research Jim . . . , *CoDesign*, No. 2. pp. 34–41.

Research Training Initiative (1996) *Research Guide: Designing and Managing a Research Project* (Birmingham Institute of Art & Design, UCE).

Research Training Initiative (1996) *Research Perspectives in Art & Design: Case Studies* (Birmingham Institute of Art & Design, UCE).

Provocative Comment, http://www.sunderland.ac.uk/~as0bgr/learnmat.html

Schön, D. (1987) *Educating the Reflective Practitioner*, chapter 2, pp. 22–40 (San Francisco: Jossey-Bass).

Tufte, E. (1997) *Visual Explanations* (Cheshire, Connecticut: Graphics Press).

Tufte, E. (1990) *Envisioning Information* (Cheshire, Connecticut: Graphics Press).

Tufte, E. (1983) *The Visual Display of Quantitative Data* (Cheshire, Connecticut: Graphics Press).

Waldrop, M. M. (1994) *Complexity: the Emerging Science at the Edge of Order and Chaos* (London: Viking).

Watson, A. (1996) Reflections on research without a white coat. In: *RADical International Research Conference Proceedings*, The Robert Gordon University, Aberdeen.

2 Mapping the terrain: methods of contextualizing research

CHAPTER OVERVIEW

2.1 The purpose and structure of a Contextual Review
2.2 Critical thinking and response: key generic skills
2.3 Locating and using reference materials for Art and Design research
2.4 Undertaking a Contextual Review: mapping the terrain
2.5 A reflective journal
The final topic, whilst relevant to the research process as a whole, is included in this chapter for its relevance to critical reflection and evaluation.

2.1 THE PURPOSE AND STRUCTURE OF A CONTEXTUAL REVIEW

Purpose of a Contextual Review

The Contextual Review is a major part of any research project, its lifespan being as long as the project itself. It is a critical and analytical activity that defines both the scope of the inquiry as well as the state of the relevant knowledge base to date. In this process, it is a 'bridge' between the identification of the research problem – the 'what?' – and researching that problem through the methodology – the 'how?' – and contributes to both. The Contextual Review prompts a number of questions.

- *Why* is your research needed and *what* evidence is there to support this? (Rationale.)
- *Who* else in the field has addressed significant aspects of your research question? (Competitors, contributors, co-operators.)
- *When* (and possibly *where*) was the research carried out? (Currency, cultural context.)
- *How* has the research been carried out, and *what* are the implications of this for your methodology and specific methods?
- *What* aspects remain unexplored or require further work? ('Gaps' in knowledge, new ground.)

The Contextual Review helps to identify precisely the nature of your own research question by gaining more information about its context, both what has already been addressed, when, where and by whom, as well as what has not yet been addressed. Through the Contextual Review, the hunch that initiated your research project becomes a tangible 'gap' in knowledge.

Structure of a Contextual Review

The Contextual Review is an ongoing activity throughout your research. At the outset, it helps to shape and position your particular research topic and connect it to other significant research, as well as identifying a specific space into which you might make a contribution. This is a mapping process – where is your research in the wider scheme of things? As your work progresses the map might expand, shrink or change shape as relevant new references are identified and reviewed, and some earlier references become less important. In the final phases of the research the Contextual Review becomes an essential section/chapter of your thesis that allows you to explain your argument in relation to selected key references. This is much more concise and directional – like a river, where the main current is your argument into which important tributaries of other research flow.

There are two distinct phases in developing an understanding of your proposed research area through a Contextual Review.

(1) Initial surveys, to establish the proposal's rationale and viability, to provide some background information, and to help focus the proposal. From these searches a set of relevant references/sources can be compiled into a bibliography and/or a 'store' of non-textual source material.
(2) The use of these references/sources to develop a critical review of your research context, leading to the identification of your own particular research question and the development of a convincing argument.

In both phases it is important to keep precise records of your inquiry so that you, and other researchers, can trace and revisit the material. It is also important to keep updating the information with new references as the field around you develops. The research habits of learning to select, record and use references are as important as the content itself.

Phase 1. Initial surveys

In Chapter 1 we examined the important stages of the research process (Section 1.2). The preliminary stages of 'planning the journey' include taking advantage of the knowledge of explorers who have visited similar areas, so that you can acknowledge their 'trailblazing' and not waste your valuable energy going over old ground or travelling towards a dead end. In the case of a PhD study, it is critical to establish that your proposed research topic has not yet been investigated (usually by accessing various databases and websites, for example Index to Theses and abstracts on university websites).

Initial surveys enable you to:

- establish the proposal's rationale – that the research is really needed, that is has professional relevance, and that it should be viable to undertake;
- gain some background information around the proposed topic, define key terms, and elicit some external feedback, perhaps through contact with other researchers/ advisors;
- focus the proposal, or in some cases refocus;
- gain information on validated research methodologies used in other completed research.

From these searches a set of relevant references can be compiled into a bibliography/ 'store'.

It is important that the scope of the inquiry is feasible, and therefore a balance has to be maintained between breadth and depth. Initially it is important to cast the net of contextual enquiry very wide and develop an overview and understanding of the field. This is the mapping stage and can help in deciding what comes within the scope of the research and, equally important, what lies outside.

Once this overview is in place, a few key references/sources will probably identify themselves as being of most relevance to your argument. The selection is made as a result of an emerging awareness of the exact nature of your own research question. (Further details on locating, selecting, reading, managing information, citing and tracing materials can be found later in this chapter, in Section 2.3.)

Phase 2. Critical review

Phase 2 involves the placement of these references/sources into a critical review of the research context to enable the identification of your own particular research question and the development of an argument. In evaluating the 'terrain' you will encounter a range of perspectives. The review allows you to acknowledge these different contributions, but also encourages you to state your responses to them – both positive and negative! Adopting a critical stance is essential and requires an open mind. You must be prepared to have your ideas challenged, and be receptive to different arguments. (For more details on this see Section 2.2.)

Hart (1998) suggests a set of quality criteria for evaluating a body of contextual information:

> Many reviews, in fact, are only thinly disguised annotated bibliographies. Quality means appropriate breadth and depth, rigour and consistency, clarity and brevity, and effective analysis and synthesis: in other words, the use of the ideas in the literature to justify the particular approach to the topic, the selection of methods, and demonstration that this research contributes something new.
>
> (*Doing a Literature Review*, Chapter 1, The literature review in research, pp. 1–2)

So these essential quality criteria – 'breadth and depth, rigour and consistency, clarity and brevity, and effective analysis and synthesis' – can help not only to evaluate what you have found in the context, but also to apply it in writing/visualizing your own review. (More details on this can be found in Section 2.4.)

At the end of this process you should be well placed to 'locate your position' within the professional context and formulate a viable research question and research strategy (this is covered in detail in Chapter 3).

Reflection and action: suggestions

- Familiarize yourself with the generic process of review by reading Chapter 1, in Chris Hart's useful book *'Doing a Literature Review'* (Hart, 1998, pp. 1–20).
- Think about the kind of 'contexts' relevant to your research ideas.

2.2 CRITICAL THINKING AND RESPONSE: KEY GENERIC SKILLS

Critical thinking and critical response are key postgraduate skills applicable across the whole research process – identifying issues, evaluating context, developing methodology, analysing and interpreting research outcomes, synthesizing and communicating research process and products. These skills will be revisited in all subsequent chapters as part of developing generic professional skills. In relation to this chapter, they are particularly important in enabling critical exploration, considerations, and responses to existing public domain information in your research context in order to make a suitably critical review of it. Understanding and applying these skills will enable you to develop a critical approach to your working context, and to develop an argument – a sustainable research proposition – which is a crucial part of any research proposal (raising a research question will be covered in Chapter 3).

What is critical thinking?

Critical thinking means thinking effectively and applying sound intellectual standards to your thinking. It involves 'meta-thinking' – thinking about your thinking – and self-evaluation. It involves not jumping to conclusions too quickly and maintaining an open mind, considering all aspects of an issue before making up your mind. It involves maintaining some degree of distance in order to prevent personal bias or prejudice interfering with your reasoning. However, this does not mean that a personal position cannot be adopted – indeed, this is the basis of developing a strong argument in relation to your research proposal. Critical thinking is creative thinking – it encourages questioning ('why's that . . . '), imagining ('what if, how about . . . '), connecting ('try linking this to that . . . '), interpreting ('could this mean . . . '), applying ('I'll try this out').

Critical thinking is essential for developing a convincing research proposition – an argument – in relation to what already exists in the research context. An argument is a process of reasoning in which you attempt to:

> . . . influence someone's belief that what you are proposing is the case. . . . Whichever way someone makes an argument they are attempting to convince others of the validity . . . of how they see the world and convince us that we should see it the way they do. (Hart, 1998, chapter 4, pp. 79–80)

Argument

By developing convincing arguments, we can propose different views and contribute to debate in our research context. Stephen Toulmin, writing in 1958, developed a model of a structure of an argument, which has four components.

- *Claim* – an arguable statement, for example formal research in Art and Design is an important activity.
- *Evidence* – data used to support the claim, for example an analysis of the Higher Education Statistics Agency data (www.hesa.ac.uk) reveals a rapid increase in completed research for higher degrees in the creative arts and design between 1994 and 2002.
- *Warrant* – an expectation that provides the link between the evidence and claim, for example formal research in Art and Design should be encouraged.
- *Backing* – context and assumptions used to support the validity of the warrant and evidence, for example formal research should be encouraged because it contributes to the rigorous investigation of practice encouraging new developments and new roles for practitioners.

Being aware of this structure helps us not only to develop our own arguments, but to recognize the arguments of others when listening to debate and reading the published research literature. It helps us to explore the reasoning behind a particular perspective, evaluate its strengths and weaknesses, and evaluate its contribution to our understanding. It is the essence of making a truly critical review of the research context.

Intellectual standards

The critical thinker bases arguments on the use of evidence and sound reasoning. There are intellectual standards[1] (criteria and related questions) that you can apply to check both your own use of critical skills and those of others:

- *Clarity* – Is a statement expressed in the best way? How else could it be expressed? Is it sufficiently elaborated? Is there too much jargon/over-specialized language? Are there relevant examples or illustrations?

  If a statement is unclear then it is difficult to say whether it is accurate or relevant, for example 'higher education is failing students'. This could be interpreted in at least two ways – either that the HE system is not providing an appropriate learning framework for students or that students are actually failing.

- *Accuracy* – Is this true? Can its accuracy be checked? Is it appropriately attributed?
  A statement can be clear but inaccurate, for example 'all research in Art and Design is practice-based'.
- *Precision* – Is there enough detail to explain the meaning? Could it be more specific or more clearly defined?
  A statement can be clear and accurate but not precise, for example 'most methods of distance learning are effective'. We need to know precisely what is meant by 'effective' – for whom and in what context – and the proportion of methods that are effective.
- *Relevance* – How is this related to the topic? Is it truly relevant? Is it out of context?
  A statement can be clear, accurate and precise but be of little relevance to the issue, for example if you were discussing the growth of practice-based research, it would be irrelevant to mention whether the researchers involved were right-handed!
- *Depth* – Are the complexities of the question addressed? Is the statement qualified by reason and evidence? Is it a superficial treatment?
  A statement can be clear, accurate, precise and relevant but superficial, for example collaborative learning is fun!
- *Breadth* – Are there issues that have been omitted? Is there another way to look at this? Are there other acknowledged perspectives on this? Is a balance provided?
  An argument can be clear, accurate, precise, relevant, have depth but still ignore other views, for example a strong argument for the effectiveness of distance learning would lack breadth if it ignored a comparison with other modes of learning or failed to consider the cost involved in buying equipment and spending time on-line.
- *Logic/reason* – Does this really make sense? How does this follow from what was said before? Is it consistent? Does this contradict the previous statement?
  In developing an argument, a range of ideas can be combined. However, if these ideas do not support each other, or are not sequenced properly, or present contradictions, then the combination is not logical/reasonable.

Critical thinking in visual practices

Unlike many other disciplines, where formal logic and serial thinking are predominant, artists and designers are usually visual, lateral thinkers. In our domain we know that there are no certainties, no 'right' answers, no simple solutions, no absolute objectivity. All views are admissible, many interpretations are possible, different 'ways of seeing' are encouraged – indeed, one might say that the ambiguity of visual language is its strength and fascination, and one reason for the persistence of visual practices. In Art and Design education we are encouraged to be critically aware (the 'crit' as a learning method is pervasive) but often we are not adequately equipped with critical skills. Often the vocabulary of critical language is not made explicit, yet we know a good painting when we see one! It could be argued that precisely because of this implicitness, complexity and uncertainty, we need to develop very strong critical skills. Fortunately, most – if not all – of the criteria we have just examined can be applied to the development of our own arguments and the evaluation of others.

Applying critical skills

Being aware of the structure of argument and the criteria of clarity, accuracy, precision, relevance, depth, breadth and reason, you can begin to evaluate the significance and value of relevant materials that might form part of your professional context. In examining the materials it is essential that you maintain an open mind – it's not a question of whether you like it or not! If you are seriously engaging in the research process you must be prepared to have your own beliefs challenged, expect the unexpected, and see 'failures' as valuable information. As we saw in Chapter 1 questioning our assumptions about research is an important part of becoming an effective researcher.

One useful critical method is to 'play devil's advocate'. This involves deliberately taking a conflicting or different (possibly uncomfortable!) position in order to see things from another perspective. It can make us aware of the limits of our own knowledge and understanding. Try to outline the strengths and weaknesses of different positions in order to explain/justify/defend your preferred position. Flexibility of thinking is a creative characteristic. Playing with ideas, adopting an 'imaginative agenda', extends our capacity for creative response and may even prompt a shift in position and an advancement of understanding.

Another useful device for making sense of, and understanding, ideas is to develop a conceptual framework. For example, if we were trying to evaluate and make sense of 'research' we could develop a framework for understanding it by using a *concept map*. The map might contain concepts such as:

- purpose of research,
- types of research,
- kinds of research questions,
- methodological assumptions,
- related literature/public output,
- scale and scope of research, and so on.

(See Hart, 1998, Figure 6.10, p. 157.)

This kind of conceptual framework allows us to develop an overview of the topic/idea and to begin to ask questions of it. The overview (or generic) framework could then be used to develop a more subject specific framework. Of course the idea of gaining an understanding of something by visually mapping it is a key method for artists and designers, and something that is considered in more detail in Sections 2.3 and 2.4.

By applying critical criteria and methods you can develop a sound understanding of your professional context, the significance and value of key arguments within it, and adopt a considered personal position, argue for it and defend it.

Critical writing

In relation to the Contextual Review, different styles of writing may need to be adopted at different stages. In the survey and mapping stages it is important to gather and record factual information; for example:

- *clear* and *precise* descriptive summaries of sufficient depth about a key reference, using *no emotive or value-laden language or jargon*;
- a *clear* description and evaluation of the key arguments (applying the set of criteria previously outlined);
- the use of *accurate* quotes (where appropriate) to illustrate a point, with *precise* references as to source (for example, section, chapter, page; website; publication date, and so on).

Naturally you will want to make your own *critical evaluation* of this information, which demonstrates some *depth* of understanding, the ways and the extent to which the arguments are *relevant* to your study, and how the arguments relate to other/different arguments (*breadth*).

At a later stage, you might revisit this initial information and develop a more reflectively critical response in an individual writing style that demonstrates the development of your argument as a *considered* and *convincing* one.

These are suggestions and are not meant to be prescriptive, but they should go some way towards helping to develop (or develop further) appropriate critical language and writing skills, which are essential in presenting a convincing argument.

Reflection and action: suggestions

- Using Toulmin's model can you outline an argument relevant to your own research proposal?
- Choose a journal article of relevance to your research interests. Can you evaluate it using the set of critical criteria described? What are the arguments put forward by the author? Are they convincing?
- Visit the 'Provocative Comment' section at: http://www.sunderland.ac.uk/~as0bgr/learnmat.html
  What kinds of arguments are being made about research in Art and Design?

2.3 LOCATING AND USING REFERENCE MATERIALS FOR ART AND DESIGN RESEARCH

This topic is very pragmatic! It provides guidelines on how to search for and select references relevant to your research proposal. Its purpose is to help you manage that information and use it to compile a 'bibliography' (including a range of media sources) relevant to your research proposal, using accurate citation protocols. The bibliography can then be used to develop a critical Contextual Review of your research area.

A bibliography comprises a set of references relevant to a research proposal. Think of the proposal as a 'magnet' to which different 'metallic objects' (different references) are attracted, some more strongly than others! The compilation of the bibliography demonstrates that the most relevant materials have been identified and summarized, and that their significance has been evaluated in relation to your research proposal. In the light of this information, the proposal may need to be modified or refocused to ensure that you are not 'reinventing the wheel', and that you have the opportunity to make an appropriate contribution to the research area.

Locate and select – the importance of keywords

Only broad guidelines can be given on searching, because the materials found will be specific to your research context, and even more specific to your particular research proposal. The *Visualizing Research* website () includes a set of useful resources and links to related sites – a good starting point for searching. However, your bibliography will necessarily be subject-specific to a great degree, and will draw on your particular professional context. It is easy to get carried away – so much information is now accessible that it is necessary to keep a reasonable focus through the use of keywords. Use a maximum of six. Your keywords are crucial in starting the search for relevant materials so it is worth reflecting on their relevance and accuracy. They provide criteria and parameters for searching, and may need to be expanded, contracted or amended depending on the results of initial searches. Orna and Stevens (1995) suggest an interesting metaphor – 'fishing' for information: where the keywords are 'hooks' (see Oma and Stevens, 1995, Chapter 3, p. 41).

In searching for information, be prepared to be simultaneously depressed and excited – depressed because you cannot find anything to match your needs exactly, and excited because this means that your line of inquiry could be unusual or even unique. Be prepared to step out of both your subject area, for example painting, and even your discipline, for example design, into related (or hitherto unrelated) disciplines (for example education, geology, history, astrophysics!). This could be likened to searching for intelligent life in the solar system and further out in the universe (see Figure 2.1).

Do not simply rely on one or two sources of information (for example Art Abstracts, ARIAD) – different resources cover different types of information. The likelihood is that you will need to combine information from many different (and possibly unlikely) sources to gain a reasonable picture of what already exists and is relevant to your proposal. In addition, do not rely on a single search – you might need to reiterate the process using new keywords or a more constrained set. Venture out into the information universe as often as possible!

Identifying a 'gap' in knowledge and providing evidence for it

Especially at doctoral levels, it is crucial to ascertain what other PhD research exists in relation to your proposed research area. Your claim of making an original contribution to knowledge will partly rest on demonstrating that there is no similar research. In reporting the results of literature surveys and other contextual searches, many research reports and PhD theses often state that there is a 'lack of research' without providing sufficient evidence to justify that statement. A useful structure to address this could be as follows.

(1) The identification of all PhD research related to your proposed research area through searches of various databases, for example Index to Theses and university websites/libraries.
(2) A similar search for MPhil and Masters level theses/dissertations.
(3) A search for other key references, most obviously books, journal articles, professional periodical articles, catalogues, and references in other media, for example documentary film.

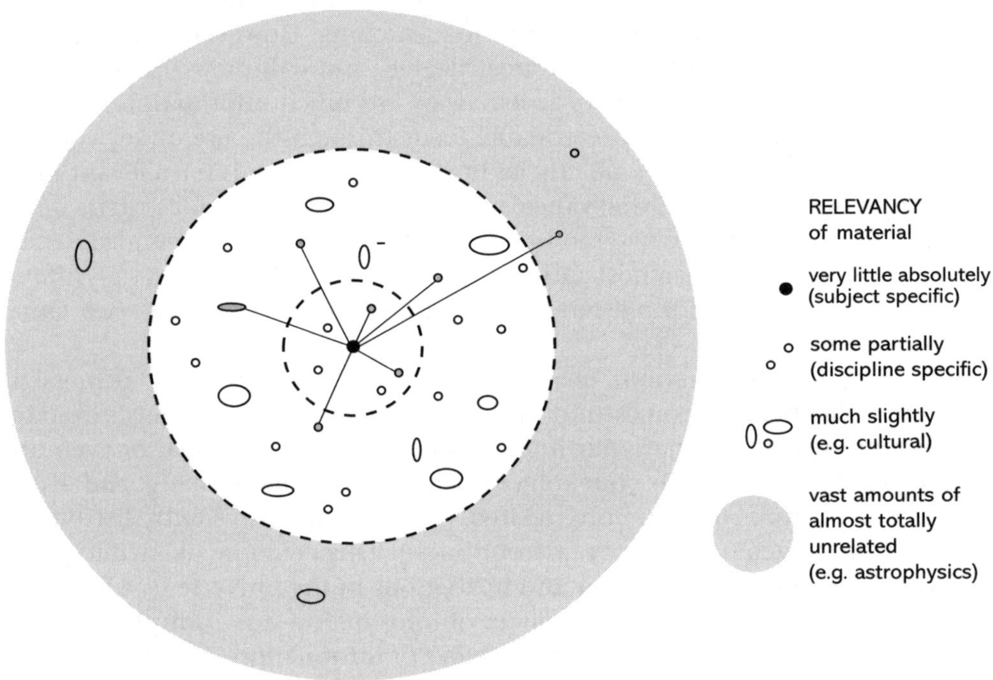

Figure 2.1 Information searching strategies: connecting material from various 'orbits' of relevance (💻)

It is important to keep track of all searches, especially names of sources, for example 'ARIAD database', keywords used, number of results. When something relevant is identified, make a copy of the reference details and the abstract. Follow up the most relevant pieces of research, that is, if possible contact the actual researcher, the institution where the research took place, obtain a copy of the complete thesis through inter-library loan. Beware of drawing major conclusions from brief abstracts.

Of course, it may be impossible to locate every relevant piece of research, especially very recent material, but in adopting a rigorous explicit approach to this task you will be able to demonstrate that you have taken all reasonable actions to find relevant material, and to justify your claim of a 'lack of research'.

Reading – but not as we know it!

Most of us enjoy reading a gripping novel, and usually we resist the temptation of peeking at the final chapter! However, reading at leisure for relaxation and pleasure is very different from reading for a Contextual Review, rewarding though the outcome might be. You will probably identify many sources of information that you need to assimilate quickly and form an opinion on. Fortunately there are several sources of advice that provide very useful suggestions and guidelines for this kind of focused reading (for example, Hart, 1998, Chapter 3, pp. 53–56). A suitable methodology might be as follows:

- obtain the reference/source material and don't forget to capture publication/public output details in your bibliography (to store information efficiently you may wish to use commercially available software applications such as ProCite or EndNote to keep a bibliography database);
- try to get a quick overview of content and structure – look at the index/chapter/section headings;
- keep your keywords/research descriptors in mind – they are like 'spectacles and sieves' to help you focus and select;
- scan and 'skim' read (try scanning down the middle section of the page) – the theory is that your peripheral vision picks up the rest;
- scan/'skim' read the introduction/abstract and the summary/conclusions;
- read more carefully the various sections that seem significant;
- if you photocopy sections, use coloured highlighters on the copy to code key content, for example key words could have different colours to help identify different types of relevant information;
- extract key information – Buzan (1999, Chapter 24, pp. 235–238) proposes an excellent technique for mind mapping a book, or you could interrogate each set of information with a consistent series of questions – what? why? who? where? how? when? (this makes comparison between sources easier);
- while you are reading/mapping, take note of the quality of the information – you could check it against critical quality criteria such as: clarity, accuracy, precision, brevity, breadth, depth, relevance, rigour, consistency, reason, effective analysis and synthesis.

It is likely that you will want to revisit certain references and read them very thoroughly to confirm your initial understanding and extend it. It is also likely you will want to update/expand your bibliography accordingly. These strategies could be adapted for reviewing other materials in other media. By adopting some of the suggestions for reading, the information universe will not seem as daunting!

Managing information

The information you derive from these searches must be carefully captured and stored (see Figure 2.2). Hart (1998) provides an interesting diagrammatic overview of the

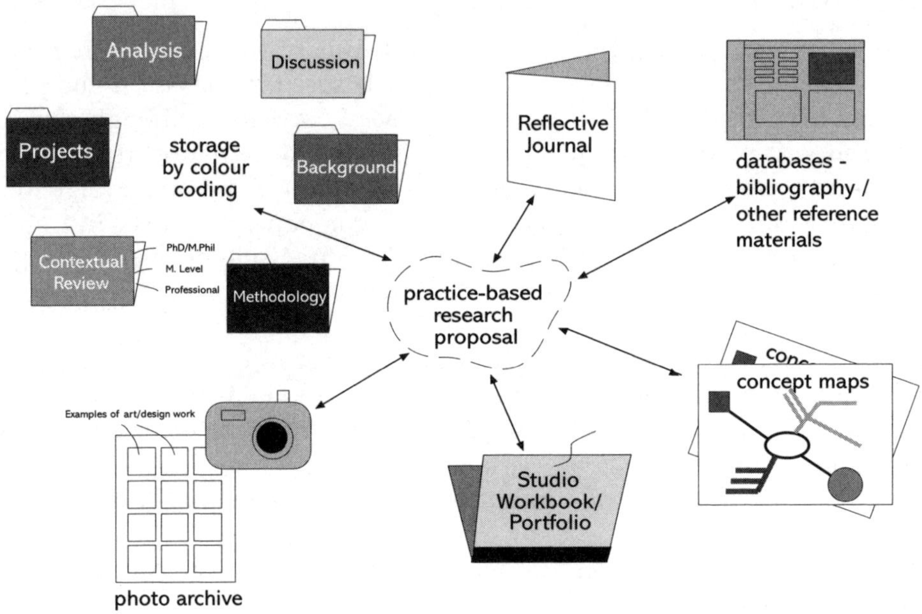

Figure 2.2 Possible methods of managing information for the Contextual Review (💻)

different kinds of devices useful in managing information, for example a 'search diary', 'memory cards', 'action plans', mind maps, quotes, correspondence and contacts, and so on (Hart, 1988, Appendix 4, pp. 215–218). Some of these techniques are described in detail and should prove helpful. In addition, Orna and Stevens (1995, Chapter 3) provide excellent advice on a range of methods for managing research information.

You may like to consider setting up your own coding system, for example using coloured highlighters for different kinds of information when reading texts – your colour coding system could extend to files, folders on your computer or even specific colours for computer disks for storing back-up files. You might consider developing other kinds of databases, for example for research contacts/correspondence, project images, and using an organizational structure such as a matrix to store information.

The importance of accurately capturing and properly managing information cannot be stressed enough. This is an essential part of the rigour of research. A convincing argument cannot be made unless your claim is backed up by evidence. Careless handling of initial data can compromise the quality of your evidence. (These issues will be expanded upon in Chapters 3, 4 and 5.)

Using bibliographic software

There are a number of commercial software applications available that will assist in compiling a database of references, for example ProCite and EndNote. The more recent versions of these applications will handle graphic information as well as text.

Alternatively, you may wish to compile your own database (for example, using FileMaker Pro) customized for your own particular purposes. In addition to the usual fields of 'publication/public output' details and 'keywords' you could include:

- a 'summary' field – a brief and accurate description of the reference (in many applications a field for an abstract is already included);
- a 'critical evaluation' field – critical statements on the significance and value of the reference to the research context and to your research in particular (most applications will include a 'notes' field);
- a 'key quotes' field – selected brief quotations that illustrate significant arguments/points;
- an 'other media' field – for the inclusion of video/audio/multimedia extracts (FileMaker Pro can handle these kinds of data).

If a sufficient level of detail is entered then this should provide a good basis from which to write the Contextual Review.

With the increasing speed of information dissemination (especially digital data) it is essential that you see the compilation of your bibliography as a dynamic task. You will need to keep a regular track of new developments in your subject area. Your bibliography will probably need revisiting regularly and may require you to update your Contextual Review as a result. This will be considered in subsequent chapters.

Citing and tracing references

An essential research skill is the accurate citing of references. Not only does this ensure that references are traceable, but equally important that research is attributed correctly to the rightful author/creator. A Contextual Review in Art and Design research can be based on a wide range of permissible material – both text and images, for example art and design objects, as long as they are traceable by a formal referencing system. Referencing protocols should be followed exactly (including use of punctuation and italics) as these ensure that a single reference can be revisited, if necessary, by any other researcher. The protocols are a shared language that therefore helps to guarantee traceability.

There are two main systems for dealing with textual publications – Harvard or British Standard (Numeric) – but whichever you choose you must apply it consistently within a document, and take particular care to follow the exact protocols. In this book the Harvard system is used. Most academic libraries will have information on various systems. In addition, Hart (1998, Appendix 2, pp. 209–212) provides excellent detail on citing protocols. There are a number of websites providing information on how to cite correctly. One such site can be found at: http://www.unn.ac.uk/central/isd/cite/ (accessed June 2003).

Citing art/design/other media works

However, the above website does not provide information on citing art/design works. There are many examples of references for art/design works – look at a range of catalogues for example. Usually they comprise the following basics:

- creator/designer/artist's name;
- title of work and/or brief description;
- date (year of origination and, if relevant, further details for development stages);
- materials (in reasonable detail);
- dimensions (metric, usually height × width × depth);
- venue/means of public access (with dates if appropriate);
- location – public/private collection, geographic;
- review/other literature/references (see standard protocols on recommended website).

In addition, depending on the particularities of the output, additional information may be required, for example exact geographic location of a piece of architecture or public art; patent or registration number; inscriptions/signatures; commissioners' details; process of commission (for example invitation, competition, tender, and so on); funding source(s); curation details; copyright information; collaborator(s); solo or group output, and any other distinguishing features! Check out the AXIS website (http://www.axisartists.org.uk) for examples.

Remember that providing the appropriate level of detail helps in revisiting the reference at a later date, helps other researchers to use the information and, most importantly, ensures that your evidence for making claims is supported by valid and accurate references.

Reflection and action: suggestions

- Which keywords (maximum of six) are most relevant for your information searches? Try them out using various databases.
- Make a list of the methods you already use for managing information.
- Can you think of other metaphors (apart from fishing and intergalactic space travel!) to describe searching for information?
- Choose three different kinds of art/design output and consider what information would be required in order to provide comprehensive citation details.

2.4 UNDERTAKING A CONTEXTUAL REVIEW: MAPPING THE TERRAIN

This topic expands on the previous brief introduction to the purpose and structure of a Contextual Review. Its purpose is to enable you to develop a critical Contextual Review of your professional working context, and to demonstrate competence in structuring and writing a critical review. However, there is no such thing as a typical Contextual Review! Different disciplines take different approaches. It very much depends on what you are trying to say and to whom. For instance, one of the purposes of a Contextual Review in a PhD thesis would be to identify a 'gap' in existing knowledge, thus providing a rationale for the new research and a context for its original contribution to knowledge. In Masters courses a Contextual Review might be directed at your professional peers and/or the people with whom you work. You may want to use it (or parts of it) for:

- demonstrating your professional awareness;
- demonstrating the value of your research to your particular working context;
- using it in an application for funding or securing resources;
- locating and relating your own particular practice;
- developing a new research project.

The structure and content are responsive to the function of the review in your research/professional context and the flow of your argument. Remember the analogy of the 'argument as river' – a moving force with a strong direction, usually starting from a small spring in high terrain (a speculative idea) and on the way being expanded and shaped by diverse contributions from tributaries (other relevant research) until eventually flowing confidently into a sea of knowledge.

Within this flow, key references may be incorporated in various ways: some references may be organized chronologically in parts of your review where you may be evaluating developments over time; some may be arranged thematically, demonstrating similarities and allowing you to make creative connections (cross-currents) between previously unrelated research; and some arranged to demonstrate comparison and contrast perhaps using a common set of criteria as an 'anchor'.

Whatever the preferred structure, the content should include:

- clear and brief objective descriptive summaries of each key reference;
- judicious use of brief key quotes to illustrate significant arguments/ideas;
- use of visual overviews and more specific visual materials, for example photographs;
- critical evaluation of the significance and value of reference material to the wider research context, and to your research proposal in particular;
- demonstration throughout of critical thinking skills and critical writing, and an attempt to develop a language appropriate for practitioner research.

In summary, what is required is a description and critical evaluation of the existing research, demonstrating a balance between a 'reasonable' response and a personal, creative, alternative view towards developing a strong and convincing argument.

Examples of Contextual Reviews in Art and Design research

Two examples of Contextual Reviews from completed practice-based PhDs are now described in terms of structure, content and style.

Example 1

A project investigating environmentally sensitive printmaking necessitated a broad-based contextual review due to the research proposition – that alternative and environmentally safer materials and processes can be used by artists/printmakers without compromising their creativity and the quality of their output. The Contextual Review therefore covered three key areas: printmaking processes/practices, the diversity of artists' approaches to printmaking, and a review of health and safety issues related to printmaking. The researcher visualized these areas in an overview diagram (see Figure 2.3):

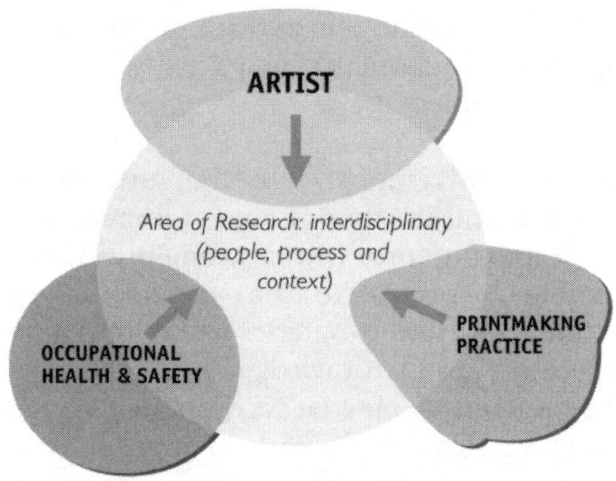

Figure 2.3 Simple visual overview of a Contextual Review (💻)
(example from Pengelly, PhD, 1997)

This structure characterized the area of research as interdisciplinary, involving people (practitioners), print processes (technologies) and the working environment (health and safety issues). In each of these three areas, key references were identified and critically evaluated. Some references supported the argument and others offered alternative or opposing views, giving the review some critical balance. The style of the review is pragmatic and written from the perspective of a practitioner for the benefit of other practitioners. It demonstrates an excellent understanding of the working context (both professional and environmental). It provides evidence from the professional context to support changes in practice and views against this, and clearly identifies a methodology for bringing about change through the research.

Example 2

A project investigating the integration of new technology into designer-maker practice also necessitated a broad review. The researcher's proposition was that the introduction of new technologies into designer-maker practice would extend, enrich and sustain those practices and help to develop a new critical framework for the crafts. This ambitious proposition was also complemented by an ambitious format – a PhD thesis in digital format, which in many ways attempted to encapsulate and visualize many of the possibilities of new technologies for practitioners. The thesis was constructed using a series of linked databases. The Contextual Review was therefore developed as an integrated database from the start of the research. This enabled thematic searching for references, enabling various ways of organizing the draft review. The scope of the review was visualized by an interactive, colour-coded map, and covered key areas such as computer technology, environmentally sensitive technology, designer-maker practice and practitioners' use of technology (see Figure 2.4).

Each section of the review presents a clear summary description and critical evaluation of each reference (or group of references), and positions are compared and contrasted in order to understand the debate about technology and craft. In the section on designer-makers, 16 practitioners are reviewed in terms of their use of technology and its impact on practice. A useful layout design was developed for this section, emphasising key visuals. The use of scrolling fields meant that the text could always be read in relation to the visuals (and their detailed captions). The writing style is clear, straightforward and effective – speaking to other design-makers and researchers. At the end of

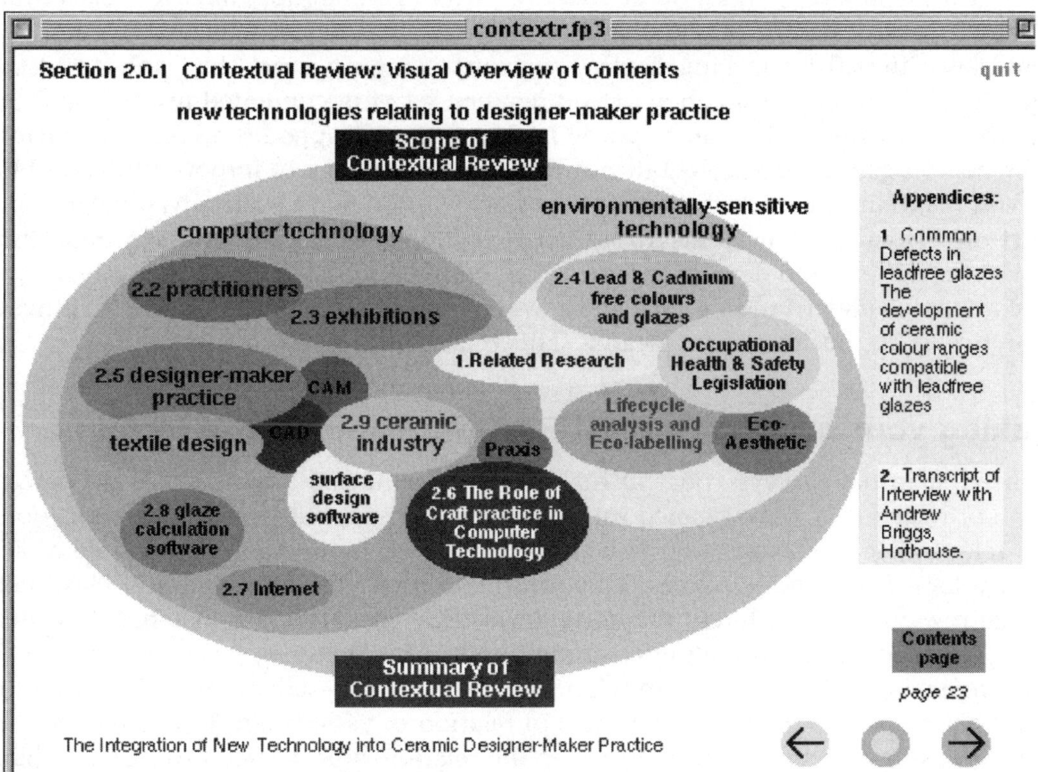

Figure 2.4 A more complex visual overview of a Contextual Review (💻) (example from Bunnell, PhD 1998)

the section there is a summary that reminds us of the key findings of the Contextual Review, and why further research is required.

Developing a good critical contextual understanding and writing about it is not easy, especially in Art and Design. Compared with other arts and humanities disciplines, which have a strong research tradition, for example History, and others for which critical writing is the main vehicle for expression, for example Cultural Studies, we are relative novices. Many artists struggle with writing, but if the practitioner–researcher adopts an honest approach to writing their enthusiasm and belief in the research will usually see them through. It is tempting to lapse into 'research speak' or 'critical theory' mode and become over complex and over intellectualized! This may be counterproductive in convincing your readers of the value of the research. The review must be clear, concise and allow you to demonstrate that you understand your context (and related ones), and that you can locate your research in relation to it.

From the two examples described (and others) it is clear that because practice-based research in Art and Design is in development and is investigating new areas of research, Contextual Reviews (for PhD at least) are by necessity wide ranging – they are trying to map 'continents' so that more local terrain can be located and understood in relation to them. For the moment, this kind of breadth is necessary, but does have its disadvantages – namely lack of depth. Many examples of Contextual Reviews in new research areas could be criticized for lacking depth – at worst being no more than annotated bibliographies. Until there is a coherent and detailed set of documented research and practice in an area this will be an ongoing problem and will present a constant dilemma. How do you gain an overview but not lose sight of a range of important details? How do you maintain brevity but demonstrate clarity and rigour? Naturally, a balance must be struck. However, our ability to visualize, to think holistically and synthetically, to make connections and develop relationships between ideas are great strengths to apply in contextual understanding. We must work hard at developing critical writing and analytical skills, but these are research skills that we will hone in time!

Making your own Contextual Review: mapping the terrain

From your initial surveys you will have probably amassed a wide range of materials, some of which may have seemed important at the time, but perhaps are now looking less relevant. It is essential that you select from your bibliography/store a core of the most relevant references/sources. This information can be organized and classified in different ways, using different mapping devices (details later). For instance, in order to get the most comprehensive understanding out of the material, you may want to map the references in different ways in relation to different criteria, for example chronology, using a 'timeline' to map key references in relation to various developments over time; thematic issues, using a mind map to see the relationships between things; comparing and contrasting references – how various authors/originators take different or similar stances in relation to an issue or a set of issues using a table or a matrix structure. A useful understanding of methodology/methods used by researchers can be gained by visualizing the different approaches and tools used – try using a network display.

By 'playing' with the references – organizing them in different ways – you could end up with several maps to help you decide how to structure your review. In order to 'see' what you have got and 'where to go with it', using different kinds of mapping techniques can be helpful in understanding the 'terrain'. Three examples of mapping techniques are now described.

Mind map

A mind map (Buzan, 1998) is a useful way of sorting out these references. In this process, your keywords should help to prioritize and locate the references: is there anything that relates directly to *all* your keywords? If so, then this (or these) is the centre of your map. Is there anything that relates to *most* of your keywords? Again this/these can be positioned relative to the main reference(s) on your map. The basis of this map could be a 'target-like' structure with concentric rings to help locate and differentiate between degrees of importance. Carry on with this process until you have located and related all your references. Some might be so far towards the edge of the map that they can be removed. You may need to go through this process several times to feel happy with your selection. There are a number of software applications available for developing mind maps, for example Inspiration (http://www.inspiration.com/). See Figure 2.5 for an example of mapping.

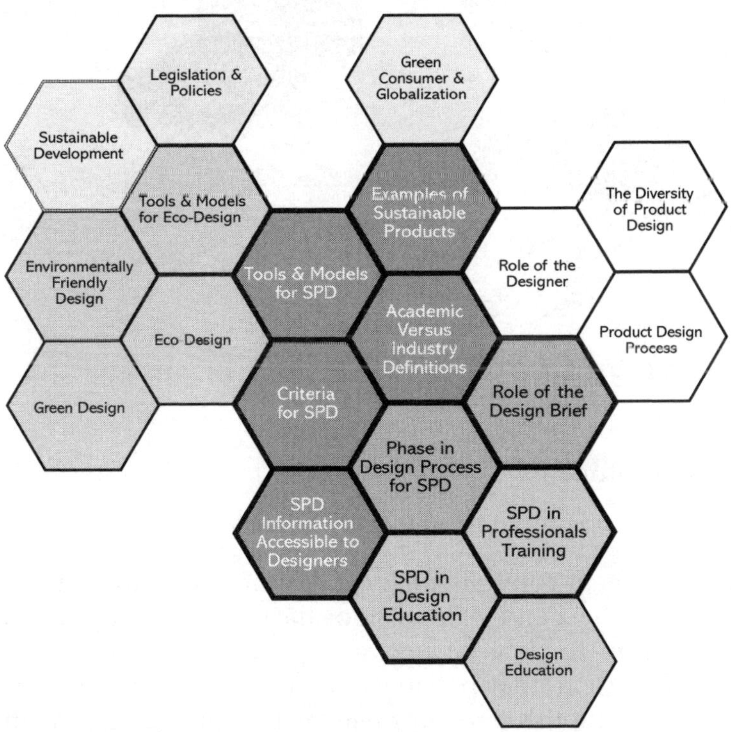

Figure 2.5 A hexagon map of sustainable design issues (💻) (example from a PhD in progress)

Matrix

A matrix comprises 'columns' and 'rows' that represent two different dimensions, concepts or sets of information, for example 'ingredient' in relation to 'cooking process'. Where these two dimensions cross a new 'cell' of information emerges, for example ingredient 'raw egg' × cooking process 'poach' = 'poached egg'! In designing a matrix we are considering how to 'partition' information (Miles and Huberman, 1994) and there are usually many different ways to do this. As with the mind map method, you may need to try out different kinds of dimensions/concepts. For the purposes of trying to understand contextual information, we might use the concepts of 'author/originator' in relation to 'content' or 'year of publication'. Different variables or component factors can be extracted from the main concepts yielding more detailed information in the intersecting 'cells', for example 'content' could be unpacked to comprise 'date', 'scope', 'key ideas/ arguments', 'links to others', 'strength of relevance', and so on. The matrix can also be a useful device for making comparisons across authors/originators.

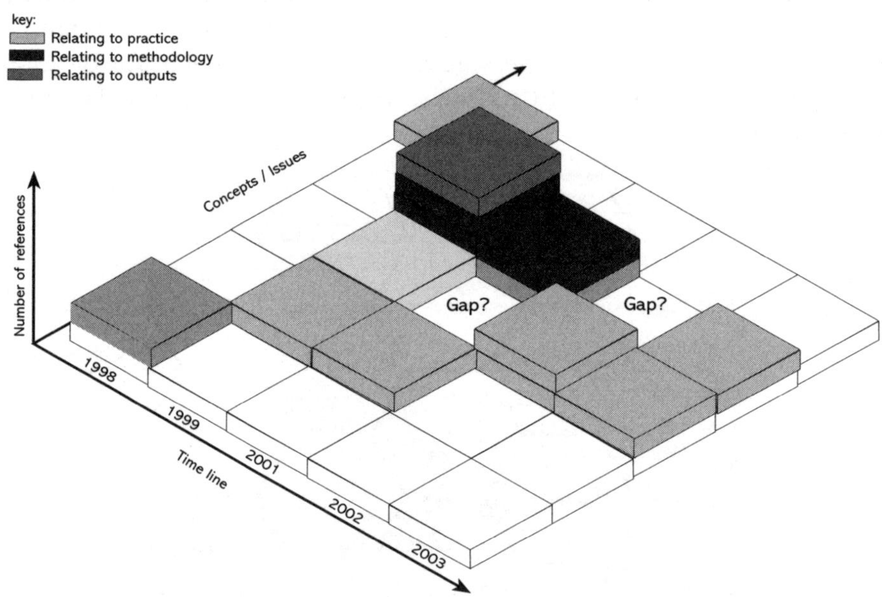

Figure 2.6 A '3D' matrix (💻)

A matrix is capable of conveying a great deal of information. For instance, in the 3D matrix in Figure 2.6 the *x* and *y* dimensions have been labelled as a set of 'concepts' or 'issues' (*x*) in relation to time (*y*) respectively. This may be all the information you require, in which case a 2D matrix (table or grid) would be fine. However, we have added a third axis representing the *number* of references found (*z*). As the matrix is built up, a 'contour map' of references on the research area begins to emerge. You can see from the matrix that, in 1996/97, one of the concepts/issues attracted quite a number of contributions. Equally interesting are the 'gaps' in the matrix. Where there are no references in relation to a concept/issue this may indicate a complete lack of research in that area, or just that further hunting for appropriate references is required. Colours have also been used to provide another way of coding the information. These colours might represent the subject area covered by the reference, for example references that relate to practice could be yellow, methodology purple, or forms of output orange. Similarly, symbols could be used to indicate different forms of output. We could have used any number of categories to label the dimensions of the matrix, such as 'method' against 'time' with 'location' in the *z* direction. You need to try out several different dimension labels to see what works best. The matrix is a very versatile tool for both information management and for analysis. We will return to these ideas in subsequent chapters.

Networks

The same kind of concepts used in a matrix can be used in a less rigid structure like a network. A network is a collection of 'nodes' (points) connected by 'links' (lines) and can be visualized as a tree structure with branches or plant with roots. Network displays are useful for examining the relationship between many variables, visualizing groups and sub-groups, and for describing an unfolding narrative. There are many different kinds of network displays, for example context charts, causal networks, hierarchical networks (Miles and Huberman, 1994). The latter is useful for classification of ideas/objects/concepts, for example subjects taught at an art school (see Figure 2.7).

There are other kinds of useful visual devices described in Hart (1998, Chapter 6, p. 156), for example a semantic map of cultural criticism. These visual methods will be revisited and expanded upon in Chapters 4 and 5, and new methods introduced.

Writing the Review

The review is a justification of your research topic and research approach. To recap, it is a description and critical interpretation of the existing research, and has a balance between a 'reasonable' response and a personal, creative, alternative view towards developing a strong and convincing argument in your research proposal. However, convincing arguments must be well planned – do not plunge into writing yet! From your 'maps of the terrain' you could make a master mind map of the structure and content of your Contextual Review. You might return to the 'river' analogy and make a visual that describes the flow of the water through different landscapes – thematic areas of research. Where do the specific tributaries join the river – to which points in your argument do certain references relate? The aim is to be highly selective and increasingly focused – a 'gathering in' of only the most essential references/sources.

If this master map is clear and focused then writing the review should be much easier. Don't forget who are your target readers – probably your professional peers/colleagues – so use clear and concise language. Bear in mind the quality criteria identified by Hart (1998): clarity, brevity, breadth, depth, rigour, consistency, effective analysis and synthesis. Essentially your review might have:

- a focused structure/sequence for the key references – your argument – with material organized in some sensible ways, for example chronologically, thematically, comparatively, and so on.

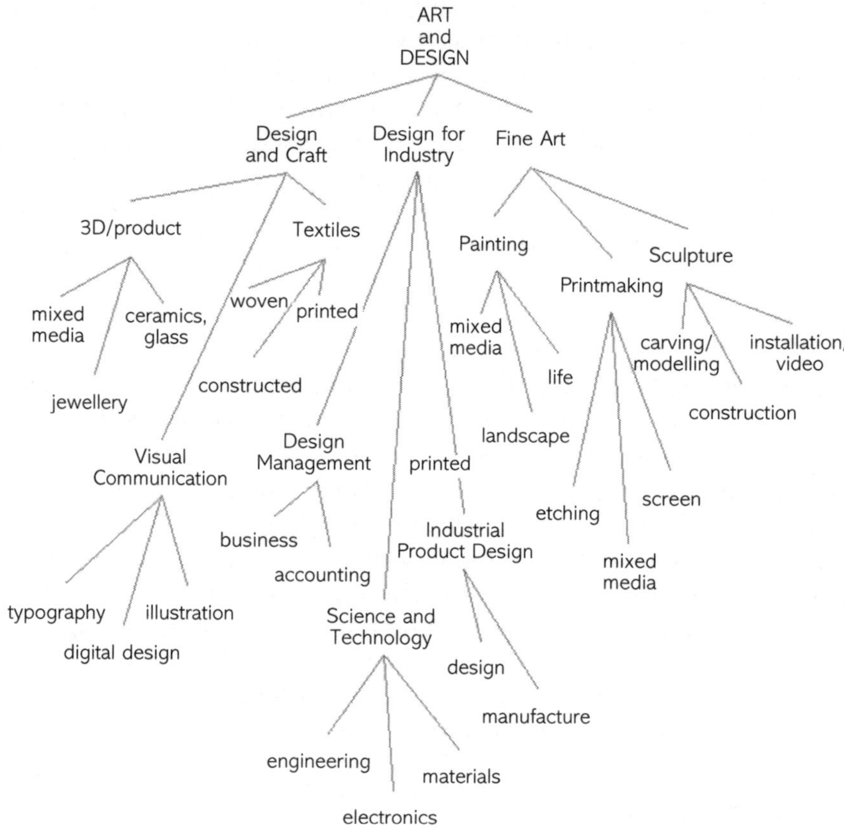

Figure 2.7 Network display: subjects taught at an art school (💻)

Within this there might be:

- overviews/previews (describing briefly the structure, content, sequence of major sections of the review);
- the most important key references should be described and critically evaluated in depth (if you have followed our advice on the use of bibliographic software you may already have captured the basis of this information in your bibliography database 'summary' and 'critical evaluation' fields);
- less relevant references may not require extensive detail but could still be mentioned as examples and selected lists (for example, Bloggs, 1986; Flintstone, 1991), which demonstrates your awareness of them and your ability to select critically;
- judicious use of brief key quotes to illustrate significant arguments/ideas – do not be tempted to 'over quote' – it is better to paraphrase;

- use of visual overviews and more specific visual materials – include illustrations of work discussed whenever possible;
- summaries/reviews to close each section (remind the reader briefly what you have said).

Your Contextual Review will never be definitive, and will probably need to be reviewed and updated during the course of your research. In this sense, it is provisional and should be 'modelled' as your research progresses and your context develops.

Reflection and action: suggestions

- Find three examples of Contextual Reviews in your research area – what are their particular characteristics, that is structure, content, style, and so on?
- How do these three reviews stand up to being evaluated using Hart's quality criteria? (You could use a matrix structure to do this evaluation.)
- Choose 12 key references from your bibliography/'store'. Map them in relation to each other, then visualize the flow of your argument. Use this to write a draft Contextual Review.

2.5 A REFLECTIVE JOURNAL

Experiential learning and 'off-loading'

In Chapter 1 we considered the important concept of 'reflective practice', and various modes of reflection. In addition to Schön's reflection 'in' and 'on', John Cowan proposes the concept of reflection 'for' future action (Cowan, 1998) see Figure 2.8.

This addition suggests a dynamic and recursive reflection process, which relates to David Kolb's experiential learning cycle (Kolb, 1984). Briefly, Kolb proposes four stages of learning from experience: do, reflect, summarize, test. McAleese (1999) has built on

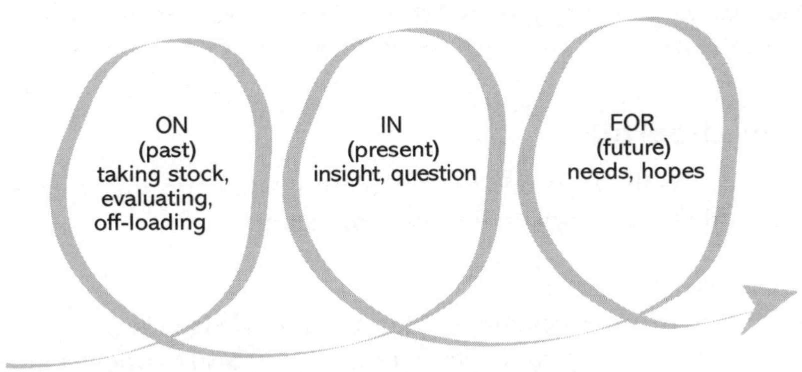

Figure 2.8 Reflection-for-action – a looping process (adapted from Cowan)

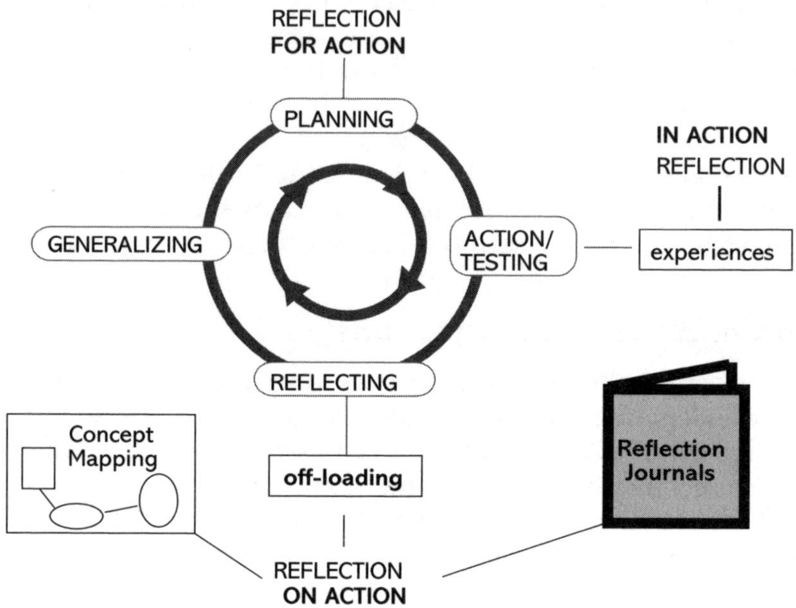

Figure 2.9 Reflective journaling as part of the 'Serious_Fun Framework' (💻) (adapted from McAleese)

this model in his research on skill acquisition, and proposes two main tools to enable and externalize reflection-on-action: concept mapping, and reflection journals. These tools are described as 'off-loading' devices – presumably because they allow the learner to take stock, evaluate and 'deposit' ideas and feelings about the learning experience. This kind of 'off-loading' enables the learner to continue the cycle 'unburdened' as it were and to be ready for new learning experiences.

The idea of 'off-loading' into a reflective journal for instance goes some way to address Schön's concern about the difficulty of articulating the 'knowing-in-action' of professional practices. As practitioners in Art and Design we can recognize the fear of losing or damaging creativity by speaking about it and, even worse, by writing about it!

Reasons to be cheerful!

However, there are compelling reasons for articulating and exposing what we do, in a professional sense and also in a personal sense. For example:

- *Developing various models of practice*
  If we as practitioners can articulate this kind of knowledge, not only are we more likely to develop clearer epistemologies of practice, but also to understand better the diversity of that practice, as well as the core characteristics. This provides extremely valuable information for practice-based research, which usually requires a descrip-

tion and evaluation of practice as a starting point for research. It has obvious implications for teaching, in illustrating a range of different approaches to practice.

- *Developing interdisciplinarity and collaboration through better communication*
  If we can articulate practice more clearly for ourselves then we are more likely to communicate better with other disciplines. By exposing ideas and practices to other professionals we can gain useful feedback. This communication can lead to the development of fruitful collaborations, and possible external support and funding.
- *Extending professionalism through self-evaluation*
  In Chapter 1 we considered the 'extended professional' whose most outstanding feature is a 'capacity for self-evaluation and self-improvement through rigorous and systematic research and study of his or her practice' (McKernan, 1998, p. 46). Unless practitioners themselves carry out this self-evaluation and make it explicit we will still be reliant on being described and represented by other disciplines, for example critics, theorists, psychologists, and so on.
- *Having better conversations with ourselves!*
  Finally, in a purely personal sense, we all know the benefits of 'talking to ourselves' – making sense of events, actions, feelings, and rehearsing for new situations. If some of your 'conversations' about practice and research can be captured and visualized this contributes to your growing understanding.

The Reflective Journal

How then can we develop various models of practice, encourage interdisciplinarity and collaboration, extend professionalism and have better conversations with ourselves? 'Reflective journalling' can provide a purposeful process and framework for contributing to these developments. 'Knowing' about professional practice is dynamic and demands a complementary method of capturing that dynamism which is flexible, responsive, improvisational, reflexive. A reflective 'journal', or something like it, is a useful device. Perhaps the word 'journal' is slightly misleading. The dictionary definition states: 'A book in which a daily record of happenings, etc, is kept' (*New Collins Concise Dictionary*, 1986). First, your 'journal' might not take a 'book' form, it is likely not to simply comprise text, and you might not use it 'daily'!

However, what is crucial about the principle of a 'journal' is that it is a store – a depository for a range of information in a range of media, which is added to and consulted on a regular basis. Of course, there are obvious benefits to the physical form of a book, as it literally binds all the material together in one place. However, it is not a 'static' store. If the journal is truly reflective then it is not a precious, self-conscious object, but an interactive device, which will probably become a bit dog-eared over time!

The 'journal' may contain different types of information – activity and development log, diary, documentation of work in progress, contextual references, information about the pace and progress of work, key points from evaluation and analysis, and any other kind of relevant 'life' information. Let us examine some of these components in more detail.

For instance, if you are making some experiments with materials and processes, this kind of information will need to have factual and precisely detailed records, so that you (or someone else) can recreate the effects. Fact, precision and detail are the characteristics of activity logs. These records may include visuals, photographs, material samples, diagrams, charts, numerical data, video/audio and, of course, text. One of the most amazing kinds of 'life log' is the architect and polymath Buckminster Fuller's 'chronofile' (Krause and Lichtenstein, 1999). As a very young man he took the radical decision to regard his life as an experiment, the failures and successes of which he would document as extensively as possible. The result was a comprehensive collection of data – letters, postcards, photos, sketches, even receipts – 'a life's transcript' (Krause and Lichtenstein, 1999, p. 14) spanning almost 75 years!

Other events and experiences may be recorded in a less comprehensive way, perhaps using more descriptive and discursive means – as in a diary. Brian Eno provides us with an interesting example of a diary in his *A Year With Swollen Appendices* (Eno, 1996). David Hockney's contribution to Stephen Spender's (1993) *China Diary* is a different kind of travel journal, with the emphasis very much on the visual. An excellent example of yet another kind of diary is the 'cyclogram' that describes the space flight of Salyut 6 from December 1977 to March 1978. (This beautiful visual can be found in Tufte, 1997, pp. 92–95.) Again other media may prove useful – the idea of a 'video diary' for some people can be attractive, to others completely intimidating! For some a 'visual diary' might take the form of a multimedia document or even a website.

The documentation of work in progress is essential for both practice and for research. For the purposes of the journal, colour photos/digital images ('snaps') are useful and relatively cheap. Of course, good quality 35 mm transparencies are standard requirements for documenting professional outputs (especially three-dimensional work), but equally important in the context of a reflective journal are all the stages of the work's development – warts and all! 'Failures' are extremely helpful in research terms. Asking why a failure has occurred is liable to reveal much more useful information in research terms than contemplating 'successful' final outcomes. This concept provides a very important insight into the difference between 'practice per se' and research. Naturally, the focus of attention, when it comes to practice, is on the final result. In research, however, the focus of attention is much more likely to be on the process and to providing an explanation as to why things have not worked, hence the importance of making the process transparent and being rigorous in the recording of procedures.

Most reflective journals would contain contextual references. Many practitioners amass a great collection of visual examples of other practitioners' work, and some selected examples could be included in the journal. However, it is not enough to simply paste in a postcard or magazine cutting – do not forget to provide details about the work and, most important, what you think of it and why it is significant (similar to the type of information you would include in a bibliographic database).

As the journal relates to your research journey, it is helpful to include information about the pace and progress of your work. A Masters student developed an interesting visual example of this kind of information. The visual very clearly and honestly describes the 'peaks and troughs' of the project's development in relation to the time scale of the course (Figure 2.10).

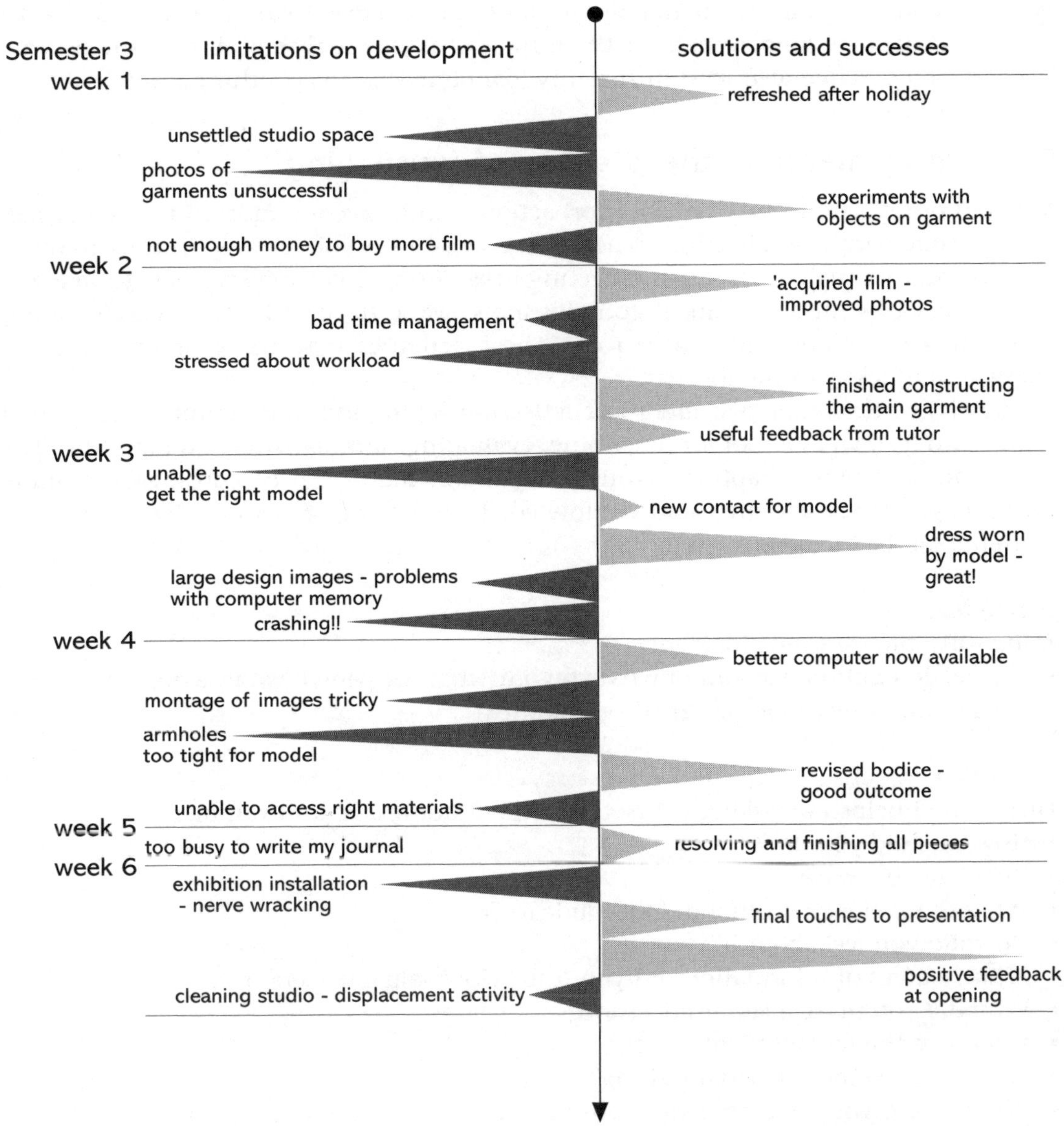

Figure 2.10 Example of visualizing the pace and progress of a project

The 'mountains and valleys' encountered in the journey also help to identify key summary points for evaluation and analysis – key incidents, events, decisions, realizations, and other kinds of relevant 'life' information. The description and 'unpacking' of this kind of visual helps to develop analytical and evaluative thinking, which Cowan (1998) suggests is the key function of a reflective journal.

We have suggested that the journal may not necessarily take the form of a book. You may want to consider a range of possible formats, which might more easily accommodate visual/actual materials, for example a large folio, a map/chart, a 3D 'container' of some kind. Whatever the format, it is essential that all the contents are labelled, dated, sequenced, and sufficiently 'contained' so that nothing is lost.

Possible elements in the process of journalling

All types of reflection ('in', 'on' and 'for' action) can be accommodated in the journal. The dynamic nature of reflection-in-action probably gives you less opportunity to interact with your journal, however, in reflecting-in-action we may quickly brainstorm ideas, talk to ourselves (in a 'stream of consciousness' way), have insights, make decisions, make changes, re-orientate, and so on. These activities may be recorded (probably briefly and quickly) in the journal.

Clearly, in the other two modes of reflection – 'on' and 'for' action – the journal comes into its own as a tool for describing, evaluating, summarizing and planning. The quick and brief 'notes' captured while reflecting-in-action can be considered in more depth, expanded, elaborated and completed. In reflecting-on-action a wide range of elements can be included.

Description
- Identification of event/incident.
- Factual description/account of what you did/what happened (what, who, why, when, where, how – methodology/methods, context).

Evaluation
This is often helped by asking yourself a series of questions, for example:
- How well did you do it?
- How valuable was it?
- What did you learn? What didn't you learn?
- How did you feel about it?
- What sources of information did you find? How valuable were they?
- Why did you make a certain decision?
- What was the most difficult thing?
- What was the most satisfying thing?
- What would you have done differently?

Summary
- List pros and cons/strengths and weaknesses.
- What does it all mean?
- What advice would you give someone?
- Identification of new key questions.

In reflecting-for-action, you should use the information gained in the previous reflection mode. In contrast to the previous mode, reflecting-for-action is much more about refinement, narrowing and focus. This mode relates to both your learning strategies for research and obviously your research proposal. A range of elements can be included in this planning mode, for example:

- the declaration of intentions and expectations;
- what if . . . ? (projection, speculation);
- the pros and cons of projections;
- the proposal of solutions or a way to obtain solutions to questions;
- the identification of scope for improvement and how to achieve it;
- the identification of most significant next step and why.

A reflective journal is essentially a personal document, and is not usually assessed (as part of any higher degree). However, it can provide you with a whole range of evidence and examples that could be useful for the development of your research project, for discussion with your supervisors and other students/peers, and for discussions with and presentations to potential collaborators.

Reflection and action: suggestions

- Consider the idea of a reflective journal. Ask yourself:
  - Why should *you* keep a reflective journal?
  - How would *you* go about it and why?
  - What kinds of content and structure might *your* journal have and why?

Looking back on Chapter 2: mapping the terrain

How can you know what's new if you don't know what already exists? How can you progress on your journey of discovery unless you are aware of the surrounding landscape and the nature of specific features of the terrain? How can you avoid dead ends or going over old ground? Answer – by making a thorough survey of what is out there and developing a critical understanding of what is directly relevant to your own research context.

Making decisions about what is an important feature of the research landscape to be explored, and what is irrelevant and why, is a key research skill requiring critical thinking and response. We have described ways of helping you evaluate the significance and relevance of existing contextual material, such as applying accepted critical criteria as well as more imaginative questioning strategies.

In attempting to get a sense of what is out there, various pragmatic strategies for searching, scanning, and surveying need to be used. Whatever is discovered needs to be carefully stored, organized, selected and prioritized, contributing to your developing view of the research terrain and identifying the unexplored spaces within it. Part of this careful surveying requires that you know how to retrace your steps – how to find your way back to some significant source and allow others to do the same.

Demonstrating your understanding of the research terrain can be achieved in different forms – there is no one right way. However, you might start off with a mapping activity making thematic groupings or clusters of similar sources, describing/visualizing the different kinds of relationships between clusters – for example, distances between, similar and contrasting features. Then, using the power and flow of your argument to make sense of your key sources, cut through the landscape like a new river, and convince us that there is indeed a void in knowledge to which your research might contribute.

Some travellers keep a 'journal' as a way of reflecting on, and making sense of the experience of exploration, through plotting key co-ordinates on their map. The reflective journal helps you to see where you've been, know where you are and, most importantly, imagine where you want to be.

REFERENCES AND FURTHER READING FOR CHAPTER 2

References

AXIS – register of practitioners and work, http://www.axisartists.org.uk.

Buzan, T. (1998) *The Mind Map Book: Radiant Thinking – a Major Evolution in Human Thought* (London: BBC Books).

Cowan, J. (1998) *On Becoming an Innovative University Teacher: Reflection in Action* (Maidenhead, Berkshire: SRHE/Open University Press).

Endnote, www.endnote.com.

Eno, B. (1996) *A Year With Swollen Appendices* (London: Faber & Faber).

Hart, C. (1998) *Doing a Literature Review* (London: Sage).

Kolb, D. (1984) *Experiential Learning: Experience as the Source of Learning and Development* (Englewood Cliffs, NJ: Prentice Hall).

Krause, J. and Lichtenstein, C. (eds) (1999) *Your Private Sky: R. Buckminster Fuller. The Art of Design Science* (Baden: Lars Müller).

McAleese, R. (1999) Skill acquisition – the curious case of information searching. *Teaching of Information and Communication Sciences, Euroconference*, September 1999, Pontificia de Salamanca, Spain.

McKernan, J. (1998) *Curriculum Action Research: a Handbook of Methods and Resources for the Reflective Practitioner* (London: Kogan Page).

Miles, M. B. and Huberman, A. M. (1994) *Qualitative Data Analysis*, Chapter 9, Matrix Displays: some rules of thumb (Thousand Oaks, CA: Sage).

New Collins Concise Dictionary of the English Language (1988) Managing editor W. T. McLeod (London and Glasgow: Collins).

Orna, L. and Stevens, G. (1995) *Managing Information for Research*, Chapter 2, Mapping the research territory: known and unknown; and Chapter 3, Managing information to support research (Maidenhead, Berkshire: Open University Press).

Procite, www.procite.com.

Spender, S. (1993) *China Diary* (with illustrations by David Hockney) (London: Thames & Hudson).

Toulmin, S. (1958) *The Uses of Argument* (Cambridge: Cambridge University Press).

Tufte, E. (1997) *Visual Explanations* (Chesire, Connecticut: Graphics Press).

Suggested further reading

Allison, B., Allison Research Index of Art and Design, 1996 (CD), and on-line at http://www.ariad.co.uk.

Booth, W., Colomb, G. and Williams, J. (1995) *The Craft of Research*, Section iii, Making a Claim and supporting it; and Chapter 13, Revising your organisation and argument (Chicago: University of Chicago Press).

Conducting a Literature Search, http://www.sosig.ac.uk/subject-guides/social_science.html.

Ennis, R. (1987) A taxonomy of critical thinking dispositions and abilities. In: Baron, J. and Sternberg, R. (eds) *Teaching Thinking Skills: Theory and Practice* (New York: W.H. Freeman).

Harrison, C. and Wood, P. (1992) *Art in Theory – 1900–1990: an Anthology of Changing Ideas* (Oxford: Blackwell).

Hart, C. (1998) *Doing a Literature Review. The Research Diary*, Appendix 4, p. 216 (London: Sage).

Jencks, C. (1993) *A Post-Modern Reader* (Chichester: Wiley-Academy).

Kuhn, D. (1992) Thinking as argument, *Harvard Educational Review*, 62(2) pp. 155–178.

Lechte, J. (1994) *Fifty Key Contemporary Thinkers: from Structuralism to Postmodernity*, (London: Routledge).

Phelan, P. and Reynolds, P. (1996) *Argument and Evidence* (London: Routledge).

Sarup, M. (1993) *An Introductory Guide to Post-Structuralism and Postmodernism*, 2nd edn (Hemel Hempstead: Harvester Wheatsheaf).

NOTE

1. Source: Critical Thinking: applying sound intellectual standards to your thinking, student resource on http://www.utas.edu.au/docs/cult/Critical_thinking.htm (accessed 16 August 1999).

3 Locating your position: orienting and situating research

CHAPTER OVERVIEW

3.1 RAISING A RESEARCH QUESTION: FROM MAPPING TO LOCATION – OVERVIEW TO YOUR VIEW

Your Contextual Review should enable you to address key questions crucial for the development of your research project proposal.

- *Why* is your research needed and *what* evidence is there to support this?
- *Who* else in the field has addressed significant aspects of your research area?
- *When* (and possibly *where)* was other relevant research carried out?
- *How* was that research carried out, and what are the implications of this for your methodology?
- *What* aspects remain unexplored or require further research?

If you are still not clear about the answers to these questions you may need to revisit your survey and review material. Don't forget that the critical review of your research context is an ongoing task essential for framing and, if necessary, re-framing your research project. Your Contextual Review should help you to focus on a viable research area and to raise an appropriate research question, which will drive your research project. The importance of focusing on specifics cannot be stressed enough.

If we take the analogy of different map scales, the process of focusing on a research question can be understood in terms of going from a large scale and not much detail, to exact location. For instance, your Contextual Review should have provided you with an overview picture and an understanding of your particular research context – a 'map of the world'. It should have enabled you to begin to locate your research proposal in relation to that context – a 'map of a country'. The identification and evaluation of the most important research and practice in that context should enable you now to focus on a particular area – a 'map of the city' – acknowledging what has already been achieved and what might still be explored and evaluated, and possibly improved upon. The identification of a specific research question is like a 'street map', where your own house can clearly be seen. But what exactly is a 'good' research question?

A good question!

It is true to say that an answer is only as good as the question (Allison *et al.*, 1996). A meaningful question can be answered by research; a non-meaningful question cannot. For example, the question 'Did God create the universe?' is unlikely to be answered by rigorous inquiry – it is essentially a metaphysical question. Similarly, the question 'is practice more important than research?' would no doubt provoke heated debate, but remains essentially an issue of personal belief. There are other kinds of questions that can be answered definitively but are not likely to make riveting research. For example, 'how many completed PhDs are there in Art and Design?' Most research questions in our discipline do not lend themselves to easily quantifiable answers, and of course they usually cannot be *proved* in the scientific sense. The best we can do is provide a credible argument based on good quality evidence.

The research questions that have been asked in Art and Design research are invariably complex and multi-dimensional, for instance:

- 'how can new technology be integrated into ceramic designer-maker practice?'
- 'in what ways can safer, more environmental processes and products be used creatively by the contemporary printmaker?'
- 'how do audiences relate to interactive artworks?'
- 'what kinds of roles do artists take on in the public realm?'
- 'how can the use of multimedia enhance artists' and designers' practices?'
- 'how can new media practices extend inclusivity?'

A research question can be used as the basis for developing a tentative proposition as the basis for an argument. For instance, the research question 'how can new technology be integrated into designer-maker practice?' can be turned into the proposition 'the use of new technology can introduce sustainability into ceramic designer-maker practice'. An argument can then be developed which persuades us, through the use of evidence, that this is indeed the case – or not. The research proposition helps to develop the plan of work, and guides the methodology and use of specific methods.

Raising a research question: various guidelines

A meaningful research question takes time to develop. It is probable that the initial questions you asked yourself about your research proposal have been re-shaped in some way by starting to undertake a Contextual Review, and have become more focused. Robson (1993, Chapter 2, pp. 27–28) gives guidance on developing research questions. He suggests three main strategies: know the area; widen the base of your experience; consider using techniques for enhancing creativity. He also points out possible pitfalls.

Know the area

Clearly, information from your Contextual Review has given you an understanding of your research context. Robson suggests that it is also helpful to demonstrate your understanding by sharing your ideas with others and getting reactions to these ideas (you could test out a few research questions with colleagues and supervisors).

Widen the base of your experience

Again, material from surveys of literature/public domain materials, especially from other disciplines, may provide useful parallels in setting research questions; you might want to identify different examples of research questions and evaluate them.

Consider using techniques for enhancing creativity

Robson suggests using brainstorming techniques (Buzan, 1998, Chapter 6) to develop questions. You could 'play devil's advocate', deliberately taking a conflicting or different position in order to see things from another perspective and so raise a range of possible research questions. Once you have a range of questions you could make use of Buzan's method for decision-making using a mind map to help you focus (Buzan, 1998, Chapter 12, see map on p. 126). Similarly using metaphorical thinking can be engaging and helpful in describing a difficult idea. For example, a horticultural metaphor has been used to describe how research can be nurtured and evolved (Gray, 1997). The use of mixed metaphors can be a creative trigger in question raising:

> Mixed metaphors, cross-over of theories . . . may provoke new questions, and provide useful insights, and suggest new ways of looking . . . (Brewer and Hunter, 1989, Chapter 3, p. 74)

'A bird in the hand, gathers no moss' – no matter how crazy this might seem, it might just generate a new view.

Donald Schön (1993) has discussed the role of metaphor in problem setting. He describes the example of a group of product development researchers who wanted to improve the performance of a new paintbrush made with synthetic bristles. After much experimentation nothing seemed to improve the delivery of the paint to a surface. Then, one of them suggested that a 'paintbrush is a kind of pump'. By seeing the paintbrush as a pump (two basically different things) they were using a metaphor – paintbrush-as-pump – as a way of generating new questions and a range of new inventions. Schön calls this process 'generative metaphor' and considers it a useful strategy not just in problem solving, but also in problem setting. In being asked to consider the paintbrush as a kind of pump, the researchers were forced into questioning 'how could that be?', 'in what ways are they similar and different?', 'how does this help us to take new approaches to the problem?'. They were forced to 're-group' and 're-name' elements of the paintbrush, so that it could be *seen as* a pump.

The use of analogy is also helpful in trying to articulate something that is poorly understood. For instance, in the Hindu story of the blind men and the elephant (in Chapter 1), analogy was used to describe the various parts of the large complex thing – an elephant. 'It's like a snake, . . . a fan, . . . a wall, . . . a rope' (Gray, 1998). You could use analogy to help you focus on a poorly defined research area and raise questions about it.

The suggestions described for raising a research question basically rely on two key factors:

- immersion in the context where the possible questions lie, and
- adopting a proactive, creative approach to identifying possible questions.

Robson also warns about possible pitfalls. These, he suggests, include avoiding non-meaningful questions – those that can't be answered by research, for example 'is there life after death?' and questions that have already been answered (you could gauge this to some extent through your Contextual Review). There are also areas of research and specific research questions, that might be considered highly inappropriate, for example raising ethical and moral issues, or possible infringements of human rights. Generally, these issues would be covered under the following categories: invasion of privacy, threats to dignity, exploitation of the vulnerable, public decency, intention to mislead, inappropriate use of technology, for example concealment of identity (on the internet), secret surveillance.

Ethical considerations

We would like to think that, in taking the decision to embark upon postgraduate research, you have:

- acknowledged that you don't know something, which is why you want to do some research in order to learn and discover new things;
- assumed a position of some humility – essential for learning anything;
- a genuine desire to carry out the research to the best of your ability with integrity and honesty;
- accepted the formal framework of academic research, complete with its ethical obligations.

If this is not the case, then stop now!

Ethics are general principles and rules of proper conduct – what one ought to do when conducting research. The most obvious contexts in which these issues arise are to be found in medical research, and researchers in these and related fields must conform to published codes of conduct or sets of principles. Academic institutions will have their own statement on research ethics, and research funding bodies, for example AHRB, usually require a response to any particular ethical issues that a research proposal might raise. There are many helpful references on research ethics that you could consult in developing your research proposal, for example Robson (1993, Box 2.4, p. 33, adapted from Kemmis and McTaggart, 1981, pp. 43–44); Booth *et al.* (1995). We briefly outline here some ethical considerations for research projects in Art and Design that necessarily involve people.

> . . . ethical dilemmas lurk in any research involving people. (Robson, 1993, p. 30)

Some projects simply cannot happen without the involvement of people, for example community arts development, user feedback in new product design, audience/artwork interaction and relationship, social interaction in design education, and so on. If your project requires the active participation of people then the following ethical principles should be adhered to.

Clarity of research framework and participants' involvement

- Make it clear from the start that you are conducting a research project for a particular purpose. Explain how you will operate as a researcher within the project, for example as a participant-observer, as a creative 'shaper', as a reflective practitioner. The issue here is that you are not the distanced observer wearing a white coat and goggles and that your participants are not 'lab rats'. Rather, together you are co-operatively developing understanding – described as 'democratic participation' (Hall, 2000).
- Discuss with your participants the kind of involvement that the project requires of them, for example the time/extent of engagement. Encourage them to be genuinely involved as creative participants, and value their input and feedback (however critical!).
- Respect the wishes of those participants who do not want to take part at any stage of the process. Take this opportunity to find out why – this could be useful research information, especially about the focus and design of your project.

Gaining permissions and access

- Make sure you have explicit (preferably documented) permission from those in authority to carry out certain aspects of the research, for example access to special archives or other bodies of sensitive information.
- Gaining permissions is essential if your research requires access to certain groups such as students on a course, the disabled, youth groups, and so on. If the research entails observation and visual documentation, be explicit about how this material will be used, for example for analysing the research and developing understanding. Ensure that your research does not exploit the participants in any way.
- Agree to keep the research material confidential until it needs to be communicated as part of the research findings. If necessary, agree to the anonymity of the participants.

Use of data/information resulting from participants' involvement

- Share your developing understanding of the research with your participants by regularly reporting progress. Get their feedback on this and integrate into the research anything that improves their accurate representation.
- Obtain permission from participants to include in research reports quotations from them or visual material in which they appear. They may wish to check this material before publication.
- In reporting your research findings, apply judgement and sensitivity so as not to misrepresent or misuse information with regard to participants (avoiding causing

offence or embarrassment). In any publication/public output, make sure you acknowledge people's participation and proper contributions.
- In designing any visualization of factual research material, for example diagrams, charts, graphs, and so on, make sure that the structure accurately represents the data (for further information see Booth *et al.*, 1995, pp. 255–258; Tufte, 1983).

Your research question (or questions) provides the basis of your project 'plan of work'. The research question can then be addressed by the use of appropriate methods for generating/gathering information, evaluating and analysing that information, and synthesizing and presenting information as research outcomes – responses to your research question.

Reflection and action: suggestions

- Identify four different kinds of research questions from completed research.
- Use these questions as a basis for developing, in your own words, a tentative research proposition for each of them.
- Suggest a few different metaphors and analogies through which you could frame your research problems.
- What kinds of ethical considerations might be raised by your research question?

3.2 METHODOLOGY REVISITED: POSSIBLE RESEARCH POSITIONS AND APPROACHES

In Chapter 1, the importance of having a broad appreciation of research methodology was described (see Section 1.3). Different philosophical approaches were described – positivism, post-positivism, critical theory, constructivism – and the development of a more 'artistic' research approach. Guba (1990) suggests that methodology is evolved through an awareness of what the researcher considers 'knowable' (what can be researched – what questions can be answered by research), and through an awareness of the nature of the relationship between the researcher (you) and the 'knowable'.

Section 1.3 described a series of emergent characteristics of practice-based research methodology. To recap:

- The kinds of research questions that have been asked embrace both positivist experimental ontological positions and constructivist interpretative and reflective ones, as well as invented hybrids involving a synthesis of many diverse approaches.
- The practitioner is the researcher, who identifies researchable problems raised in practice, and responds to these through practice (or aspects of it); the researcher's role is multifaceted: sometimes the generator of the research material; sometimes the self-observer through reflection and through discussion; sometimes the observer of others for placing the research in context, and gaining other perspectives; sometimes the co-researcher, facilitator and research manager, especially of a collaborative project.

- Characteristics of 'artistic' methodology are a pluralist approach and the use of a multi-method technique, tailored to the individual project. Methodology should be responsive, driven by the requirements of practice and the creative dynamic of the art/design work. It is essentially qualitative, naturalistic and reflective. It acknowledges complexity and real experience and practice – it is 'real world research', and all 'mistakes' are revealed and acknowledged for the sake of methodological transparency. Increasingly, this has involved the use of various media (and multimedia) to integrate visual, tactile, kinaesthetic, experiential data into 'rich' information. Projects can be collaborative and inter-disciplinary, either by design or necessity, and this may be as a result of the complexity of Art and Design research questions. It also demonstrates a willingness to examine other fields and make sensible connections. It requires an outward-looking attitude and an awareness of other research cultures and paradigms.

It is important to consider these issues and the implications they have for how you structure and describe your research project proposal.

Useful existing approaches to inquiry

There are various existing methodological approaches from 'new paradigm research'[1] which researchers in Art and Design have found productive and have adapted/extended for their own particular research requirements.

Naturalistic inquiry: an approach for real situations

As part of the development of post-positivistic research paradigms, Lincoln and Guba (1985) described a set of characteristics of what they termed '**naturalistic inquiry**'. This is suggested as a particularly appropriate research strategy where research happens in real situations rather than in laboratory controlled conditions (Robson, 1993, Chapter 3). Robson's table (Robson, 1993, p. 61) describes fourteen characteristics of naturalistic inquiry. These have been adapted for ceramic design research providing a helpful example of how an artist or designer can relate these concepts to practice-based research (Bunnell 1998, Methodology section 3.2.2).

In Figure 3.1, Bunnell interprets some of the key characteristics of naturalistic inquiry by using an engaging flower image as a metaphor for the 'natural':

- she equates the *natural setting* with the studio/workshop environment, where the researcher is at the heart of the research;
- she acknowledges the importance of intuitive *tacit knowledge* for artists and designers (similar to Schön's knowing-in-action – the kind of knowledge we have in doing something);
- practice-based methodologies are *emergent*, that is the research strategy grows and unfolds from the practitioner's interaction with the research question and context, and the research is grounded;

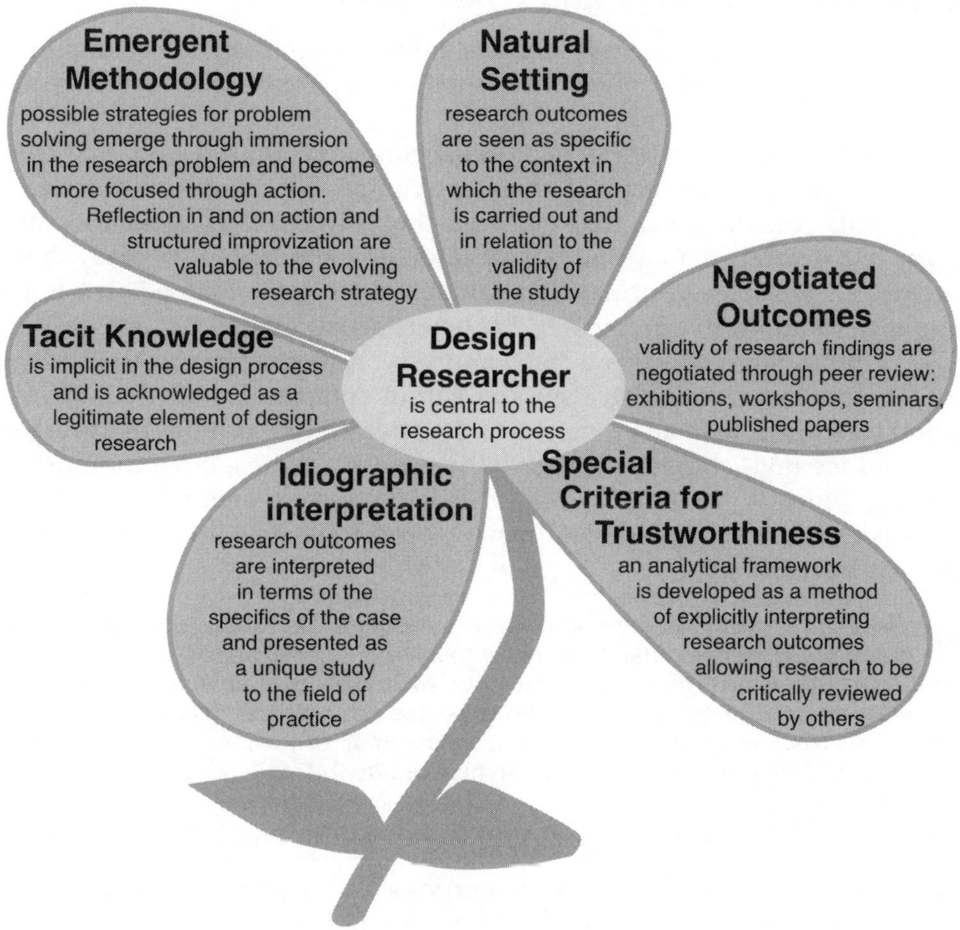

Figure 3.1 Characteristics of naturalistic inquiry (💻) (interpretation by Bunnell from Robson)

- the criteria for evaluating the research are generated again in relation to the research question and context – *special criteria for trustworthiness;*
- the research outcomes are interpreted as particular to the situation, and might only be generalizable in principle – *idiographic interpretation;*
- *negotiated outcomes* – critical assessment of the research can be carried out through peer review and meaning and value negotiated.

You may wish to think about how these characteristics might relate to your own research setting and develop a different interpretation.

The 'bricoleur': collage and construction

Brewer and Hunter (1989) suggest that qualitative research essentially employs a multi-method approach. By adopting a multi-method approach, the qualitative researcher uses a set of interpretative practices, and has been described as a 'bricoleur' – a kind of professional 'do-it-yourself' researcher! (Denzin and Lincoln, 1994, pp. 2–3. Their quotes are used extensively here because their description can hardly be bettered or paraphrased.) This does not mean that the researcher is in any way an amateur, haphazard or is any less rigorous than a counterpart undertaking quantitative study, but that the researcher '. . . produces a bricolage, that is, a pieced-together, close-knit set of practices that provide solutions to a problem in a concrete situation'. Neither does this mean that the use of multiple methods is a 'pick and mix' research strategy that mingles paradigms. The bricoleur works 'between and within competing and overlapping perspectives and paradigms' with an awareness of the research implications of those paradigms. The various methods chosen, adapted or invented are related, often forming a developmental set, which is coherent. By acknowledging that research takes place in the 'real world' – is complex and sometimes 'messy', open to change, interaction and development – the bricoleur uses:

> . . . the tools of his or her methodological trade, deploying whatever strategies, methods, or empirical materials are to hand . . . If new tools have to be invented, or pieced together, then the researcher will do this. The choice of which tools to use, which research practices to employ, is not set in advance. The choice of research practices depends upon the questions that are asked, and the questions depend on their context . . . what is available in the context, and what the qualitative researchers can do in that setting.

The outcomes of the research can be seen as a 'bricolage' – an emergent construction:

> The product of the bricoleur's labor is a bricolage, a complex, dense, reflexive, collage-like creation that represents the researcher's images, understandings, and interpretations of the world . . .

The notion of the bricoleur is an interesting one for researchers in Art and Design. It suggests that methodology is derived from, and responds to, practice and context, and the use of terms such as 'tools', 'collage', 'construction', 'reflection' and 'interpretation' are completely familiar to us as practitioners.

Action research: designed to make a difference

Some kinds of research in Art and Design have been called 'action research', or an interpretation of it. Originating in group dynamics and educational research, the definition of action research varies with time, place and setting; however, action research is situational – intervening, diagnosing and solving a problem in a specific real-world context, for example a school (McKernan, 1998). It requires the co-operation of the 'inhabitants'/participants of the potential action context, and is self-evaluative with modifications ongoing, where the application of the results is part of the methodology. Its aim is ultimately to improve practice in some way.

Action research has been applied in many different contexts, for example social reform, occupational therapy, urban planning, and also in Art and Design – specifically product design, human-computer interface design, space planning (ref. ARIAD search using the term 'action research'). 'Participatory action research' (PAR), as the name suggests, values and uses the 'lived experience of people' (Reason, 1994, p. 328) as a way of democratizing inquiry and in some cases empowering marginalized groups. In Art and Design research, this kind of approach has been used to investigate the use of new media to explore issues of inclusivity (Hall, 2000). Similarly, community development strategies (stemming from 'appreciative inquiry') have been used in research on the re-mapping of post-colonial land ownership and use (Renwick, 2003). Appreciative inquiry is an optimistic strategy for change that identifies the best of 'what is' to imagine 'what could be'. In early forms of action research, intervention might have been considered threatening or condescending, whereas appreciative inquiry encourages democratic participation, imagination and innovation, using a four-stage model of discovering, dreaming, designing and delivering (Cooperrider and Whitney, 1999).

Soft systems: understanding the complex whole

'Soft' systems methodologies (SSM) is derived from the domain of 'hard' information systems (usually computer-based) and was developed by Checkland (1981). SSM is concerned with improving problem situations and learning from the problem-solving process. It is a collaborative process that involves 'system' members/users in explorations of, and debate about, their system, which could be any kind of complex, changing situation or context. Taking a 'systems view' of something involves gaining a holistic understanding of the whole, as well as an understanding of the parts, and how these integrate into a whole. As a whole, properties of the system emerge which may not be obvious in examining the parts. SSM uses various visual techniques for mapping and communication, for example diagrams, graphs, pictures, animation, charts, and so on. These visualizations are known as 'rich pictures' (see Jayaratna, 1994, Chapter 10, p. 186).

Cornock's (1978) research, 'The concept of systems as a paradigm in the domain of the artist', was probably the first in Art and Design to involve a systems methodology. The study involved two commissioned interventions to explore the organization of the art world and people's 'tacit knowledge' of it. Other research projects in Art and Design have used 'soft' systems ideas, for example considering a bilingual publishing context and culture as a system; considering a 'framework' of safer practice for the printmaker as an integrated system, especially in relation to risk assessment.

Inquiry by design: design and research – parallel processes?

Zeisel (1984) in his book *Inquiry by Design* considers design itself as a mode of inquiry. The title suggests that inquiry is deliberately constructed to affect change or improvement, the subtitle is 'tools for environment-behaviour research'. He focuses on the design process in relation to the built environment – practitioners and researchers in architecture, planning and the social sciences. Zeisel suggests 'there is a close kinship between design images and research concepts, design presentations and research hypotheses, and tests in both disciplines'. Zeisel (1984, pp. 10, 14) sees the design inquiry process as having a spiral structure, in which empirical knowledge is developed as a result of 'imaging', 'presenting', 'testing' and 'reimaging'. This cycle might be likened to the research process of raising a research question and developing a working proposition; developing and presenting an argument; testing and evaluating it; and using feedback to develop further the thesis or revise it.

Similarly, Press and Cooper (2003) in their book 'The Design Experience' highlight the close relationship between the design process and the process of applied research:

> The commonalties are obvious in that both go through a process of identifying a problem, undertaking a series of steps to investigate that problem and provide a useful solution. Each step involves research or a process of searching for knowledge, which will inform all those stages of the creation process. Indeed for designers engaged in practice, design research is primarily about the process of searching in the three following areas. Searching for understanding . . . ideas . . . solutions. (Press and Cooper, 2003, p. 102)

They identify four basic categories of the design process: formulation, evolution, transfer and reaction, making the point that:

> Research, the designer's activity of searching and the design process are therefore interrelated and iterative, a constant process of learning and knowledge management. (Press and Cooper, 2003, p. 107)

We have also examined how 'artistic' models of inquiry have developed in both design and fine art practices, and suggest common factors between these and the generic research process (Gray and Malins, 1993).

There are interesting and imaginative connections to be made between recognized qualitative approaches and research involving practice through considering:

- the creative processes involved in both practice and research;
- the contexts for research – real situations that are usually complex and changing, requiring flexibility and responsiveness;
- an active approach using 'collage' and 'construction' to design a research project that will make a difference.

Reflection and action: suggestions

- Find an example of the use of 'naturalistic inquiry' in Art and Design research.
- Can you think of any other 'artistic/design' terms to describe what the 'bricoleur' does?
- Find an example of the use of 'action research' in Art and Design.
- In what ways might the 'systems' concept be useful to your research? If the concept is not relevant say why not?

3.3 STRUCTURING AND WRITING A RESEARCH PROPOSAL

The importance of a proposal

In undertaking any kind of research, whether a modest short-term project or a sustained long-term research for PhD, a clear project proposal is essential. The proposal is an important thinking and focusing tool, and a useful communication tool for discussing ideas with others, for instance potential collaborators and any group who may help generate/gather information. Not least, it is important for securing resources for your research, as potential funders/supporters need to be convinced of the viability, value and usefulness of the research.

It is common for any research proposal to go through several draft versions. Most PhD proposals take from three to six months to develop and be approved. Although this may seem like a long time it is not time wasted. Any researcher needs to carry out a certain amount of background research in preparation for actually undertaking any project. Furthermore, proposals are difficult to formulate by simply working alone. The process of discussion, draft, feedback, negotiation and revision is very much a peer group activity. This is an extremely useful process to engage in, as it is used in most professional contexts when considering the allocation of funding (for example arts councils, research councils, local enterprise companies, and so on).

In Chapter 1 we considered the standards and criteria for graduate study (see Appendix 1 and Appendix 2). Although broad and generic, these are valuable in helping to develop a research proposal of a standard appropriate for masters through to doctoral levels. Consider the kinds of competencies expected at each level and for each learning 'assessment domain', for example organization and planning. It would be sensible to ensure that the structure and content of your research project proposal enables you to demonstrate your learning in relation to these 'domains' (see Section 6.1). A careful consideration of criteria for postgraduate degree awards at this proposal stage should help to build in appropriate standards and quality.

Once a final version of your proposal is complete it provides you with a 'bearing', which helps you to remain 'on course' in the face of potentially distracting information and developments on the 'journey'. It also provides your supervisors and institution with a framework for monitoring and evaluating your project's progress. However, a proposal is exactly that – a projection – which is not set in stone. As your research progresses the proposal may necessarily need to be remodelled to accommodate shifts in your thinking and also important contextual factors, for example, newly published research, real-life circumstances. Again this reshaping can benefit from peer group feedback.

Finally, the proposal is extremely useful in providing an outline structure and content for a research report, a presentation, and the basis for another proposal for funding/support.

Possible structure and content of a research proposal

As with most things in Art and Design there is no definitive structure and content of a research proposal. However, any proposal should answer the basic questions what? why? how? so what?

If you examine various proposal proforma examples (for example the Arts and Humanities Research Board Research Grant scheme[2]) there are basic headings to which you should respond, for instance:

- project title, aim, objectives – what?
- rationale, context – why?
- methodology – how?
- outcomes – what's new?

Let us examine each of these in further detail.

Title of Research Project

Choosing an appropriate project title is not easy! The title is an extremely important element as it must convey very clearly the focus of the research. It is the first piece of information for project collaborators, participants and funders/supporters, and as such should not cause a furrowing of the brows! You could start with a working title that can be amended as the research develops. At the proposal stage, the working title should not be restrictive, that is make presumptions or be too specific. The specificity will develop as the research progresses and focuses.

Try to make the title describe the research accurately, for example *An Investigation of the Use of Multimedia for Practitioners in Art and Design*. This title provides at least four pieces of information:

(1) where the research is located, that is the sector Art and Design;
(2) who its users are, that is practitioners – fine artists and designers;
(3) identification of the content of the research, that is multimedia and its usefulness;
(4) suggests a purposeful and rigorous approach, that is an investigation.

Aim of the project

The aim – a single aim – should encapsulate your research question(s), for example in what ways could multimedia be useful to artists and designers? It also reflects a hunch (an untested belief, a proposition) that multimedia could have a profound impact on the ways in which visual practitioners develop and to show ideas and working process. The aim could be written as follows:

> This research aims to investigate how multimedia technology can enable practitioners to develop new working processes in order that visual practices might be enhanced.

This example aim also identifies what the element of innovation might be (new working processes) and what might be affected (enhancement of visual practices). The aim should also attempt to indicate the scope of the research if possible, for instance using parameters of time scale (common in historical research), reference to location/context, defining users/audience, drawing other relevant limits. It is crucial that the scope of the inquiry is feasible. The most common criticism of most research proposals (whatever the level) is that the aim is too ambitious (a life's work!) the scope is too wide (parameters/limits are not drawn tightly enough), and that, given the actual time available, the project is not viable.

Objectives

Objectives are specified actions that enable you to realize your aim. For instance, taking the example aim, we could suggest that we would need to:

- understand the use of multimedia in Art and Design to date in order to establish its use and value to date;
- investigate multimedia technology in order to gain an understanding of its benefits and limitations to practitioners;
- evaluate the use of multimedia technology with visual practitioners in order actually to experience how potential users might engage with the technology.

Objectives are usually sequential (but could be simultaneously carried out) and usually developmental, that is each one informs the others. Both the aim and the objectives should indicate purpose – 'in order to . . .'. It is advisable to limit your objectives to say three or four. A long list suggests that the scope, and therefore viability, of the project is unrealistic.

Rationale and context for the research

This section must present a convincing argument as to why the proposed research is required, and how it relates to the professional context. This could draw on a number of sources of information and evidence.

- Your own professional experience, knowledge and understanding of your context, which, whilst this may be derived from 'tacit' subjective knowledge, discussions with colleagues, and perhaps anecdotes, can suggest a 'hunch' and provide a personal rationale for the research. For example, your specific geographic location may be the starting point for a project on remote rural visual arts practices.
- Your Contextual Review should be providing you with the kind of 'objective' evidence essential for the establishment of an external and wider rationale for the research. This evidence should enable you to present a clear argument (with key references), answering the following questions:
  - Why is your proposed research needed? Who needs it?
  - Who else has addressed aspects of your proposed research and to what result?

- In what areas and in what ways could development/improvements be made?
- Who might benefit from and use the research (apart from yourself!)?

For any research proposal, the rationale should be concise. A good rationale should demonstrate that you have a viable relevant research proposition that can be developed into a realistic research project.

Plan of work

This section is the driver of your proposal. The plan of work should enable you to carry out your objectives in order to realize your aim. To reiterate, the scope of the project must be feasible, with clear parameters. It is useful to point out what the project does not attempt to cover and why.

Any project should take into consideration the actual time available, be it full or part-time study, a Masters level semester or several years for a higher degree (see Figure 3.2 for an example of a typical MPhil/PhD time scale). It is essential to work out the actual amount of time you can devote to the project, basing this on your personal circumstances and patterns of preferred study so far. Part-time research degrees are very common, so it is crucial to consider carefully how you will integrate the research with other work, family and various kinds of social obligations (Kember, 1999). Therefore any project should be realistically structured considering all these things.

Again there is no prescription for the plan of work, but it should answer questions such as 'how? who? when? where?'. It should include a strategic overview of the research project, with key milestones, related to your objectives. You need to identify, specifically for your project, the key points for the start and completion of various aspects of work, as well as key points for evaluating project progress. It is always helpful to visualize this by some kind of time chart, for example a Gantt chart or some other kind of time plan. This overview can then be broken down into 'nitty-gritty' information on month-to-month and/or even week-to-week tasks.

The plan of work should have a description of the general methodological approach and assumptions, for example inquiry through practice, the use of multiple methods, and so on (Figure 3.3). Whilst this would not be considered necessary in most other disciplines (because research methodologies are established and widely understood), in Art and Design it is still important to declare a methodological position. Within this 'position' statement your role and the roles of others should be briefly described, for example researcher as practitioner, collaborators, other participants. You may want to refresh your understanding of these issues by revisiting various sections in Chapter 1, and Section 3.2 in this chapter.

The main part of the plan of work must describe how the project objectives will be realized by the use of proposed research methods. For instance, let us re-examine the example objectives.

- To understand the use of multimedia in Art and Design to date in order to establish its use and value to date.

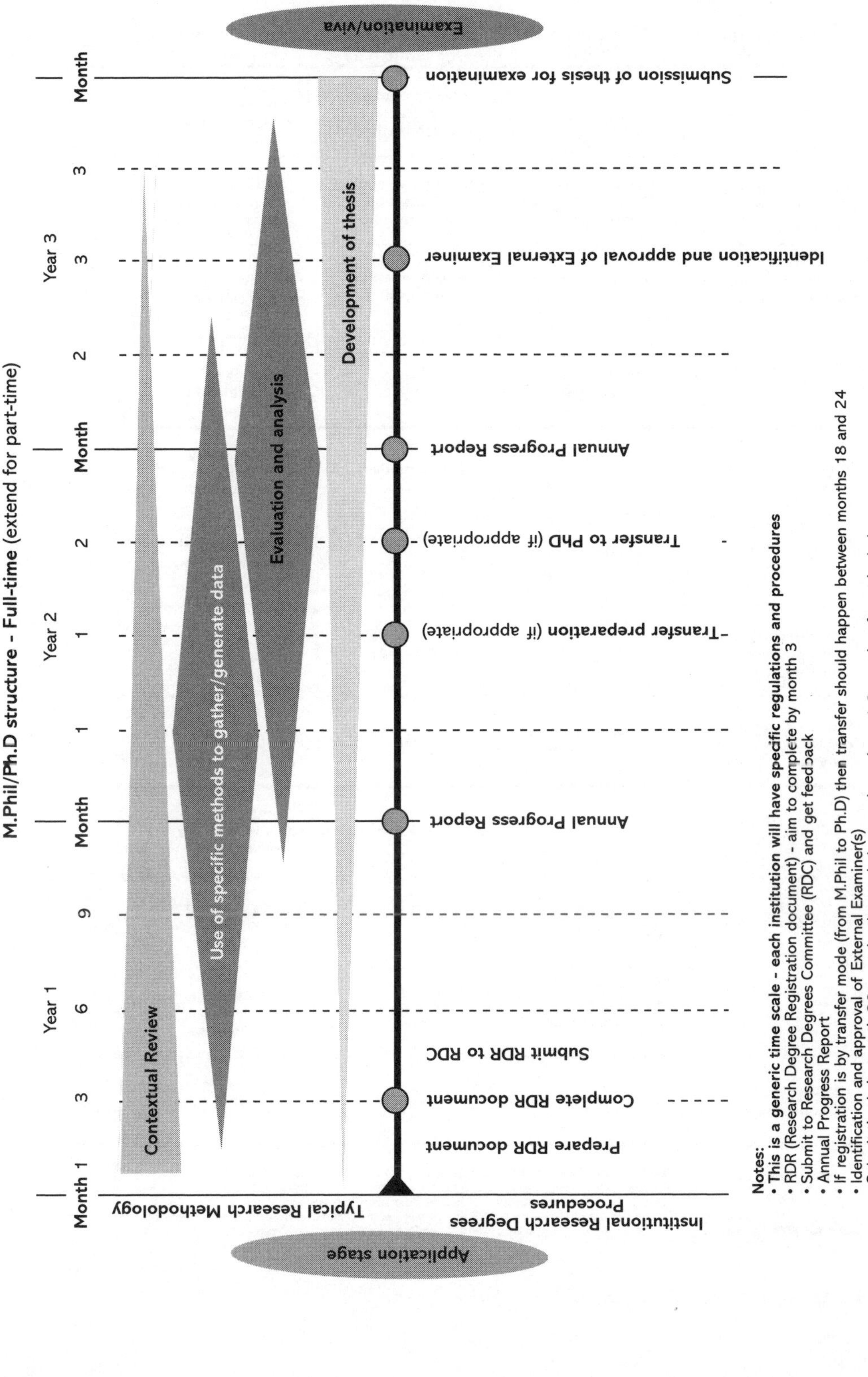

Figure 3.2 Typical time scale for MPhil/PhD study

Development of Thesis	Evaluation and Analysis	Use of specific Methods to gather /generate data	Contextual Review	TASKS / TIME
• outline argument		• search/survey - possible research methods	• search/survey - relevant material	1
• consider possible thesis formats	• search/survey - possible analytical approaches	• identify potential methods from existing research	• build bibliography / organize key reference material	3 (Year 1)
• evaluate completed thesis formats	• consider possible analytical strategies	• try out potential methods	• iterative mapping of key references	6
• outline structure of thesis	• evaluate potential methods		• critical review of key references	9
• refine argument		• use methods	• search/survey - to check for new developments	Month 12
	• evaluate outcomes from methods		• update critical review structured by argument	1 (Year 2)
• transfer stage (if appropriate) - summary of progress		• use methods		1
• submit transfer material - possible examination/viva	• evaluate outcomes from methods			2
• finalize structure of thesis		• final use methods	• search/survey - to check for new developments	Month 24
• finalize argument	• analysis of research outcomes		• update critical review of key references	2 (Year 3)
	• final analysis and conclusions		• final check on new relevant contextual info/literature	3
• colllate/conclude submission				3
Submission of thesis				Month 36

Preparation for Viva

Examination/viva

Notes:
Develop in conjunction with 'Typical MPhil/PhD structure' - Appendix 3 - and your institutional research degree procedures
Example tasks shown - replace with your own specific tasks and break down in detail
Remember research is not simple and linear - some tasks are interactive/simultaneous - this is a plan - it should be amended/updated as the research develops.

Figure 3.3 Example of a possible plan of work (💻)

If we ask the questions 'how? by what means?' we are prompted to propose specific methods 'to understand . . . ' by, for example, undertaking a literature/contextual survey and making a critical review, and carrying out a 'pilot' survey of multimedia practitioners as a means of orientating the research.

- To investigate multimedia technology in order to gain an understanding of its benefits and limitations to practitioners.

Again, asking the questions 'how? by what means?' we could 'investigate . . .' by, for example, using our own multimedia practice as a key research method, and/or by involving other practitioners in collaborative practice and as case studies.

- To evaluate the use of multimedia technology by visual practitioners in order actually to experience how potential users might engage with the technology.

Finally, asking the questions 'how? by what means?' we could 'evaluate . . .' by, for example, seeking the opinions of other practitioners through a survey questionnaire, and/or through structured interviews with practitioners, and/or by working directly with some of them as case studies.

Even though the objectives are laid out sequentially for the purposes of clarity, it is possible that the first two could be carried out simultaneously, and affect the development of each other. In interrogating the objectives we have arrived at a set of proposed methods:

- a literature/contextual survey,
- a critical review of the research context,
- a 'pilot' orientation survey,
- practice as a means of directly exploring and experiencing multimedia ideas and technology,
- collaborative practice with other practitioners to see how others use the technology,
- case studies involving practitioners,
- questionnaire for a range of multimedia users,
- structured interviews with 'expert' practitioners.

These particular methods were used in a PhD programme lasting several years. In a Masters level project, a more modest set of methods should be used. You must also consider the range of tasks associated with the use of each method. For instance, conducting a structured interview requires a considerable amount of preparation and post-interview evaluation and analysis. This might involve tasks such as identifying key questions, selection of interviewees, development of an interview schedule, organising the actual event, recording/documentation of the event, transcription of audio/video tapes/disks, content analysis, summaries. So realism must rule!

It is often the case that only when you get down to a sufficient level of detail do you realize that what you have proposed is scarily impossible! Then you know it's time to revisit your aim and objectives. Back to the drawing board!

Resources/support

As a consequence of the plan of work, questions will be raised as to how the research is to be resourced and supported. This is an essential part of any research proposal and keeps the aim of the project firmly in touch with reality! Most academic research projects supported by a research funding body (for instance the AHRB) require a detailed financial breakdown – costs for research staff, travel, consumables, outputs, dissemination, and so on. This level of costing may not be required for your research project, but it is essential that you consider the general resource implications in order to carry out your project.

Resource requirements might include negotiating access to facilities, for example, studio, workshop, specialist equipment, better IT resources, and so on. There may be costs associated with these, which providers might waive if they are acknowledged and their support credited in any dissemination of the research project findings. Likewise, you may need to draw on the expertise and experience of advisors, whose time may be precious (and possibly costly). You might also need to consider particular requirements for collaboration and participation, and you must remember to address any ethical considerations in your proposal. Usually the main 'costs' are time related, which, assuming there is a willingness to be involved in the research, most people are happy to donate. Usually, it is acceptable and courteous to feed back/share your research findings with advisors, collaborators and participants, as long as the research is not confidential; that is, in the case of it being supported by a particular commercial concern (your academic institution should have guidelines on Intellectual Property Rights and commercial sensitivity and confidentiality issues). There may be other resource issues specifically related to the nature of your project, for example specialist materials, travel, and so on.

In considering the resource implications, it may again be necessary to return to the drawing board and revise the aim and objectives accordingly! The key thing to keep in mind is the scope and viability of the project within your research time scale and your personal circumstances.

Probable outcomes of the research

It is almost impossible to state with any certainty just how the research will develop and what the outcomes will be. However, it is important to speculate – to have some kind of 'vision' of the desired outcomes, not least for considering any future research strategy. Obviously, the outcomes must relate to the project aim, and go some way to addressing your research questions. Let us return to our example aim.

> This research aims to investigate how multimedia technology can enable practitioners to develop new working processes in order that visual practices might be enhanced.

This example aim attempted to identify what the element of innovation might be – 'new working processes' – and what might ultimately be improved – 'enhancement of visual practices'. These are vague terms that clearly would need to be clarified in the process of carrying out the research. However, it is helpful to speculate just what 'new working practices' and 'enhancement of visual practices' *could* be. Perhaps multimedia could provide artists and designers with new ways of developing ideas, which bring together information from many diverse sources into a single working environment to make previously unrelated creative connections. Perhaps visual practices could be enhanced by the use of a multimedia environment as an analytical space, and as a powerful medium for presenting and communicating art and design methodologies.

An analysis of completed practice-based research (for PhD) reveals that there are usually outcomes beyond the stated aims. This tends to concern aspects of the development of practice-related methodology – development of these kinds of research strategies, adaptations of methods and innovative methodological tools.

It is also helpful to suggest how the outcomes might be physically realized. For example, through a body of art/design work (possibly peer reviewed), supported by an illustrated document (paper-based, multimedia, web), and/or other complementary materials.

Reflection and action: suggestions

- Discuss the 'quality standards' appendices with your supervisor(s) and how you might use them to develop your research proposal.
- Find some other examples of project aims, objectives, rationales and evaluate them in terms of the advice offered in this section.
- Make a draft plan of work and discuss it with your supervisor.
- Organise a 'peer review' session – with a colleague exchange your draft 'plans of work' and review each other's in terms of the advice offered in this section.

3.4 MANAGING RESEARCH PROJECT INFORMATION

A rigorous process

In Chapter 2, the importance of accurately capturing and properly managing information was stressed as being an essential part of the rigour of research (see Section 2.3). This rigorous approach to information management needs to be considered as part of your project plan of work. Chapter 4 will present information about a range of research methods that might be suitable for your project. However, it is helpful as part of your project proposal to consider possible methods of generating and gathering information, and to anticipate how that information can be organized efficiently, so that it can be used effectively as evidence for evaluation and analysis, and of course used in presenting your project outcomes as a coherent argument.

Both Orna and Stevens (1995, Chapter 4), and Hart (1998, Appendix 4, pp. 215–218) provide useful general advice for managing information. Here, more specific advice is offered in relation to managing project information involving practice.

Managing project information involving practice

It is likely that a range of different types of information will be acquired or generated during your research. If you can anticipate and prepare now, to some extent, what that might involve, then organizing, storing, retrieving and using the information can be made more manageable. Simple, but often overlooked, things can apply to all kinds of information management, and ultimately impact on time management and sanity! For example:

- an organized space conducive to action and reflection with a project map/strategic overview of the project, large scale calendar/diary marked with deadlines, meetings, and so on; wall and floor space for working and laying out ideas/results; storage and shelving;
- accessible and safe storage (using colour coded folders, lever arch files, box files, plan chests, filing cabinets, portfolios, slide wallets/slide library cases, digital equivalents to folders, and so on);
- accurate labelling for clear identification – topics, date(s), other 'locating' details, for example '1 of 6 related folders'.

Practice

If your practice, or aspects of it, is to be part of your research project, then you need to take great care in the documentation of it. If practice is part of your body of evidence from which to make research claims, then good quality documentation is essential. You will probably already have various tried and tested ways of managing information related to, or derived from, practice, for example studio 'tools' such as workbooks/sketchbooks, portfolios, 35 mm slide documentation, photographs, digital images, 3D models, material samples, scrapbooks, video and audio tapes/disks, magazine cuttings, reference materials, postcards, and so on. However, if this kind of information is to be used for research then it needs to be organized in a purposeful way in relation to the stages of the research process (see Chapter 4, Section 4.3) and the particular structure of your research proposal, for example information relevant as:

- background/introductory material,
- contextual material/evidence,
- information on the use of various methods and evidence from their use,
- information/evidence for evaluation and analysis,
- material for conclusions and discussion.

Colour coding project information

Colour coding information is a simple but helpful strategy for quickly identifying different types/sections of information. You may also want to consider using colour coding for 'tagging' different information and materials as they relate to different areas of your particular research project. For instance, if you have colour coded various thematic areas of your contextual review, then any new information can be colour coded and more easily related to the appropriate section.

Use of icons/symbols

In a similar way to coding project information by colour, you might develop your own set of icons or symbols. Bunnell (1998) used various icons in the analysis of her research to indicate information related to different groups of new technologies (see Figure 3.4).

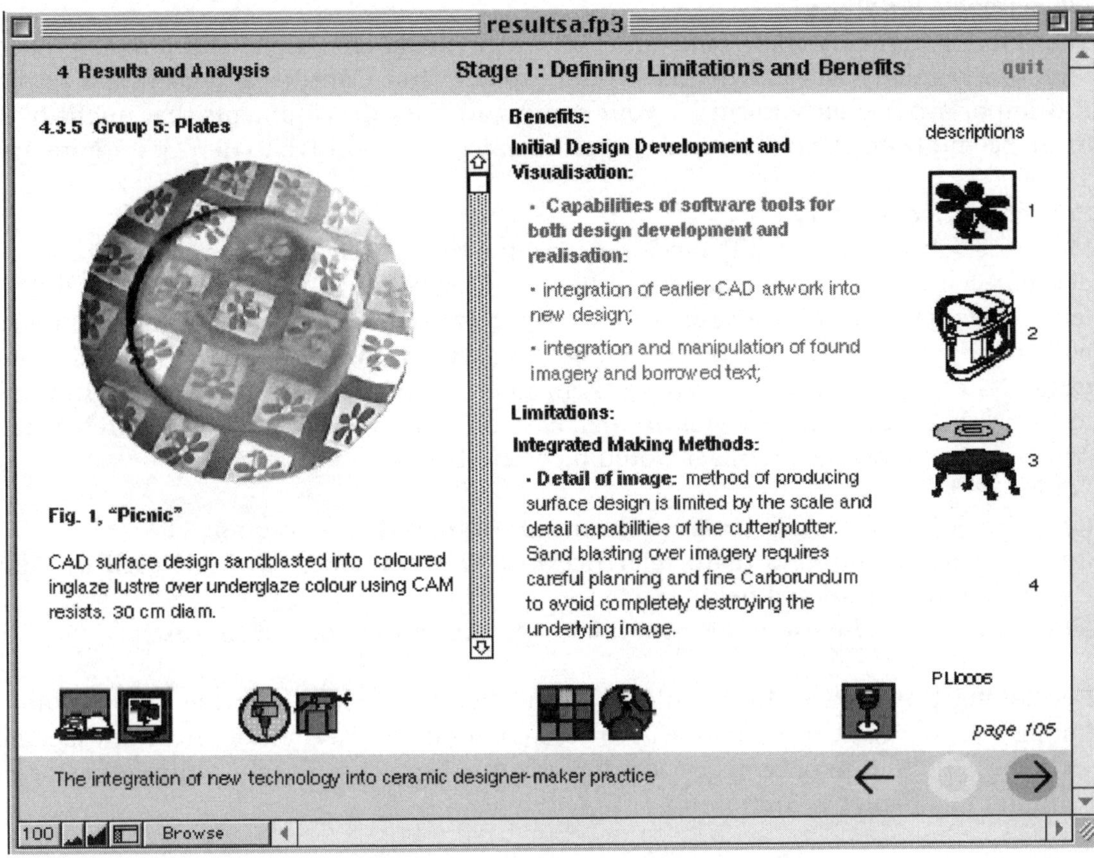

Figure 3.4 Example use of icons ( )
(Bunnell, 1998 – thesis in digital format)

Reflective Journal

Your journal (in whatever form it takes) should now be a key tool for planning, describing, evaluating, summarizing your thoughts and feelings about your research. (You might want to revisit Section 2.5 in Chapter 2.) Your reflective journal may contain different kinds of information. It can be an important device for storing studio/workshop activity information – an activity log; at other times it may function as a diary; it may also contain documentation of work in progress, in which changes and developments can be seen as we progress through the journal; it certainly should help you to contextualize your project, and link your ideas to those of other practitioners and researchers; and it could contain some indication of the pace and progress of your project. Although the journal may contain a diverse range of information, the value of having all the material in one place is very helpful when it comes to evaluation and analysis.

Bibliographic database

Your bibliographic database (and 'store' of other media references) will probably need revisiting regularly and may require you to update your Contextual Review as a result. It is important regularly to survey your context for new developments that might help to shape and reshape your research. Good research is responsive to new developments.

Project specific glossary

Most research projects usually need to define the terms used in the research in order to develop clarity and shared understanding. This may range from specialist/technical terms, new terms you have coined in a speculative sense to develop an idea, to those which are generally familiar but which are being used in a very specific sense in your research project, that is you are giving them a particular interpretation. You might want to think about developing a glossary database of terms specific to your research topic. As you come across new terms it would be useful to:

(a) find out what the dictionary definition is (if indeed there is one);
(b) give a few examples (with references) of how the term has been used in your research/professional field;
(c) say how you are using the term in the specific context of your research.

Developing this kind of information will be useful in communicating your research findings. It is not uncommon for the written component of a thesis to include a specific section on 'definition of terms'. (More information on sections of the written thesis can be found in Chapter 6, Section 6.2.)

Other databases

As your project progresses you will probably want to make new databases, for example for contacts and correspondence, resources, images/other media. Storing and managing information in a database allows for easy searching and retrieval of information, as well as the ability to group and re-group information – essential processes in evaluating and analysing your research project outcomes.

Software for managing research information

A number of useful software applications are available for the storage, organization and management of a range of digital information (including visuals/multimedia) and its subsequent analysis, for example Atlas.ti, HyperRESEARCH, NVivo. More information can be found at www.scolari.co.uk.

Proformas

Devising simple proformas can be a good way of storing and organizing notes on meetings, exhibition visits and other events. The use of a consistent structure can serve to remind you of your key objectives, as well as provide a means of comparing information from one similar event to the next. Again, this will be useful in evaluating and analysing your project information.

Visual devices

You will probably need to visualize your project ideas in a range of ways, for example mind maps, matrices, network displays, other diagrammatic devices and visualizations, posters as summary devices, PowerPoint sequences. (See references to Buzan, Tufte, Klee and various other references on mapping and visualization in Chapter 2 and Chapter 4.) These visual methods will be explored in more detail in subsequent chapters.

Documentation related to other research methods

For each particular research method you might use, there will be specific ways of capturing, storing, organizing and retrieving information (a range of methods is presented in Chapter 4). The use of photography, video and audio as methods of data capture, analysis and presentation requires careful attention.

- Photography – for research purposes the photograph alone is insufficient. It needs annotating – labelling and expanding with key information on who?, what?, when?, where?, why?, how? and so on. (For more information on annotation see Zeisel, 1984, Chapter 8; an example of an annotated photograph is included in Chapter 4, Section 4.3.)
- Audio/video recordings on tape/disks – again these need simple clear labelling, perhaps with a short summary of the content on the library case. Both kinds of recordings will usually need transcribing – verbatim transcription is a time-consuming task, but for most research absolutely necessary (more information on these media, especially in relation to interviewing methods will be included in Chapter 4).

Considering some of these information management issues as you develop your project proposal/plan of work will encourage you to anticipate, to some extent, task organization in relation to time management. If you look at Figure 3.3 you can see how various project tasks might need to be sequenced and distributed in time in order to be manageable and achievable so that things do not clash or pile up.

Reflection and action: suggestions

- Think about your information management skills. What aspects might you need to improve to ensure a more effective organization of research evidence?
- Devise a simple proforma/matrix for logging some aspects of your information gathering or research training, for example exhibition visits, seminars/events, meetings with supervisor(s).

Looking back on Chapter 3: locating your position

Once you have a clear overview of the terrain you are more likely to be able to clarify, hone and locate your particular research questions in relation to a space of potential contribution. The development of a 'good' question requires ethical and creative thinking. Bringing the questions into sharp focus helps to set limits/parameters for the research proposal and suggest ways to proceed.

In revisiting methodology, various new paradigm research approaches relevant to Art and Design are described. These may eventually be dismissed, however they offer up important ideas that could help shape an appropriate research approach: the notion of the natural and organic; the acknowledgement of the complexity and connectedness of reality; the excitement of action, design and creative construction; the value of lived experience and listening to stories as a way of making sense of the world; the optimism of appreciating what is best, turning problems into challenges; the responsibility of being sensitive and responsive to the research situation.

A research proposal is exactly that – a projection of a way forward. The naming of the journey (project title) and the destination (aim) are necessary declarations. The key steps/stages (objectives) and clear reasons for setting off (rationale) give some purpose. Sensible suggestions on how to proceed and the equipment required (methodology, methods and resources) make the plan seem more real and achievable. Speculation as to new ground and a different position (outcomes) spur us on. Having a detailed plan is, in some ways, comforting as long as we acknowledge that responsiveness is required to the unexpected twists and turns of the journey.

Many kinds of research evidence may be generated on the way. Some forethought should be given as to how this valuable material might be rigorously managed. Often very simple methods are the most effective and help to prevent lost luggage!

REFERENCES AND FURTHER READING FOR CHAPTER 3

References

Allison, B., Hilton, A., O'Sullivan, T., Owen, A. and Rothwell, A. (1996) *Research Skills for Students* (London: Kogan Page).

Brewer, J. and Hunter, A. (1989) *Multimethod Research: a Synthesis of Styles*, chapter 3 formulating research problems (Newbury Park, CA: Sage).

Booth, W. C., Colomb, G. G. and Williams, J. M. (1995) *The Craft of Research* (University of Chicago Press).

Bunnell, K. (1998) *The Integration of New Technology into Designer-Maker Practice*. PhD thesis, The Robert Gordon University, (on CD Rom) (Methodology, Section 3.4).

Buzan, T. (1998) *The Mind Map Book*, Chapter 12, Making Choices (useful for focusing) (London: BBC Books).

Checkland, P. (1981) *Systems Thinking, Systems Practice* (Chichester: Wiley).

Cooperrider, D. and Whitney, D. (1999) *Collaborating for Change: Appreciative Inquiry* (San Francisco, CA: Berrett-Koehler).

Cornock, S. (1978) *The Concept of Systems as a Paradigm in the Domain of the Artist.* M.Litt. De Montfort University Leicester (formerly Leicester Polytechnic).

Denzin, N. and Lincoln, Y. (1994) *A Handbook of Qualitative Research* (Thousand Oaks, CA: Sage).

Denzin, N. and Lincoln, Y. (1998) *The Landscape of Qualitative Research: Theories and Issues* (Thousand Oaks, CA: Sage).

Gray, C. (1997) Grow your own: evolving research at Gray's School of Art. CHEAD Conference, Edinburgh.

Gray, C. (1998) *Inquiry Through Practice: Developing Appropriate Strategies. No Guru, No Method? Discussions on Art and Design Research* (Finland: UIAH).

Gray, C. and Malins, J. (1993) *Research Methodology/Procedure for Artists & Designers, Principals and Definitions* (Winchester School of Art).

Guba, E. (1990) *The Paradigm Dialog* (Thousand Oaks, CA: Sage).

Hall, R. (2000) *Practising Inclusivity with New Media: Young People, Digital Technology and Democratic Cultural Participation.* PhD thesis, University of Central England.

Hart, C. (1998) *Doing a Literature Review,* Appendix 4, pp. 215–218, Diagrammatic overview of devices for managing information (London: Sage).

Jayaratna, N. (1994) *Understanding and Evaluating Methodologies,* Chapter 10, Critical evaluation of 'soft' systems methodologies (London: McGraw Hill).

Kember, D. (1999) Integrating part-time study of the research with family, work and social obligations, *Studies in Higher Education,* Vol. 24, No.1 p 109–124.

Lincoln, Y. and Guba, E. (1985) *Naturalistic Inquiry* (Newbury Park, CA: Sage).

McKernan, J. (1998) *Curriculum Action Research: a Handbook of Methods and Resources for the Reflective Practitioner,* Chapter 1 (London: Kogan Page).

Orna, E. and Stevens, G. (1995) *Managing Information for Research,* Chapters 4 and 5 (Maidenhead, Berkshire: Open University Press).

Press, M. and Cooper, R. (2003) *The Design Experience: the Role of Design and Designers in the Twenty-first Century* (Aldershot: Ashgate).

Reason, P. (1994) Three approaches to participative inquiry, in Denzin, N. and Lincoln, Y. *Handbook of Qualitative Research* (London: Sage).

Renwick, G. (2003) *Spatial Determinism in the Canadian North: a Theoretical Overview and practice-based response.* PhD thesis, University of Dundee.

Robson, C. (1993) *Real World Research: a Resource for Social Scientists and Practitioner Researchers,* Chapters 1 and 15 and Appendix A, Writing a Project Proposal, pp. 464–469 (Oxford: Blackwell).

Schön, D. (1993) Generative metaphor: a perspective on problem-setting in social policy, in: A. Ortony, *Metaphor and Thought,* 2nd edn, chapter 9 (Cambridge University Press).

Tufte, E. (1983) *The Visual Display of Quantitative Information* (Cheshire, Connecticut: Graphics Press).

Zeisel, J. (1984) *Inquiry by Design: Tools for Environment-behaviour Research* (Cambridge University Press).

Suggested further reading

Bell, J. (1993) *Doing Your Research Project.* Chapter 2, Planning the Project (Maidenhead, Berkshire: Open University Press).

Cohen, L. and Manion, L. (1994) *Research Methods in Education,* Chapter 9, Action Research (London: Routledge).

McKernan, J. (1998) *Curriculum Action Research: a Handbook of Methods and Resources for the Reflective Practitioner,* Part 1, Curriculum Action Research, Chapter 1, Action Research – Historical and Philosophical Background (London: Kogan Page).

Orna, E. and Stevens, G (1995) *Managing Information for Research,* Chapter 4, Keeping the Record Straight: Documenting the Research; Chapter 5, Managing the Time Available (Maidenhead, Berkshire: Open University Press).

Research Training Initiative (1996) *Research Guide: Designing and Managing a Research Project* (Birmingham Institute of Art & Design, University of Central England).

NOTES

1. Denzin and Lincoln's (1998) *The Landscape of Qualitative Research* provides an excellent summary of recent developments in 'new paradigm research', including chapters on critical theory, cultural studies, and feminist research methodologies.
2. Application proformas for this and other schemes can be downloaded from www.ahrb.ac.uk.

4 Crossing the terrain: establishing appropriate research methodologies

CHAPTER OVERVIEW

4.1 A CASE FOR VISUAL INQUIRY

Leonardo – visual researcher

> The eye, which is said to be the window of the soul, is the primary means by which the 'sensus communis' of the brain may most fully and magnificently contemplate the infinite works of nature. . . . Now, do you not see that the eye embraces the beauty of all the world? The eye is the commander of astronomy; it makes cosmography; it guides and rectifies all the human arts; it conducts man to the various regions of this world; it is the prince of mathematics; its sciences are most certain; it has measured the height and size of the stars; it has generated architecture, perspective and divine painting. Its excellence places it above all other things created by God. (Notebook extract by Leonardo da Vinci (circa 1500), in: Kemp, (1989, Chapter 8, p. 116)

Leonardo provides us with an excellent model of a 'practitioner-researcher', who used visual thinking to consider a wide range of problems in fields as diverse as fluid dynamics, mechanics, anatomy, botany, ballistics, town planning, optics, and so on. His notion of art – 'arte' – meant skill, while that of science – 'scienta' – meant knowledge, and he considered both to be interdependent.

From initial observations – a classic research method – he developed his responses to problems through sketches – organizing, analysing and shaping thought. These sketches were called 'pensieri' ('thoughts' in Italian) – thoughts made visible by drawing and enhanced by annotated comments – descriptive, analytical comments and poetic reflections demonstrating a dialogue with himself, and also communicating to others through their clarity and elegance. His drawings in notebooks/sketchbooks display a concern for the following:

- detail, accuracy and analysis,

- understanding of structure and form,
- exploration of function and interaction,
- sensitivity towards the nature of phenomena and materials, and their characteristic qualities,
- dynamic expression and composition,
- appropriate use of media – pen, chalk, wash, and so on,
- correction, reformulation and sometimes contradiction of an earlier idea, resulting in a build-up of information over a number of years, evidencing a consistent investigative process.

The 'pensieri' completely lack self-consciousness; they are rigorous, honest, and display a passion for knowledge, integrity and humility crucial for any kind of real research. We can smile now at his attempts at understanding optics and fluid dynamics, but at the time they were incredibly adventurous visualizations of what could not be seen – the invisible – and a real attempt at inquiry using visual tools. Leonardo's sketchbooks, drawings, models and writings represent, perhaps, the first coherent example of what might be called a 'visual research methodology'.

Almost all disciplines – Physical and Natural Sciences, Social Sciences, Humanities, Creative and Performing Arts – use visuals in some way to:

- gather and/or generate data,
- organize, describe and communicate ideas,
- explain or understand a phenomenon or situation,
- propose and persuade,
- evaluate, analyse and interpret,
- resolve and communicate findings.

Many scientists, for example Faraday, Einstein, Feynman, as well as (quite naturally) visual artists, are familiar with the processes of visual thinking. However, no one has perhaps done more to investigate and legitimize visual thinking than the psychologist Rudolf Arnheim (1969, 1986) whose main concerns are epistemological in nature, exploring how the mind interfaces with the world of reality. Visual perception and, by extension, visual thinking is considered by Arnheim as the 'dominant instrument' of this exploration. He suggests that all truly productive thinking takes place in the perceptual realm. Perceptual thinking tends to be visual, vision being the only sensory mode in which spatial relations can be represented with sufficient precision and complexity. It is this concern for adequately expressing complex phenomena, ideas and relationships that drives researchers in the visual arts to consider the potential of multi-sensory/ multi-media methods in their modes of inquiry.

'In the beginning was the word . . . '

Historically, research (for a PhD and the presentation of the thesis submission itself) has been dominated by the written word. Although visuals are widely accepted in a supportive role in the thesis, they remain very much as illustrations for concepts in the text, and are rarely used as a primary means of expression. One might say that this is hardly surprising as the visual could be open to wide interpretation and ambiguity, and text is considered to be more precise than visuals (Ziman, 1978).

However, the sole use of written language for many disciplines is restricting: it is 'language doing the work of eyes' (Tyler, 1986 (anthropologist) in: Clifford and Marcus, 1986, p. 137) or ears for that matter. Inevitably when an idea is translated from one medium to another it loses some of its meaning and power. The verbal description of a Mozart symphony is obviously qualitatively different from hearing the actual music. The closer one can get to the medium of the original idea or experience the more likely it is to have impact and meaning. The word 'idea' is closely related to the Greek verb 'to see' – how often do we say 'see what I mean'?

Certainly part of PhD training must be concerned with the skills of clear and concise expression, yet the written medium is only one form, and the ability to communicate verbally and visually are equally important. However, we have yet to experience and be convinced by a purely visual argument. The 'self-explanatory' object/artefact constituting a complete research report remains a challenge (Friedman, 2002). On the other hand, the inclusion of different kinds of visual evidence as components of an argument is entirely reasonable.

New technologies, new research paradigms

The development of technology has led us to a point where we are inundated with instruments and devices that allow us to sense, experience, collect, store, analyse and communicate far more information than ever before. The vast range of 'tools' for investigation has expanded the range of existing research methodologies and methods, and made possible new ones.

Through technology and our creativity, we are able to perceive new kinds of information: we can make the invisible visible (Gleick, 1988). Technology is capable of dealing with large volumes of data from a range of media; data from diverse sources can be manipulated and processed in complex and relational ways, into a range of visual and audio outputs; through digital processing, data can be enhanced, replayed and interrogated. Data can be transformed into 'rich' information. For example the use of powerful computers enabled the development of the sciences of Complexity (Waldrop, 1994), revealing their visual and dynamic nature (Figure 4.1).

The development of the media and communications technologies impacts on how we interact with each other, encouraging a closer and more involved interaction. This, in turn, impacts on how we do research, especially into human inquiry. In the Social Sciences, 'alternative' research paradigms (Lincoln and Guba, 1985) celebrate this communication and involvement with the 'subject' rather than the traditional scientific distanced observation of the 'object'.

Our task as researchers in the visual arts is to try and develop more appropriate research methodologies: this will not be accomplished without risk, without error, but certainly will not be accomplished by repetition and regurgitation of orthodoxy.

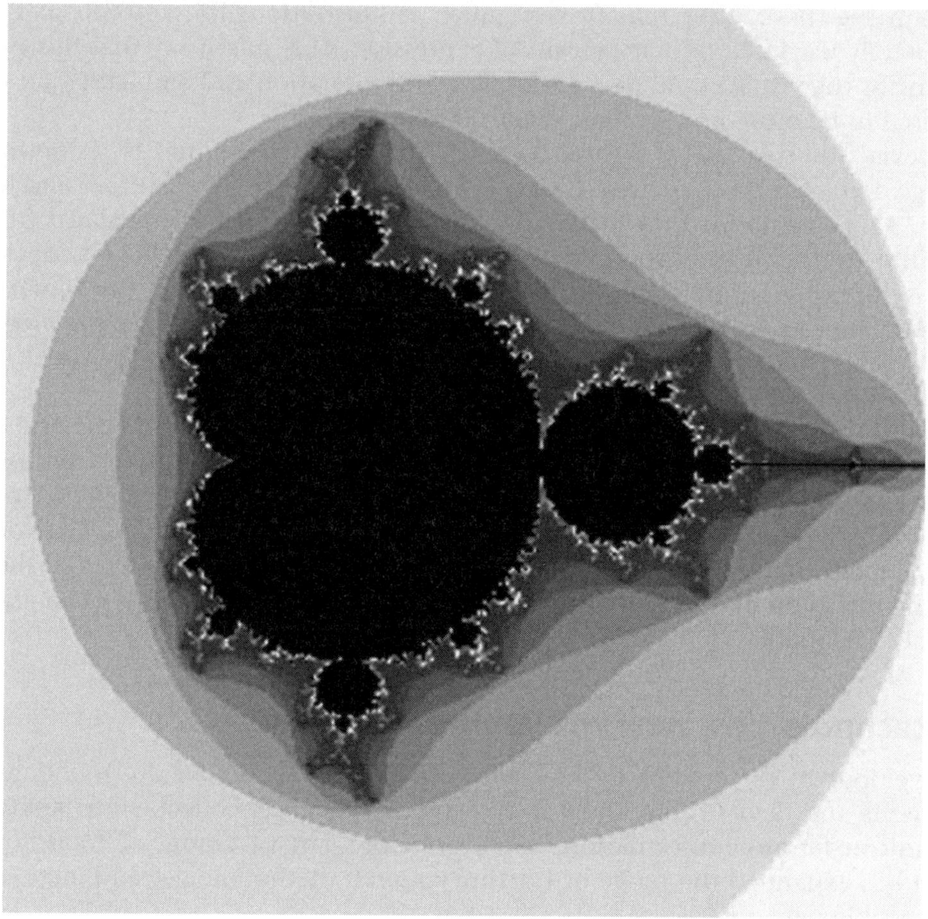

Figure 4.1 Fractal image

Einstein recommended a research strategy of 'loose opportunism', and Feyerabend (1988) reinforces this:

> For what appears as 'sloppiness', 'chaos', or 'opportunism' . . . has a most important function in the development of those very theories which we today regard as essential parts of our knowledge. These deviations, these errors, are preconditions of progress. . . . Without 'chaos', no knowledge. Without a frequent dismissal of reason, no progress' (Feyerabend, 1908, p. 164)

Research methodologies should take advantage of current cultural contexts and technologies. This can help us to extend the range of existing methods – to use multi-media, multi-sensory methods. Galileo invented the telescope so he could see further, explore further, extend knowledge – if a research tool is required why not invent it? As researchers we should be concerned about conveying information in the most accurate and convincing way, and not necessarily settling for the next best thing – the word.

Implications for research

The argument in this topic has been for a wider acceptance of the visual in the research process, especially for researchers in the visual disciplines, but also in others where it might be appropriate, for example engineering, information sciences. The logical conclusion to this is the development of a more visual research methodology, and an accessible range of visual or 'artistic' methods in response to a growing need for alternative research paradigms. Ironically, it has taken 500 years since Leonardo's poetic plea for the visual to be seriously considered as a powerful potential research methodology, and without doubt, given the historic time scale for the development of research methodologies, it may take another 500 years for a visually oriented research methodology to be fully realized.

However, 'without "chaos", no knowledge.'

Reflection and action: suggestions

- Identify three quotes about 'visual' issues relevant to research.
- Identify some examples of people who have made a contribution to knowledge through a visual approach. How have they achieved this?
- What do you think are the benefits and limitations for research in adopting a visual research methodology?

4.2 DATA, EVIDENCE, CLAIM: THE BASIS FOR ARGUMENT

In Chapter 2 we explored the idea of 'argument' – convincing others of your view. We examined Toulmin's structure of argument:

- a claim – an arguable statement,
- evidence – data used to support the claim,
- warrant – an expectation that provides the link between the evidence and the claim,
- backing – context and assumptions used to support the validity of the warrant and evidence.

Therefore, a research argument must be based on claims that can be supported by evidence. Evidence is gathered and/or generated by the application of appropriate research methods in the particular research context. Evidence can be defined as:

> information, whether in the form of personal testimony, the language of documents, or the production of material objects, that is given to establish the fact or point in question. *New Collins Concise Dictionary of the English Language* (1986)

Information is composed of data – that which is given (Latin 'dare' – to give). Data (plural, singular 'datum') only become information when used, questioned and interpreted in particular contexts. Context gives meaning – think about Duchamp's *The*

Fountain. The context in which the evidence is being used is important, as what counts as evidence in one particular context may be unacceptable in another. Any evidence must be carefully examined and its relevance to the particular argument considered.

Different kinds of research methods can use and/or generate different types of data: for example, an audio interview may yield personal opinions, attitudes and beliefs; an archival search, a set of texts or statistics; an archaeological dig, objects of material culture; practice, a body of art/design work. Different types of data can provide different kinds of evidence which, when seen as a whole, can provide a 'rich picture' of the issue being investigated. However, we cannot assume that when all the evidence is brought together the research question can be neatly and simply resolved. In discussing 'varieties of data', Coffey and Atkinson state:

> The more we examine our data from different viewpoints, the more we may reveal – or indeed construct – their complexity. We encourage the exploration of alternative strategies precisely in order to encourage the recognition and exploration of such complexity. We thus reject what might be called vulgar triangulation while endorsing a sensitive approach to complexity and variety. (Coffey and Atkinson, 1996, p. 14)

This suggests that we need to be open minded and critical about evidence, recognizing that whilst there may be corroborating evidence, there may well be conflicting or ill-fitting information. Disappointing and difficult though this may be, it is essential that this be acknowledged and discussed, and some sense made of it. In some situations there may be an opportunity to try out another research method, or to take the findings back to participants/collaborators for discussion. It is far more important to understand and acknowledge the complexity of a research issue than try uncritically to 'paper over the cracks' of a less than perfect investigation!

Primary and secondary data

There are two kinds of data – primary and secondary – both of which may be used together as evidence for constructing a research argument. Secondary data already exist, are usually publicly available and have probably already been processed in some way, for example archive texts which may have been interpreted in different contexts; statistics applied to support various arguments; art/design collections that have been classified in 'periods' or movements ('isms'). With secondary data, it is sometimes difficult to take a fresh view of the material because of the convincing arguments that have already been made. However, the whole point of making research data available (whether primary or secondary) is so that different analyses and interpretations can be made by others (this is the function of appendices in a thesis). It is entirely possible that an independent and original contribution to knowledge can be made by the reinterpretation of existing data (see Chapter 6, Section 6.1).

Primary data are those discovered or generated as a result of the application of research methods. Primary data are sometimes 'raw', provide only a partial view, and are possibly incomplete, for example fragments of ancient pottery, experimentally generated scientific data, opinion polls, design prototypes. It could be said that primary data are more 'risky' because they are new (that is, they have been discovered or created) and have not been subject to scrutiny beyond the particular research project. This is why it is essential that the discovery/generation of this kind of data needs to be very rigorously developed and documented (perhaps using different media) and described in detail through some text. Without this degree of rigour, its value as an authentic credible 'data set' open to the scrutiny and possible use by other researchers (transferability) is jeopardized.

Good quality data, derived by the rigorous application of appropriate research methods, are the bedrock of any research argument. For both primary and secondary data, it is important to be critical of their authenticity and dependability, taking consideration of their source and context, and, with secondary data, how they might have been previously used. A flawed argument will usually have 'feet of clay'!

Reflection and action: suggestions

- Within your research project, what is your argument?
- What are the claims on which it is based?
- What existing and/or emerging evidence is there to support your claims?
- What data are there which can be used as evidence?

(You may only be able to answer the last two questions towards the end of your research project.)

4.3 CROSSING THE TERRAIN: VEHICLES FOR EXPLORATION

Some journeys are straightforward – hop in a plane and land at your destination, almost oblivious to the landscape you have crossed. Others are more difficult, especially if you do not know exactly where you are going, and want to see and experience as much as possible en route. The journey of research is rarely straightforward: the destination is usually not clearly fixed, although you have a proposed route; the terrain you encounter may make you alter your route and may require you to travel using several modes of transport and various forms of all weather gear!

Your research project proposal shows your route across the terrain of your chosen research area. In this chapter, we will introduce a range of appropriate research methods to gather and generate information to help you address your research question.

Stages of the research process and relevant methods

In Chapter 1 we described the typical stages of the research process (Figure 4.2). Here, we consider how various visual methods might be used in each stage (see Sections 4.3 and 5.3 for details of methods). We acknowledge of course that some methods can be used in all stages, for example mind mapping. Some tools can be used in different ways at several stages, for example photography and video can be tools for acquiring data, for analysing information, and for presenting findings.

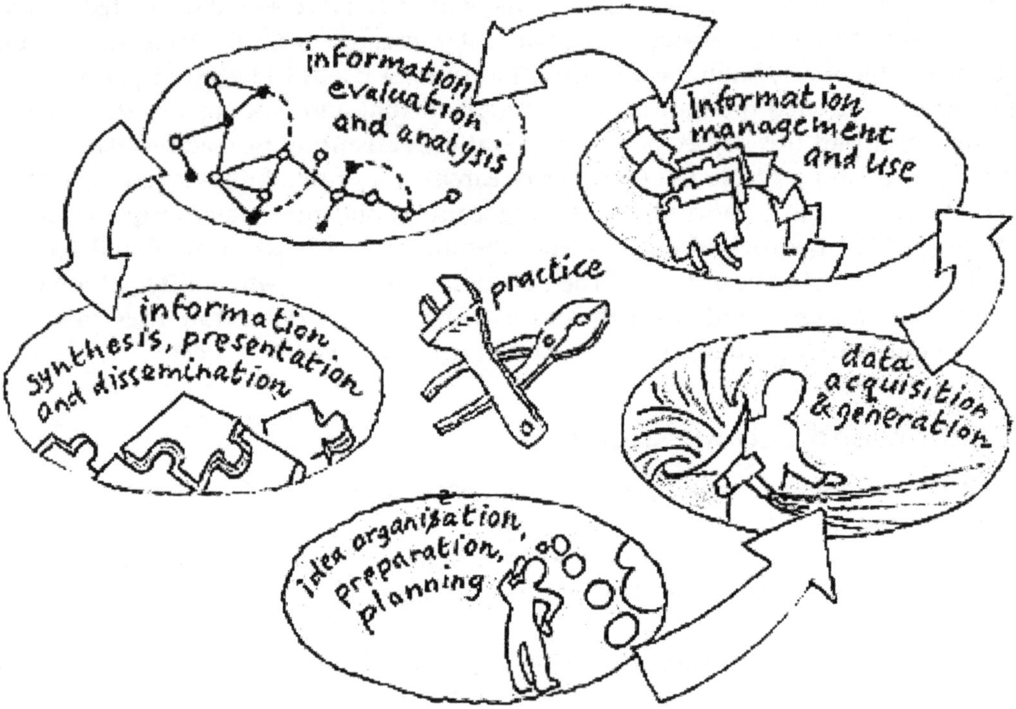

Figure 4.2 Stages of the research process – overview (💻)
(the multimedia version of this unpacks each stage to suggest various visual/creative methods)

- Idea organization/research planning and preparation – visual thinking, mapping and projection techniques (what if?), for example concept maps, flow charts, story boards.
- Data acquisition and generation – observation/generation and capture, for example objective and expressive drawing, diagrams, notation/annotation, photography, video, sound, 3D sketching/modelling, archives, web searches.
- Information management – electronic and/or paper-based storage and 'tagging'/coding, for example databases (relational/linked), card indexes, visual classification/taxonomy, colour/shape/size/symbol, sketchbook/workbook, reflective journal.
- Information evaluation/analysis – assessing value/worth and making sense (through pattern recognition), for example graphs, charts, matrices, networks, arrays showing the relationship of variables, for instance space, time, change, scale, development, and so on; photography, video, sound; aesthetic evaluation techniques (semantic differential, multiple sort); multidimensional measurement and analysis (for example cluster analysis); personal construct maps; visual impact analysis.
- Information synthesis, presentation and dissemination – making a credible accessible argument, for example overview visuals, multimedia (integration/juxtaposition of various media), structure/format of thesis responsive to content; dissemination/public outputs, for instance exhibitions, catalogues, papers, artefacts, conference presentations, performances, web-based outputs, and so on.

In developing your specific project proposal and the various stages of investigation, you will have considered various examples of methodologies and methods used in other research, especially through your Contextual Review. This information is important in the 'design' of your research methodology and the methods employed within it – for this is a design task. Think of it as a piece of work – a composition: it has an overall structure, and elements within it that must work independently, and work well together as a whole. Just as in the development of any composition you will need to try things out, evaluate them and make some preliminary sense of them, and maybe alter things. This process of 'piloting' is extremely important for checking the appropriateness of individual methods and your general methodology. A few hours spent doing a 'dry-run' with a particular method will be time well spent, and should prevent problems later.

Depending on your project proposal, it is likely that you will need to employ several research methods to realize your objectives. In Chapter 1 we briefly considered some research methods that have already been validated both in formal research in Art and Design, and in other disciplines, for example Social Science. However, it is essential that your specific research context and particular circumstances finally suggest which methods are appropriate.

Vehicles for research: existing 'wheels'!

In the more established research areas of Science and Social Science, researchers can usually select from a range of validated methods, again depending on their particular paradigm of inquiry and the research proposition. For instance, in quantitative research, a controlled scientific experiment in laboratory conditions involving pre- and post-testing may be appropriate; in qualitative research, anthropological fieldwork involving a case study of a particular social episode may provide the most relevant outcomes. These methods are likely to yield useful data for those particular research contexts respectively, data capable of being analysed and interpreted.

Sometimes an established method might need to be adapted or extended in some way to meet the needs of a different or unusual research situation or context, for example the re-contextualization and modification of 'action research' for research involving practice in Art and Design (Prophet, 1995). In the case of adapting/extending a particular established method, it is essential to acknowledge and describe the context in which that method has been used, and in what ways you are adapting it and why, for example the re-casting of 'case study' to involve the entire commissioning process for site-specific artwork (Wheeler, 1996).

Finally, in the tradition of 'methodological trailblazing', a completely new method or tool might need to be invented and developed. For instance, Galileo invented the telescope in order to gain new and more reliable evidence about astronomical matters (Feyerabend, 1988, pp. 84–86); the educational researchers Edwards and Westgate (1987) invented 'bubble dialogue – a novel technique for capturing dialogue and reflection in role-play situations (Cohen and Manion, 1994, pp. 215–218).

Vehicles for research: inventing new 'wheels' for artists and designers!

In the absence of an established and validated set of research methods in Art and Design, we have had to be similarly adaptive and inventive; for example, a participatory 3D 'game' as a means of externalizing teaching styles (Gray, 1988); experimental object making in exploring issues of 'chance' and 'choice' in sculpture (Watson, 1992); site-specific commissioned artworks for investigating the feasibility of architectural ceramics (Wheeler, 1996); curation of a major exhibition on interactive art, and the production of an interactive artwork in order to allow the audience/user direct experience of the research concepts (Graham, 1997). Although these methods have been adapted or invented and may appear idiosyncratic they have been validated, at least within the framework of formal research, and in most cases with user groups. They have all been carefully documented and described, and some of them applied in other research, for example use of exhibition projects (Silver, 1999), participatory action research (Ross, 2001), use of experimental object making (Bunnell, 1998). New methods, as with any new product design, need to be used widely in different contexts and their rigour and robustness tested in order to become a validated research tool.

In summary, the critical considerations for the application of any research method are that the method should be:

- responsive to the research context and appropriate for use in it (relevant and ethical);
- valid – acceptable to other researchers; useful in reality; meaningful to users within a particular context ('internal validity'); wherever possible generalizable to wider contexts ('external validity'); as dependable and trustworthy as possible (for details on these issues please see Robson, 1993, part 2, pp. 66–75);
- used with the utmost rigour (applied consistently, with discipline and care);
- documented and described thoroughly and clearly in any report of the research, so that it might be usable by other researchers (accessible, explicit and transparent).

Crossing the terrain: some useful research methods

To date, there is no definitive published single source on research methods for artists and designers. The following methods are drawn from a range of sources, most importantly from validated completed formal research in Art and Design (main sources: ARIAD – www.ariad.co.uk; British Library's Index to Theses – www.theses.com, Higher Education institutes' published information), as well as useful examples of research projects in non-formal frameworks (for example, industry, commerce, education, and so on) as reported in various journals and professional publications. An examination of some of these examples would no doubt lead to 'classic' references to various 'design methods' publications by, for example, Archer (1965), Jones (1980), Cross (1984), and so on; and important research by Cornock (1978, 1983, 1984) on Fine Art methodology. During recent years, many more examples of practice-based research have become accessible. Many have already been cited in previous chapters and more are cited in this one.

These methods are particularly useful if your own practice forms part of the research methodology.

Other methods described come from Social Science research, for example www.sosig.ac.uk (accessed 15 August 2003); Denzin and Lincoln (1994); and some specifically from educational research, for example Cohen and Manion (1994), McKernan (1998). These are particularly relevant for human inquiry related to Art and Design, for example the study of an individual's practice, and user feedback for designed products. In some circumstances, particular areas of design, for example industrial design, a more scientific approach may be appropriate, in which case 'design methods' may be useful. Documented examples of projects using design methods can be found in the journal *Design Studies* – www.elsevier.nl/locate/destud (accessed 16 June 2003).

The range of methods outlined is by no means definitive or completely comprehensive, and they cannot be described here in any great detail. If you think that a particular method described in this book would be useful in your project then you should discuss it with your supervisor. You should always follow up the references and examples given in order to appreciate the context in which the method was used. As you become more familiar with various methods you will realize the kind of tasks involved in applying them. Once you have identified these tasks, build them into your plan of work. Research methods development relies on researchers (including you!) adding further detail and modifying as a method is tried and evaluated.

The methods information is presented in tabular format and follows a pattern:

- Definition/function: a description of the method and its purpose.
- Context for use: examples of research situations where/when the method has been or could be used.
- Tools: specific equipment, techniques and processes – considerations involved in using the method.
- Advantages: possible benefits and positive aspects of the method.
- Disadvantages: possible limitations and negative aspects of the method.
- Ethical considerations: good research conduct, avoidance of questionable activities.
- Further references: usually key texts/sources, and examples of validated research in which the method has been used.
- Where appropriate, a visual example of the method/tools.

You might like to set up a similar structure for the description of your chosen/adapted methods.

Research methods: from validated completed formal research in Art and Design

It is likely that you will be conducting part of your research through some element of practice, and so we start our description of methods here.

Practice usually initiates research questions, provides the context for investigation, may provide various research methods, and is usually involved in the creative visualization and dissemination of the research. 'Practice' could have a range of interpretations, for example:

- practice as individual creative activity, perhaps the most obvious interpretation – 'making' in its broadest sense;
- practice as facilitation and dissemination – activities related to visual arts/design/craft/new media, for example education, administration, and activities such as curating, commissioning, critical writing, and so on;
- practice as a collaborative activity, involving other practitioners, participants and professionals from other disciplines, and/or external bodies, for example industry, commerce, voluntary sectors, and so on. This approach could involve making, facilitating, disseminating, as well as negotiating, fundraising, and so on.

Although complex in their own right, the first two interpretations of practice are probably well enough understood: as 'makers/creators' (designers, crafts-persons, fine artists, new media practitioners, and so on) and/or as 'facilitators' and 'disseminators' you can use your practice or aspects of it as a research tool for actually generating new information and gathering and structuring existing information, and use your professional situation for critically evaluating that information.

Increasingly creative opportunities are structured around collaborations of different kinds, and it is almost impossible to carry out research without working with others, to some degree, on some aspect of research. There are some useful examples of collaboration as a research strategy: Ross (2001) examined the changing role of artists operating in various organizational contexts. Working collaboratively with other professionals she used a participatory action research methodology undertaking a number of case study projects. She adopted different participatory roles in these – sometimes as artist, sometimes as observer, reporter, evaluator, consultant. In this research the artist acted as a 'cultural intermediary'. (See also Scopa's research in the matrix in Section 1.5.)

	Practice
Definition/function	Developing and making creative work as an explicit and intentional method for specific research purposes, for example gathering and/or generating data, evaluation, analysis, synthesis, presentation, communication of research findings.
Context for use	Research for higher degrees, distinct from 'practice as usual' in its use of practice within an academic research framework, which is accessible, transparent and transferable (in principle if not specifics); the work might embody research concepts, provide visual evidence and/or illustrate research findings in some way.
Tools required	Any of the tools/techniques used in the development and making art/design work; essential to document the process, for example through a reflective journal, photography, video, audio, and so on; may involve a range of methods described later; essential to have explicit criteria for evaluation and analysis, which relate directly to the research question.

Advantages	A means of generating new data through real experiential activity – researching and learning through doing to develop 'deep' understanding; the practitioner-researcher has an informed perspective on issues relating to practice.
Disadvantages	Open to criticisms of indulgence and over-subjectivity if not placed securely within the formal framework, and if lacking in methodological transparency; many debates exist against a submission for a higher degree that attempt to present an argument in a purely visual form.
Ethical considerations	Ethical considerations: as research is (usually) a publicly funded activity taking place within an academic framework the practitioner-researcher is morally obliged to make the practice publicly accessible; requires a high degree of integrity and honestly in evaluating and communicating the outcomes from practice (this might be resolved by inviting views from different perspectives).
Further references	• Polanyi, M. (1958) *Personal Knowledge: Towards a Post-critical Philosophy* (London: Routledge and Kegan Paul). • Douglas, A. and Scopa, K. (2000) Research through practice: positioning the practitioner as researcher – http://www.herts.ac.uk/artdes/conex/res2prac/ (and other papers on this site about research into practice) • Design plus Research conference proceedings (2000) – http://pcsiwa12.rett.polimi.it/~phddi/uk/01/dpr00/intro.htm • Recent and current debate on practice-based research, for example http://www.jiscmail.ac.uk/lists/phd-design.html • British Library Index to Theses – www.theses.com • Research Training Initiative – http://www.biad.uce.ac.uk/research/index.html – case studies of completed research for higher degrees • Completed formal practice-based research cited in previous chapters and this one.
Examples of the role of practice in research for higher degrees – some 'models'	For example, practice – through action and reflection – provides a means of: • Investigating the subject/content and context of one's own creative activity in order to advance or innovate; understanding one's own creative process (in relation to others'); making explicit the practitioner's tacit knowledge; as a result of greater self-knowledge being able to contribute to the wider development and understanding of research methodology involving practice. • Discovering new practices or methods/processes/techniques and materials by experimentation; re-discovering/revitalizing/revising traditional practices in new/contemporary contexts; reconstructing artwork/artefacts to bring about new understanding/insight through the experience of making/re-making. • Understanding a range of different practices – using one's own practice to contrast/compare those of other practitioners. • Being a catalyst in participatory action research where creative practice can actively involve, inform and inspire others. • Using the skills of the artist/designer to visualize and understand complex processes (perhaps in other fields) – making the invisible visible. • Providing knowledge transfer of mutual benefit between different 'worlds' of practice and research, for example art/design higher education and industry.

All/any of the following methods could be part of practice-based methodology or independently used as a research method.

	Observation
Definition/function	To watch something/someone/an environment/situation closely and accurately record in some way the activities/situation in order to capture data relevant to the research project issues.
Context for use	A classic research method in Science, Social Science and Art and Design. In Art and Design, objective, analytical drawing is a core skill and an important method for acquiring primary data in order to understand the world. Artists/designers have observed themselves making work (usually through video) in order to become more aware of their creative processes (self-observation – SO). In Social Science there are two kinds of observation: non-participant observation (NPO) and participant observation (PO). In NPO, the researcher attempts to remain objective (neutral), and detached from the object/person/situation being observed. In PO the researcher engages in the very activities he/she sets out to observe; becomes involved, empathizes, observes through the experience of engagement.
Tools required	A diverse range of qualitative and quantitative techniques including analytical and expressive drawing, mapping and/or making diagrams of what is being observed, video, photography; taking notes, counting objects/instances, timing events/movements; using checklists/schedules, scorecards, rating scales, and so on; augmented by various instruments for enhancing vision (and also other senses) or experience of the situation/context, for example optical devices such as binoculars, telescope.
Advantages	Direct visual experience and capture; relatively easy and unobtrusive; makes use of developed visual skills.
Disadvantages	All kinds of observation, especially PO and SO can both suffer from being obtrusive to 'natural' activities, perhaps causing changes in behaviour because of the act of being observed (that is, the Hawthorne effect); PO requires trust to be gained from other participants; self-observation can be too self-conscious, unless it is carried out regularly.
Ethical considerations	Possible invasion of privacy – obtain permission/authorization before you observe; ensure confidentiality; ensure permissions have been given for public use of data. Should be used with integrity and care.
Further references	• McKernan, J. (1998) *Curriculum Action Research: a Handbook of Methods and Resources for the Reflective Practitioner*, Chapter 3 Observational and Narrative Research Methods, (Kogan Page). • Popham, A. E. (1964) *The Drawings of Leonardo da Vinci* (London: Jonathan Cape). • Robson, C. (1993) *Real World Research*, Chapter 8, Observational Methods; Chapter 2, Ethical Considerations, pp. 29–35 (Sage). • Spradley, J. P. (1980) *Participant Observation* (London: Holt, Rinehart & Winston). • Zeisel, J. (1984) *Inquiry by Design*, Chapter 7, Observing Physical Traces, and Chapter 8, Observing Environmental Behaviour (Cambridge University Press).

	Visualization
Definition/function	Visual thinking; making visible ideas through a range of techniques in order to explore research project issues and/or present research findings.
Context for use	In practice-based research, making use of visual expertise to externalize and communicate concepts, interpretations, evaluations, and so on; in collaborative research as a means of sharing information, gaining feedback and generating new ideas.
Tools required	Drawing (in all forms, for example objective/analytical, expressive), diagrams, concept maps/mind maps, flow charts, storyboards, matrices, network displays, and so on; employing colour, tone, line, plane, shape, scale, symbol, and so on; the use of metaphor and analogy can stimulate visualization, for example practice-based research is like an elephant; increasing use of computer-aided visualization, for example Inspiration (www.inspiration.com) and through interactive multimedia and other applications, for example collaborative mind mapping using whiteboards.
Advantages	Visual overviews of complex material (a picture is worth a thousand words!); encourages discussion between people; encourages creative response, for example brainstorming/lateral thinking; use of a range of graphic techniques for making visible all stages of the research process; the increasing importance of the visual in 21st century life.
Disadvantages	Lack of technical and aesthetic expertise may hinder the communicative power of a visual; the possible or deliberate ambiguous nature of some visual material, for example abstract work!
Ethical considerations	All images are socially and technically constructed – visualizations should not deliberately mislead; should be used with integrity and care.
Further references	• Buzan, T. (1998) *The Mind Map Book* (BBC Books). The use of mind maps as a methods of data acquisition, for instance in notation of observation. • Spiller, J. (ed.) (1973) *The Notebooks of Paul Klee Volume 1: The Seeing Eye* (Lund Humphries). • Miles, M. B. and Huberman, A. M. (1994) *Qualitative Data Analysis* (Sage). Information on matrix displays, network diagrams. • Tufte, E. (1983) *The Visual Display of Quantitative Information* (Graphics Press). • Tufte, E. (1990) *Envisioning Information* (Graphics Press). • Tufte, E. (1997) *Visual Explanations: Images and Quantities, Evidence and Narrative* (Graphics Press).
Visual	See Figure 4.3

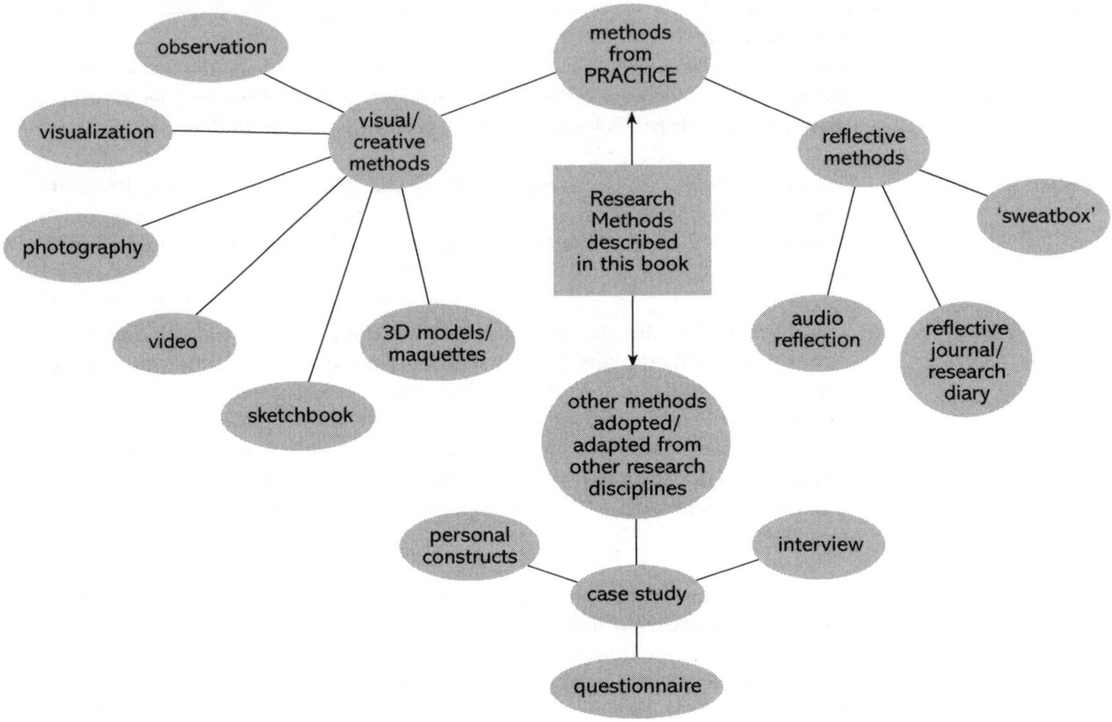

Figure 4.3 Mind map providing an overview of methods discussed in this section (💻)

	Photography
Definition/function	Technology for capturing and producing a static image of an object/person/environment, providing evidence of particular significant features related to the research project issues.
Context for use	In practice-based research or other research situations/environments for: acquisition of visual data, storage/management of visual information, analysis of visual data, and the presentation of research findings; involves the selection and framing of a particular section/aspect of the activity/environment; for research purposes photos need to be annotated, identifying the kinds of data presented in order to be useful evidence, for example textual information (as appropriate) on who (specify key people), what (specify focus of frame/action/event), where (context), when (date/time), how, why?
Tools required	35 mm SLR camera and/or digital still camera; tripod essential for long exposure shots; appropriate type of film/output media, for example colour slides to give greater sense of space; print for drawing on and display purposes; digital for image manipulation and projection, and for inclusion in multimedia documents/web pages; proforma for annotation (standard proformas can help to make comparisons across a series of photographs – see Chapter 3 topic on *Managing Research Project Information*).

Advantages	Ubiquitous technology – relatively easy to use and cheap; can present complex detail and realistic representation.
Disadvantages	As a research method, needs to go beyond the 'happy snap'! Therefore, as an acquisition method (and to aid later analysis) annotation is essential.
Ethical considerations	Possible invasion of privacy – obtain permission/authorization before you take photographs; ensure confidentiality; ensure permissions have been given for public use of data; all images are socially and technically constructed – edited work should not deliberately mislead (editing can present an extremely selective, and possibly distorted, view); should be used with integrity and care.
Further references	• Ball, M. S. and Smith, G.W. H. (1992) *Analysing Visual Data* (Sage). Use of photography in anthropology. • Banks, M. (2001) *Visual Methods in Social Research* (Sage). • Collier, J. (1967) *Visual Anthropology: Photography as a Research Method* (Holt Rinehart & Wilson). • Emmison, M. and Smith P. (2000) *Researching the Visual: Images, Objects, Contexts and Interactions in Social and Cultural Inquiry* (Sage). • Zeisel, J. (1984) *Inquiry by Design* (Cambridge University Press). See Chapter 7, Observing Physical Traces, and Chapter 8, Observing Environmental Behaviour, for Two examples of annotated photographs, p. 125.

Visual

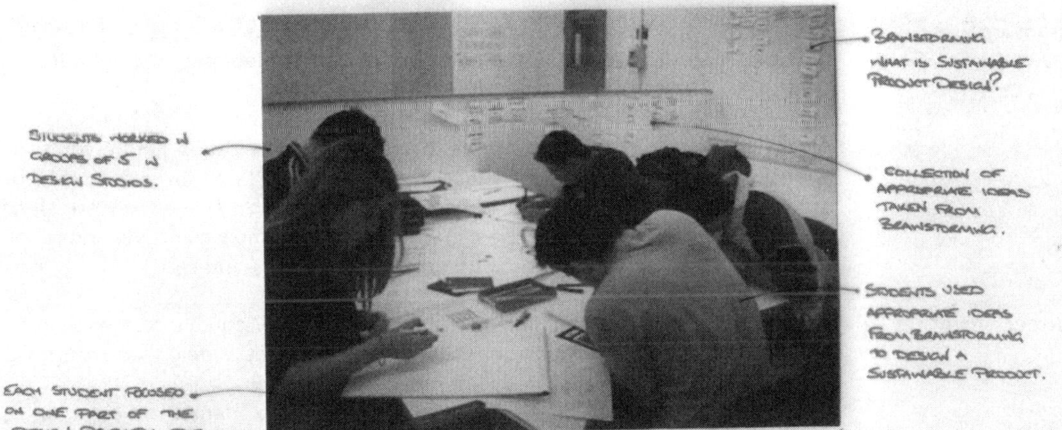

Figure 4.4 Annotated photograph from a PhD project in progress (💻)

	Video
Definition/function	A visual technology that enables the capture of dynamic information, for example simultaneous movement and sound and emergent qualities such as 'atmosphere', relevant to the research project issues.
Context for use	In practice-based research where dynamic information is required/available, for example kinetic artwork, performance, collaborative working. Like photography, can be used for data acquisition, storage/management of visual information, and analysis of visual data. By editing and the use of spoken commentary and captions, a way of presenting complex and dynamic research findings, for example interactions, sound/noise, environments, installations, dynamic visual qualities.
Tools required	Video camera; tapes/memory cards; tripod essential for most situations to eliminate camera shake; additional lighting and microphone useful in some situations; playback equipment and/or access to editing facilities/software.
Advantages	In its raw state yields more 'objective' data, that is captures data straight, including things we may unconsciously 'filter out' of our perception, for example ambient noise, background actions, and so on. Date and time coding is possible. Play and replay possible of both sound and vision, even frame by frame, forwards and backwards – a good analytical tool, especially digital video; multiple sound tracks available (for combined audio information, for example ambient sound, commentary, music).
Disadvantages	Ease of use may lead to the collection of large volumes of visual data, which requires time to review, log and edit (2 minutes of video may take 2 hours to edit!).
Ethical considerations	Possible invasion of privacy – obtain permission/authorization before you use video; ensure confidentiality; ensure permissions have been given for public use of data; all images are socially and technically constructed – edited work should not deliberately mislead (editing can present an extremely selective, and possibly distorted, view); should be used with integrity and care.
Further references	• Lozios, P. (2000) Video, film and photographs as research documents, in: G. D. Gaskell, and M. W. Bauer, (eds) *Qualitative Researching with Text, Image and Sound: A Practical Handbook for Social Research* (Sage). • Graham, B. (1997) *A Study of the Relationships with Interactive Computer-based Visual Artworks in Gallery Settings, through Observation, Art Practice and Curation.* PhD thesis, University of Sunderland. CD Rom version includes video clips from the *Serious Games* exhibition.

	Sketchbook
Definition/function	A portable book or bound collection of sheets that contain the development of ideas over time, and subsequent reflection and analysis; may include a range of visuals and notes, and other contextual references; a 'digital sketchbook' may be more appropriate for some practices
Context for use	In practice-based research, to capture and store a range of visual ideas, data and information, but not necessarily in an ordered, sequenced way; to encourage visual thinking (ref. Leonardo's 'pensieri'); dating input useful; could be seen as the artistic/designerly equivalent to a laboratory log book for recording experiments.
Tools required	Ready made book and various mark-making tools; small computer notebooks, for example PalmPilot, iBook, and relevant software, for instance Painter, Illustrator, and so on.
Advantages	Availability/accessibility in most situations (handiness); non-preciousness – a space for experimental thought; capacity for tracking developments over time; reflective/analytical space.
Disadvantages	Some practitioners may prefer a more haptic/hands-on approach through 3D 'sketching' with actual material – there are limits to two dimensions and sequential structures!
Ethical considerations	Possible reluctance to make accessible such a personal document, but if used as a research method must be accessible; should be used with integrity and care.
Further references	• Burt, I. (2000) *The Use of Multimedia for Practitioners in Art & Design*, PhD thesis, The Robert Gordon University. Methodology, section 3.5.0: practice-based investigations – The Electronic Notebook, 3.5.2.1 – 3.5.2.4. • Kemp, M. (1989) *Leonardo da Vinci* (South Bank: Hayward Gallery). • Klee, P. (1968) *Pedagogical Sketchbook* (London: Faber & Faber). • Oldenburg, C. and van Bruggen, C. (1988) *A Bottle of Notes and Some Voyages* (Leeds: Northern Centre for Contemporary Art/Henry Moore Centre). • Renwick, G (2003) *Spatial determinism in the Canadian north: a theoretical overview and practice-based response*. PhD thesis, University of Dundee. (Use of 'collaborative sketchbook').
Visual	See Figure 4.5.

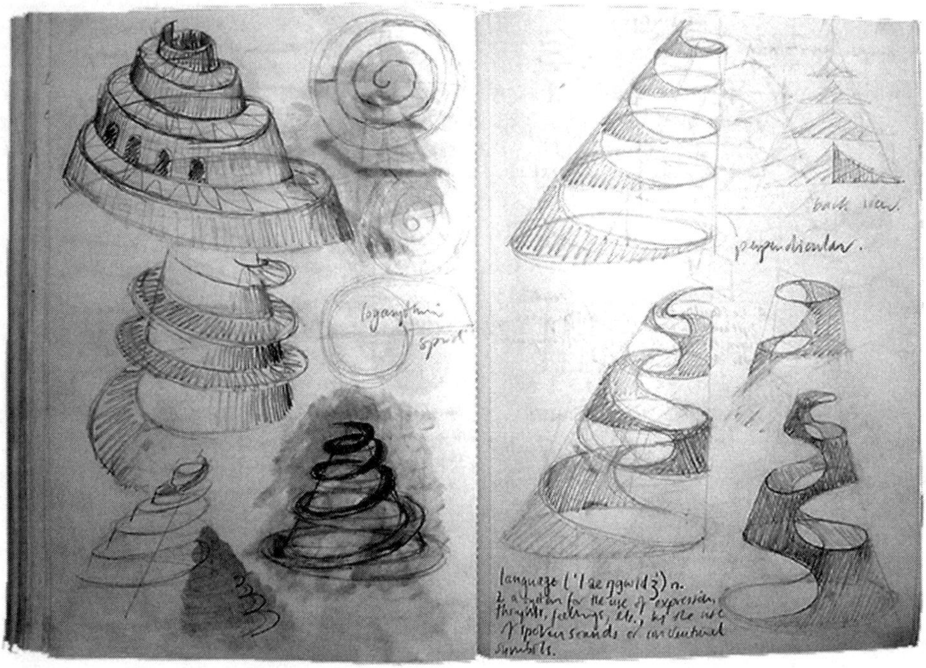

Figure 4.5 Example pages from a sketchbook exploring possible three-dimensional forms (💻)

	3D Models/maquettes
Definition/function	Three-dimensional experimentation of the research project issues with materials and processes (3D 'sketching', envisioning) that may result in a range of 'approximations' (various versions of maquettes) towards a more resolved construction/object; in some instances a scale model may be required. Increasing use of technology allows sophisticated computer modelling.
Context for use	In practice-based research, where two-dimensional information is insufficient for understanding and communicating complex ideas, structure, form, texture, and so on. For example product design, architecture, sculpture, fashion, craft. Increasing use of technology, for instance computer-aided design and manufacture (CAD/CAM) for experimentation with forms impossible to derive by other methods, and for visualizing large scale objects.
Tools required	Any relevant material and process, for example paper/card, metal, stone, wood, clay, plastic, and so on; construction, carving, modelling, rapid prototyping, simulated modelling using computer software, such as Amapi, Rhino, FormZ, ProEngineer, Autocad, and so on.
Advantages	Allows the exploration and presentation of spatial and tactile data, for example actual material qualities, surface texture, weight, and so on. Virtual models can be animated, stored in databases and shared over networks, digital information can be re-purposed both to document objects and make real objects using rapid prototyping technologies.

Disadvantages	Models/maquettes take up space! Almost always needs to be documented (photo, video). Virtual modelling often requires a steep learning curve and specialist training in order to manipulate the software confidently; some software and output technologies can be very expensive.
Ethical considerations	Should not deliberately misrepresent, for example through misleading scale model, manipulated digital model.
Further references	• Bunnell, K. (1998) *The Integration of New Technology into Designer-Maker Practice.* PhD thesis, The Robert Gordon University. (Experiments and prototypes investigating the integration of new technologies in making.) • Douglas, A. (1992) *Structure and Improvisation: The Making Aspect of Sculpture.* PhD thesis, Sunderland University. (Experiments with improvisation – ref. On the Notion of Test, see Chapter 5, section 5.2.) • Oldenburg, C. and van Bruggen, C. (1988) *A Bottle of Notes and Some Voyages*, (Leeds: Northern Centre for Contemporary Art/Henry Moore Centre). (Documentation of Oldenburg's maquettes for large scale sculptures.)

Visual

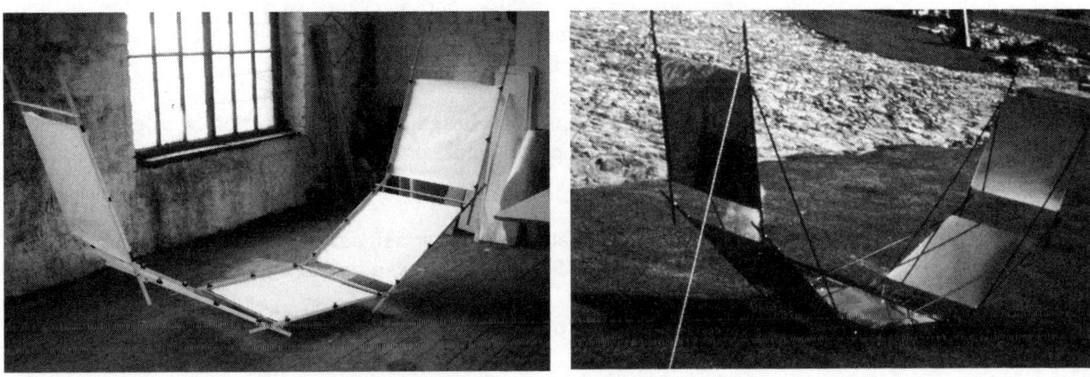

Figure 4.6 Examples of a full scale model in 'sketch' materials and the actual sculpture (💻)

The following are practice-based methods that encourage and enable reflection.

	Reflective journal/Research diary
Definition/function	Reflective journalling goes beyond the use of the sketchbook in that it is a much more structured and deliberate research method. It is a purposeful process and framework for helping to expose and explore various models of practice, encourage interdisciplinarity and collaboration, extend professionalism and have more effective conversations with ourselves. The journal/diary itself is a store – a repository for a range of information in a range of media – which is added to and consulted on a regular basis, and which may be related solely to a particular research project. The 'journal' may contain different types of information.

Context for use	In practice-based research, to help capture the dynamic and reflexive nature of practice, for example for planning (reflecting for action), for capturing action (reflecting in action whilst doing something), and describing and evaluating (reflecting on action). Invaluable for the regular documentation of the application of methods and evaluation of their outcomes.
Tools required	An off-the-shelf large format diary (at least one A4 page a day), or a home-made version; alternatively a digital version may be more appropriate, for instance a web diary or some other format, for example a 'video diary', a large folio, a wall map/chart, for example a 'cyclogram', a 3D 'container'. The 'journal' may contain different types of information to provide you with a whole range of evidence and examples: for example activity and development log (fact, precision and detail through material samples, diagrams, charts, numerical data), diary (descriptive and discursive writing), documentation of work in progress and completed (a sequence of visuals, including 'failures', 35 mm transparencies), contextual references (visual examples of other artists' and designers' work as postcards and magazine cuttings and details about the work, and its significance to your research), information about the pace and progress of work (as a 'peaks and troughs' chart), video/audio transcripts, key points from evaluation and analysis, and any other kind of relevant 'life' information. It is essential that all the contents are labelled, dated, sequenced, and sufficiently 'contained' so that nothing is lost.
Advantages	A comprehensive store of practice-based thought and action, with evidence and example. Could form an important part of a 'portfolio' of research evidence/learning.
Disadvantages	An idiosyncratic (and probably very personal) set of information, possibly of little use to others in specifics, but of value as an example of a reflective tool.
Ethical considerations	Should provide an honest picture of development and progress.
Further references	• Krause, J. and Lichtenstein, C. (eds) (1999) *Your Private Sky: R. Buckminster Fuller. The Art of Design Science* (Lars Müller). (pp. 13–14 the Dymaxion Chronofile.) • Newbury, D. (2001) Diaries and field notes in the research process, *Research Issues in Art, Design and Media*, Issue No.1, Autumn. • Eno, B. (1996) *A Year With Swollen Appendices* (London: Faber & Faber). • Hart, C. (1998) *Doing a Literature Review* (Sage). (The Research Diary, Appendix 4, p. 216.) • Renwick, G. (2003) *Spatial Determinism in the Canadian North: a theoretical overview and practice-based response*. PhD thesis, University of Dundee. (Use of 'visual journal'.) • Tufte, E. (1997) *Visual Explanations* (Graphics Press). (Example of a 'cyclogram' of Salyut 6 space flight, pp. 92–95.) • Chapter 2, section 2.5, A Reflective Journal.

	Audio reflection
Definition/function	Talking out loud to yourself whilst making work/thinking about it, especially in relation to research project issues.
Context for use	In practice-based research situations, in order to capture reflection-in-action and spontaneous spoken thoughts (stream of consciousness, reflection in action); can capture expressive qualities of voice – intonation, phrasing, pausing, reactions (for example gasp, laugh), and so on – all possibly useful data; needs to be done regularly so that the process becomes as 'unconscious' and natural as possible.
Tools required	Small wearable/pocket audio recorder, ideally digital (for high quality) and voice-activated; tapes/disks and batteries.
Advantages	Capable of capturing spontaneous thoughts 'on the move' at any time.
Disadvantages	Too self-conscious; could generate hours of tape to review and/or transcribe; people may think you are mad!
Ethical considerations	Should not deliberately mislead/misrepresent.
Further references	• Schön, D. (1983) *The Reflective Practitioner* (Basic Books). • Watson, A. (1992) *An exploration of the principle of chance as a stimulus to the creative activity known as sculpture.* PhD thesis, The Robert Gordon University. (Use of audio to capture reflection-in-action and on-action, section 3.25, Appendix 3, Tape transcripts of Experiment B.)

	'Sweatbox'
Definition/function	The 'sweatbox' is a studio-based video set-up, used by architects and artists to capture 'master class' presentations, that is an eminent practitioner talking about and reflecting on their practice and/or solving a particular problem, using various visual means, for example drawing, mapping, models.
Context for use	In practice-based research (in action, perhaps in response to a particular task) in order to capture reflection-in-action and on-action through the sharing and description of process and spontaneous spoken thoughts, sometimes augmented by drawing/sketching ideas.
Tools required	Video studio; two video cameras – one focused on the reflecting practitioner, and one mounted directly over a drawing table to capture visual outputs; wearable microphone to capture audio clearly; mixing desk to inter-cut material from both cameras.
Advantages	Although a formal situation, it does encourage 'off-loading' (ref. McAleese, 1999, Chapter 2, Section 2.5); captures valuable examples of process, perhaps not usually accessible.

Disadvantages	Formal studio set-up may be difficult to arrange or be too costly to hire; reflective practitioner may be too self-conscious.
Ethical considerations	Presenter must have given permission/authorization before recording; ensure confidentiality; ensure permissions have been given for public use of data; edited work should not deliberately mislead – editing can present an extremely selective, and possibly distorted, view; should be used with integrity and care.
Further references	• Schön, D. (1983) *The Reflective Practitioner* (Basic Books). • Silver, S. (1999) *The role of artists in the public realm: an investigation into artists' generative process in context.* PhD thesis, The Robert Gordon University. • Silver, S. and Lucas, M. (1997) *Hospitals Talking Art: Recording the Visual Dialogue* (The Robert Gordon University).

Visual

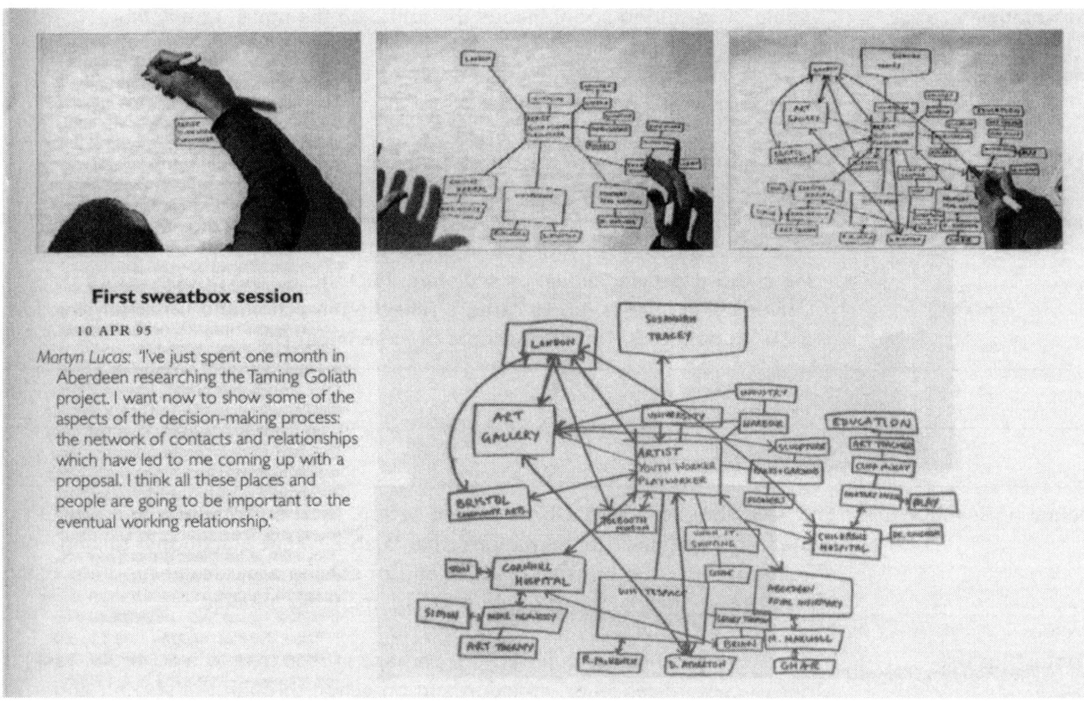

Figure 4.7 Example of a 'sweatbox' session from *Hospitals Talking Art: Recording the Visual Dialogue* (💻)

There are no doubt other methods that you use as part of your practice and the reflection on it. These should be written up and illustrated as part of your research project. Once the project is examined and validated the method(s) should be publicly disseminated. Other researchers may then adopt/adapt or extend the method, thus adding to the body of knowledge on research methods related to practice.

RESEARCH METHODS: SOCIAL SCIENCES

Research methods in Art and Design have been augmented with useful Social Science methods, usually adapted and/or re-contextualized in some way. These methods are not described in detail here – numerous texts are available (and referenced). However, their application in practice-based research in Art and Design is highlighted. For a good overview of qualitative methods see Denzin and Lincoln (1994).

	Case study
Definition/function	Case – a single instance or example of something. 'A formal collection of evidence presented as an interpretative position of a unique case . . . reports on a project or innovation or event over a prolonged period of time by telling a . . . story as it has evolved' (McKernan, 1998, p 74).
Context for use	In Social Science research, where a complex something/someone/situation needs to be studied qualitative, intensively, in-depth and comprehensively. Similarly, in Art and Design research where the case may be a practitioner, an environment, for example a studio/workshop, a project, a commission, a consultancy, a learning setting, and so on.
Tools required	May use any/all of the methods outlined below, and other more visual methods previously described. Case evidence may include all types of data, for example audio/video recordings and transcripts, field notes, diary entries, letters, other documents, visuals, objects of material culture, artefacts, and so on. Researcher may take the role of participant observer.
Advantages	Affords detailed study in depth and breadth – 'strong in reality'; use of multi-method aids corroboration and validation; produces credible and accurate account of setting and action.
Disadvantages	Specific and idiosyncratic example/case, therefore generalizations beyond the specific case cannot be made (unless a reasonable number of cases are studied); extremely time consuming; critical view sometimes difficult (researcher can be influenced by respondents).
Ethical considerations	Permission/authorization required; ensure confidentiality; ensure permissions have been given for public use of data; should be used with integrity and care.
Further references	• Cohen, L. and Manion, L. (1994) *Research Methods in Education*, Chapter 5, Case Studies (Routledge). • McKernan, J. (1998) *Curriculum Action Research: a Handbook of Methods and Resources for the Reflective Practitioner*, Chapter 4, Observational and Narrative Research Methods, pp. 74–83 (Kogan Page). • Wheeler, E. (1996) *The role of architectural ceramics in contemporary site-specific art*. PhD thesis, University of Northumbria, Newcastle. (Site-specific commissions as case studies.) • Yin, R. (1984) *Case Study Research* (Sage).

Within a case study many different methods may be used, for example:

	Interview
Definition/function	A key method in seeking the particular opinions of others about an identified research topic. A purposeful conversation initiated by the interviewer and focused by him/her on content specified by research objectives.
Context for use	In case study research where a particular and in-depth view is required; helpful in the exploratory stages of research to elicit views, identify variables, important factors as a method of structuring further research.
Tools required	Recording equipment, for example audio, video, plus tapes/disks; a quiet space; interview schedule (identified questions or prompts); notebook or schedule proforma for taking notes on responses (verbal and non-verbal). Several types of interview, for example structured, semi-structured, unstructured, focused. Various types of software for content and discourse analysis, for example NUD*IST, ATLAS (visual analysis), NVivo, HyperRESEARCH (text and multimedia data) – all by Sage publications.
Advantages	A good way of finding out a person's values, preferences, attitudes, beliefs and feelings; opportunity for direct verbal interaction, encouraging in-depth response – a discursive method, can be done at a distance using telephone or internet 'chat' tools.
Disadvantages	Could be prone to subjectivity and bias (leading questions!); the setting for the interview can influence the quality of the responses, for example formal or informal; time-consuming (event itself and transcription); if recording tools and notes are not used the interviewer could have poor recall.
Ethical considerations	Participant(s) must have given permission/authorization before recording; ensure confidentiality; ensure permissions have been given for public use of data; edited work should not deliberately mislead – editing can present an extremely selective, and possibly distorted, view; should be used with integrity and care.
Further references	• Cohen, L. and Manion, L. (1994) *Research Methods in Education*, Chapter 13, The Interview (Routledge). • McKernan, J. (1998) *Curriculum Action Research: a Handbook of Methods and Resources for the Reflective Practitioner*, Chapter 4, Non-Observational, Survey and Self Report Techniques (Kogan Page). • Robson, C. (1993) *Real World Research*, Chapter 9, Interviews and Questionnaires (Blackwell). • Keats, D. M. (2000) *Interviewing: a Practical Guide for Students and Professionals* (Open University Press). • Used in many practice-based research degrees, for example Scopa (2003), Wheeler (1996)

	Questionnaire
Definition/function	A key method in seeking the general opinions of many others about an identified research topic. A purposeful survey in order to gather data at a particular point in time to (a) describe the nature of existing conditions, or (b) identify standards against which existing conditions can be compared, or (c) determine the relationship that exists between specific events.
Context for use	In Social Science research, the questionnaire is one of the most commonly used descriptive methods; useful for identifying trends in large populations; can yield good generalizations. In Art and Design research, it has been used, for example, in longitudinal studies to track national graduate career development.
Tools required	Paper-based (or increasingly web-based, linked to a database) proforma for questions and responses (fax/e-mail back a good way of eliciting response); most simple form is a tick box or 'yes/no', 'true/false'; always take the opportunity to seek clarification/extension on a simple answer by including a 'further comments' section; design should be simple but engaging; sampling and size important – who are involved and why?
Advantages	Capacity for a large and widely distributed sample; more economical in time and money than interviewing; anonymity of respondents may encourage greater honesty; allows for quantitative data to be collected.
Disadvantages	The larger the sample the more generalized the response; the larger the sample the more time it will take to analyse; low return rates (20% is considered good!); no clarification of responses possible; responses may be questionable either because of poor question design or as a result of 'questionnaire fatigue' on the part of the respondent; if quantitative data are selected then statistical analysis is often required in order to establish whether the results are statistically significant.
Ethical considerations	Questionnaire must include information about the purpose of the research and how the resulting data will be used; ensure confidentiality; should be used with integrity and care.
Further references	• Cohen, L. and Manion, L. (1994) *Research Methods in Education*, Chapter 4, Surveys (Routledge). • McKernan, J. (1998) *Curriculum Action Research: a Handbook of Methods and Resources for the Reflective Practitioner*, Chapter 4, Non-Observational, Survey and Self Report Techniques (Kogan Page). • Robson, C. (1993) *Real World Research*, Chapter 9, Interviews and Questionnaires (Blackwell).

	Personal constructs
Definition/function	Developed by George Kelly in the 1950s, personal constructs are dimensions that we use to conceptualize aspects of our day-to-day world and make sense of ourselves in our world(s). Events are only meaningful in relation to the ways that are construed by the individual.
Context for use	In psychology, a sensitive approach in the evaluation of personality or an individual's perception of their environment, or to map personal relationships.
Tools required	Personal construct Repertory Grid Test (RGT, Kelly) is a method of quantifying the relationship between elicited constructs and illustrating the internal structure of an individual's repertoire of constructs – the individual's phenomenal world is left intact (the idiographic approach) and no attempt is made to slot him/her into categories determined by a researcher. Various techniques have been developed from Kelly's initial RGT, for example Hinkle's Laddering technique. In clinical psychology drawing has been used to visualize personal constructs and relationships between people – 'personal sphere models' (Schmiedeck, 1978).
Advantages	An adaptable method of encouraging people to externalize their understandings of the world or whatever the focus is, for example artistic identity, collaborative relationships, design values, learning styles, and so on.
Disadvantages	Use of bi-polar constructs (good–bad, rich–poor, engaged–detached) could be seen as simplistic, reductive and positivistic!
Ethical considerations	Participant(s) must have given permission/authorization; ensure confidentiality; ensure permissions have been given for public use of data; should be used with integrity and care.
Further references	• Cohen, L. and Manion, L. (1994) *Research Methods in Education*, Chapter 14, Personal Constructs (Routledge). • Hall, E. (1978) *Using Personal Constructs: Rediguide No.9* (University of Nottingham School of Education). • Gray, C. (1988) *Teaching styles in higher art education*. PhD thesis, University of Aberdeen. (Personal construct theory informed the development of Gray's teaching style 'game'.) • Kelly, G. (1955) *The Psychology of Personal Constructs* (New York: Norton). • Schmiedeck, R. A. (1978) *The Personal Sphere Model* (Grune & Stratton).

Research methods: Sciences

There are many established and validated research methods in the Sciences. It is beyond the scope of this book to describe such methods in detail. We simply refer you to a few key texts that provide philosophical and practical information. It will be clear from an examination of early examples of completed formal research in Art and Design that more positivist methods have sometimes been used (for example, quasi-experimental methods in Stonyer's 1978, PhD *The development of kinetic sculpture by the utilization of solar energy*). Indeed, there are design research areas that require more scientific methodologies and methods, for example industrial design. However, it is important for you to be aware of the different paradigms of inquiry and what the methodological implications are for each (you may wish to re-read Section 1.3, *A route map: the importance of methodology*).

Further references

Capra, F. (1983) *The Turning Point: Science, Society and the Rising Culture* (London: Flamingo).

Graziano, A. M. and Raulin, M. (1993) *Research Methods: A Process of Inquiry* (New York: HarperCollins College Publishers).

Kuhn, T. S. (1970) *The Structure of Scientific Revolutions*, 2nd edn (Chicago: University of Chicago Press).

Popper, K. R. (1991) *Conjectures and Refutations: The Growth of Scientific Knowledge* (Routledge).

Ziman, J. (1978) *Reliable Knowledge: an Exploration of the Grounds for Belief in Science* (Cambridge University Press).

Convoy! The use of multiple methods

In Chapter 1 (Section 1.5) the concept of 'triangulation' was described as a way of achieving a more meaningful and balanced understanding of a research issue by the use of two or more research methods. Triangulation helps us to get a 'fix' on something in order to understand more fully the complexity of issues by examining them from different perspectives, and generating data in different ways by using different methods. The more information we have from varying perspectives, the more able we are to test our ideas and eliminate bias that might arise from each method.

The concept of multi-method also suggests multi-media, not only in its information technology sense (multimedia/hypermedia), but its value in using and integrating different kinds of media to provide different kinds of sensory information. The involvement of practically all our human senses, as well as other independent sensory instruments, is more likely to give us a comprehensive and 'rich' perspective on the research issue being explored.

It is important to state the rationale for using several methods, and to describe clearly how they interrelate. Some research projects might use a developmental methodology where one research method prompts the next in a simple sequential order. Others might use several methods almost simultaneously. In both cases, in addition to thoroughly describing in text the use of each method, it is useful to visualize the use of various methods within the methodology as a whole (Figure 4.8).

This visualization describes four key methods in a developmental research methodology (Burt, 2000). There are two versions of this – a static 2D version presented here and also a multimedia version with a spoken commentary on the book's website.

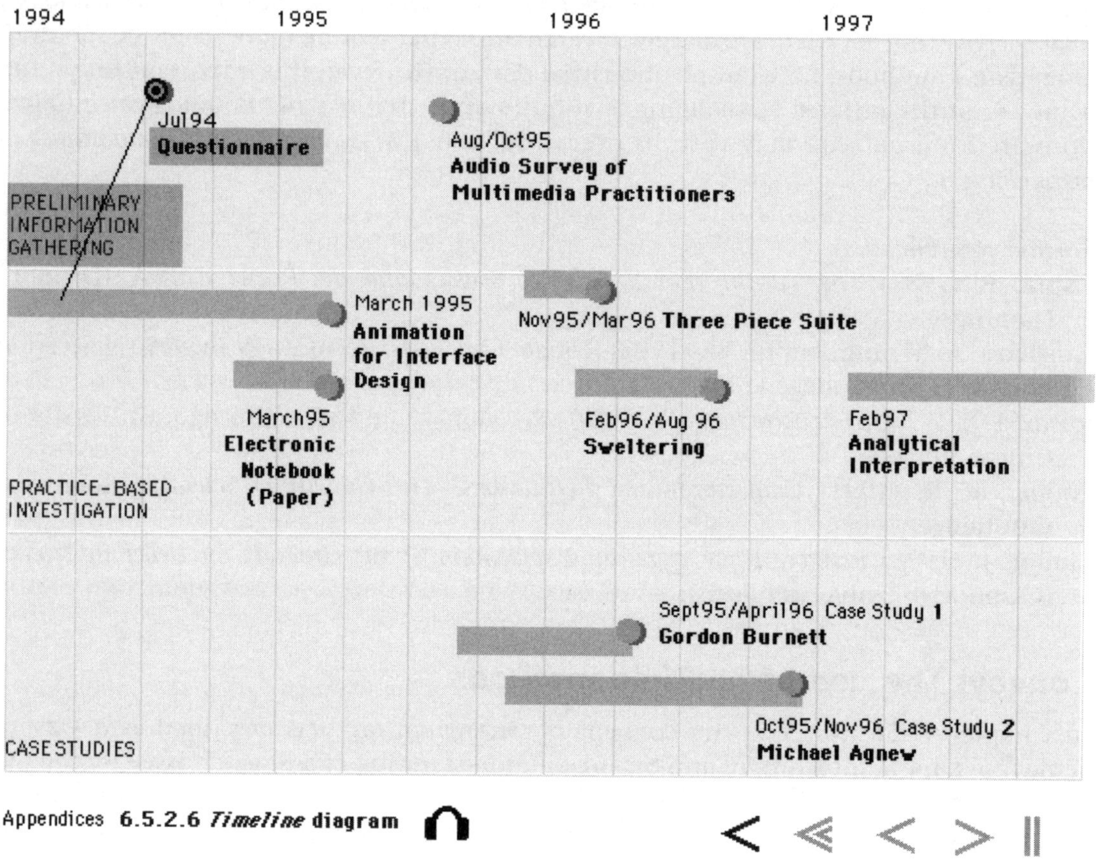

Figure 4.8 Visualization of methods used and their relationship to each other (💻)

Such visuals are helpful in planning the research as well as presenting the research findings, in which a clear description of the whole methodology and the specific methods employed is essential. They attempt to map out, or explain more fully, the richness and complexity of an issue, by studying it from more than one perspective.

An expanding battery of appropriate specific methods and tools have now been rigorously used, validated, or are currently being tested. We shall return to some of these methods in Chapter 5 to examine aspects of them in terms of their usefulness as methods of evaluation and analysis, and of course introduce some new methods for making sense of your research journey and interpreting the map.

Reflection and action: suggestions

- What established methods are you likely to select and why?
- What methods might you need to adapt and why?
- What kind of new methods might you need to invent and why?

4.4 CONSIDERING PRELIMINARY EVALUATION AND ANALYSIS

There is a distinction between evaluation and analysis. To 'evaluate' is to ascertain the value of something and to judge or assess its worth. To 'analyse' is to examine something in detail in order to discover its meaning; in a more scientific sense, it is to break something down into components or essential features. Although Chapter 5 focuses on specific methods of evaluation and analysis for artists and designers, you probably have already applied these two key activities in your critical evaluation of contextual references and what they mean for the development of your research, and critical debate on, and analysis of, research issues.

A key text in Chapter 5 will be Coffey and Atkinson's (1996) *Making Sense of Qualitative Data*. In the first section of their book they suggest that analysis is a 'reflexive activity' (Coffey and Atkinson, 1996, p. 6) that is 'pervasive throughout the life of the research project' (Coffey and Atkinson, 1996, p. 11) even though in the retrospective reporting of research it may form a separate section towards the end of the report or written thesis element. Certainly reflective practice requires a regular and critical evaluation and analysis of thought and action. Robson also promotes this view that considerations about evaluation and analysis should be an integral part of the design of any research investigation. In particular in relation to case study he states that:

> . . . it makes sense to start this analysis and interpretation when you are in the middle of the enquiry because, generally speaking, data in their raw form do not speak for themselves. The messages are hidden and need careful teasing out.
>
> (Robson, 1993, pp. 305–306)

In any kind of developmental methodology, at least some preliminary evaluation of the use of any method and the data from it must take place in order to advance to the next stage. For instance, in recent research on the use of multimedia for practitioners in Art and Design (Burt, 2000 – see also Figure 4.8) four methods were used: a preliminary survey by questionnaire helped to focus the direction of the research; in the light of this a more in-depth series of audio interviews with multimedia practitioners were conducted; these interviews raised issues which the researcher explored through practice; and finally, case studies were used to evaluate the transferability of the researcher's practice-based investigations into two different kinds of practice – one in Fine Art and one in Design. Naturally, there was some overlap and simultaneous use of these methods, but evaluations took place on a continuous and iterative basis.

Coffey and Atkinson suggest that there are many ways to analyse qualitative data, and that researchers should 'enjoy and explore' the diversity of approaches and should 'experiment and play' with analysis. As there are many kinds of data (textual, visual, material, and so on) a wide variety of analytic strategies are required. However, the common concern should be with transforming and interpreting data in a rigorous and scholarly way. They state that: 'In dealing with qualitative materials analysts *make* problems, grounding them in everyday realities and meanings rather than *taking* problems from others' (Coffey and Atkinson, 1996, p. 5).

You should begin to evaluate the appropriateness and usefulness of methods early on in your research and, if necessary, modify/remodel your methodology accordingly. You should also begin to 'play' with data derived from the various methods you are using, questioning its usefulness (validity, trustworthiness, reliability) and try to make some sense of it – deriving initial meaning. 'Playing' with data might include:

- sorting/organizing the data in as many different ways as possible (do not discount anything initially);
- making data as visual as possible (using colour coding, symbols, mapping, and so on) so that patterns can be seen, for example recurring themes/leitmotifs;
- discussing the data with participants/collaborators for feedback.

These methods and other will be explored in more detail in Chapter 5, as will the importance of raising criteria for evaluation and analysis. We agree with Coffey and Atkinson that analysis is a playful, creative, constructive activity – the principles of which practitioners are already familiar.

Reflection and action: suggestions

- In what ways might you start to 'play' with your data?
- Considering your objectives, what might be your key criteria for evaluation and analysis?

Looking back on Chapter 4: crossing the terrain

As a 'visual researcher', Leonardo inspires us to visualize our thoughts and ideas, make the invisible visible, the implicit explicit, and creatively envision that which we cannot yet see or fully understand. At the beginning of the 21st century we have to hand a range of new technologies to engage various sensory modes, not least the visual, to provide explorers with potential new research methodologies and methods.

Before setting off, we remind ourselves that we could be on shaky ground if we make claims that are not supported by evidence derived from the rigorous use of robust research methods. A giant redwood tree only stands tall and steady because of its extensive and tenacious system of anchoring roots.

In crossing the terrain, a variety of vehicles for exploration might be required, providing us with different means of evidence collection and different perspectives of the issues. Some, although familiar, need to be used in more deliberate and explicit ways. Some need to be adapted or even invented in response to new kinds of terrain. In many cases we need to test drive the vehicles to be fairly convinced that they will get us towards our final destination. Some we need to acknowledge just aren't that reliable and we abandon them in the dust. As well as vehicles for going forward we need ones that help us look back and take stock of the experience so far.

As we generate and gather evidence, we need to be constantly weighing up its value, quality and potential significance. We may need to go back over the ground to check that we have not missed anything that could be eventually valuable. We need to keep an open mind and be critical in order to avoid only seeing those things we want to see – a mirage of an oasis in the desert!

REFERENCES AND FURTHER READING FOR CHAPTER 4

References

Allison Research Index of Art & Design (ARIAD – www.ariad.co.uk).

Archer, L. B. (1965) *Systematic Method for Designers* (London: Design Council).

Arnheim, R. (1969) *Visual Thinking* (Berkeley: University of California Press).

Arnheim, R. (1986) A plea for visual thinking, in: *New Essays on the Psychology of Art* (Berkeley: University of California Press).

Ball, M. S. and Smith, G. W. H. (1992) *Analysing Visual Data* (Thousand Oaks, CA: Sage).

Banks, M. (2001) *Visual Methods in Social Research* (London: Sage).

Bunnell, K. (1998) *The Integration of New Technology into Designer-maker Practice.* PhD thesis, The Robert Gordon University.

Burt, I. (2000) *The Use of Multimedia for Practitioners in Art & Design.* PhD thesis, The Robert Gordon University.

Buzan, T. (1998) *The Mind Map Book* (London: BBC Books).

Capra, F. (1983) *The Turning Point: Science, Society and the Rising Culture* (London: Flamingo).

Coffey, A. and Atkinson, P. (1996) *Making Sense of Qualitative Data* (Thousand Oaks, CA: Sage

Cohen, L. and Manion, L. (1994) *Research Methods in Education* (London: Routledge).

Collier, J. (1967) *Visual Anthropology: Photography as a Research Method* (New York: Holt, Rinehart & Winston).

Cornock, S. (1978) *Notes Towards a Methodology for Students of Fine Art* (Leicester Polytechnic Monograph).

Cornock, S. (1983) Methodology for students of fine art, *Journal of Art & Design Education*, 2(1), pp. 81–99.

Cornock, S. (1984) Strategies in Fine Art, *Journal of Art & Design Education*, 3(2), pp. 141–159.

Cross, N. (ed.) (1984) *Developments in Design Methodology* (Chichester: Wiley).

Denzin, N. and Lincoln, Y. (1994) *Handbook of Qualitative Research* (Thousand Oaks, CA: Sage).

Douglas, A. (1992) *Structure and Improvisation: The Making Aspect of Sculpture*, PhD thesis, Sunderland University.

Douglas, A. and Scopa, K. (2000) Research through Practice: Positioning the Practitioner as Researcher, in: *Research into Practice*, July 1999 – www.hert.ac.uk/artdes/conex/res2prac/.

Edwards, A. D and Westgate, D. P. G. (1987) Investigating classroom talk. Falmer in: Cohen, L. and Manion, L. (1994) *Research Methods in Education* (London: Routledge).

Emmison, M. and Smith P. (2000) *Researching the Visual: Images, Objects, Contexts and Interactions in Social and Cultural Inquiry* (London: Sage).

Eno, B. (1996) *A Year With Swollen Appendices* (London: Faber & Faber).

Feyerabend, P. (1988) *Against Method*, revised edition (London: Verso).

Friedman, K. (2002) Design thinking prize. Discussion list – phd-design@jiscmail.ac.uk (19 April, 2002).

Gleick, J. (1988) *Chaos: Making a New Science* (London: Cardinal).

Graham, B. (1997) *A Study of the Relationships with Interactive Computer-based Visual Artworks in Gallery Settings, through Observation, Art Practice and Curation*. PhD thesis, University of Sunderland.

Gray, C. (1998) *Teaching Styles in Higher Art Education*. PhD thesis, University of Aberdeen.

Graziano, A. M. and Raulin, M. (1993) *Research Methods: A Process of Inquiry* (New York: HarperCollins College Publishers).

Guba, E. G. (ed.) (1990) *The Paradigm Dialog* (Thousand Oaks, CA: Sage).

Hall, E. (1978) *Using Personal Constructs: Rediguide No. 9* (University of Nottingham, School of Education).

Hart, C. (1998) *Doing a Literature Review* (London: Sage).

Jones, J. C. (1980) *Design Methods: Seeds of Human Futures* (New York: Wiley).

Keats, D. M. (2000) *Interviewing: a Practical Guide for Students and Professionals* (Maidenhead, Berkshire: Open University Press).

Kelly, G. (1955) *The Psychology of Personal Constructs* (New York: Norton).

Kemp, M. (1989) *Leonardo da Vinci. Exhibition Catalogue* (South Bank Centre, London: Hayward Gallery).

Klee, P. (1968) *Pedagogical Sketchbook* (London: Faber).

Krause, J. and Lichtenstein, C. (eds) (1999) *Your Private Sky: R. Buckminster Fuller. The Art of Design Science* (London: Lars Müller).

Kuhn, T. S. (1970) *The Structure of Scientific Revolutions*, 2nd edn (Chicago: University of Chicago Press).

Lincoln, Y. and Guba, E. (1985) *Naturalistic Inquiry* (Thousand Oaks: Sage).

Lozios, P. (2000) Video, film and photographs as research documents, in: G. D Gaskell, and M. W. Bauer (eds) (2000) *Qualitative Researching with Text, Image and Sound: A Practical Handbook for Social Research* (London: Sage)

McAleese, R. (1999) Skill acquisition – the curious case of information searching. *Teaching of Information and Communication Sciences, Euroconference*, September 1999, Pontificia de Salamanca, Spain.

McKernan, J. (1998) *Curriculum Action Research: a Handbook of Methods and Resources for the Reflective Practitioner* (London: Kogan Page).

Miles, M. B. and Huberman, A. M. (1994) *Qualitative Data Analysis* (Thousand Oaks, CA: Sage).

New Collins Concise Dictionary of the English Language (1986) Managing editor W. T. McLeod (London & Glasgow: Collins).

Newbury, D. (2001) Diaries and field notes in the research process, *Research Issues in Art, Design and Media*, Issue No.1, Autumn.

Oldenburg, C. and van Bruggen, C. (1988) *A Bottle of Notes and Some Voyages* (Leeds: Northern Centre for Contemporary Art/Henry Moore Centre).

Polanyi, M. (1958) *Personal Knowledge: Towards a Post-critical Philosophy* (London: Routledge and Kegan Paul).

Popham, A. E. (1964) *The Drawings of Leonardo da Vinci* (London: Jonathan Cape).

Popper, K. R. (1991) *Conjectures and Refutations: The Growth of Scientific Knowledge* (London: Routledge).

Prophet, J. (1995) *Taste, Teaching and the Utah Teapot: Creative, Gender, Aesthetic and Pedagogical Issues Surrounding the Use of Electronic Media in Art and Design Education, with Particular Reference to Hypertext Applications*. PhD thesis, University of Warwick.

Renwick, G. *Spacial Determinism in the Canadian north: a Theoretical Overview and Practice-based Response*. PhD thesis, University of Dundee.

Robson, C. (1993) *Real World Research: a Resource for Social Scientists and Practitioner-researchers* (Oxford: Blackwell).

Ross, J. (2001) *The Role of the Artist in Environmental Change – An Investigation into Collaborative, Interactive and Participative Art Practice in Organizational Contexts*, PhD thesis, Glasgow School of Art.

Scopa, K. (2003) *The Development of Strategies for Interdisciplinary Collaboration from within the Visual Arts*. PhD thesis, The Robert Gordon University.

Schmiedeck, R. A. (1978) *The Personal Sphere Model* (New York: Grune & Stratton).

Schön, D. (1983) *The Reflective Practitioner* (New York: Basic Books).

Silver, S. (1999) *The Role of Artists in the Public Realm: an investigation into artists' generative process in context*. PhD thesis, The Robert Gordon University.

Silver, S. and Lucas, M. (1997) *Hospitals Talking Art: Recording the Visual Dialogue* (The Robert Gordon University, Aberdeen).

Spradley, J. (1980) *Participant Observation* (London: Holt, Rinehart & Winston).

Spiller, J. (ed.) (1973) *The Notebooks of Paul Klee, Volume 1: The Seeing Eye* (Lund Humphries).

Stonyer, A. (1978) *The Development of Kinetic Sculpture by the Utilisation of Solar Energy*. PhD thesis, De Montfort University (formerly Leicester Polytechnic).

Tufte, E. (1983) *The Visual Display of Quantitative Information* (Cheshire, Connecticut: Graphics Press).

Tufte, E. (1990) *Envisioning Information* (Cheshire, Connecticut: Graphics Press).

Tufte, E. (1997) Visual Explanations: Images and Quantities, Evidence and Narrative (Cheshire, Connecticut: Graphics Press).

Tyler, S. A. (1986) Postmodern ethnography: from document of the occult to occult document, in: J. Clifford and G. F. Marcus (eds) *Writing Culture: the Poetics and Politics of Ethnography*, pp. 122–140 (Berkeley: University of California Press).

Waldrop, M. M. (1994) *Complexity: The Emerging Science at the Edge of Order and Chaos* (London: Penguin).

Watson, A. (1992) *An Exploration of The Principle of Chance as a Stimulus to the Creative Activity known as Sculpture*. PhD thesis, The Robert Gordon University.

Wheeler, E. (1996) *The Role of Architectural Ceramics in Contemporary Site-specific Art*. PhD thesis, University of Northumbria, Newcastle.

Yin, R. (1984) *Case Study Research* (Thousand Oaks: Sage).
Zeisel, J. (1984) *Inquiry by Design* (Cambridge University Press).
Ziman, J. (1978) *Reliable Knowledge: an Exploration of the Grounds for Belief in Science* (Cambridge University Press).

Suggested further reading

Brewer, J. and Hunter, A. (1989) *Multimethod Research: a Synthesis of Styles, Chapter 4, Collecting Data with Multiple Methods* (Newbury Park, CA: Sage).
Crickmay, C. L. and Jones, J. C. (1972) *Imagination and Method: Designing as a Response to Life as a Whole. Technology Foundation Course Units 32–34* (Maidenhead, Berkshire: Open University Press).
Eisner, E. W. (1991) *The Enlightened Eye: Qualitative Inquiry and the Enhancement of Educational Practice* (New York: Macmillan).
Evans, K. M. (1978) *Planning Small Scale Research* (Windsor: NFER).
Glaser, B. G. and Strauss, A. L. (1967) *The Discovery of Grounded Theory: Strategies for Qualitative Research* (New York: Aldine).
Jorgenson, D. L. (1989) *Participant Observation: A Methodology for Human Studies* (Thousand Oaks, CA: Sage).
Lawson, B. (1990) *How Designers Think: The Design Process Demystified*, 2nd edn (London: Butterworth Architecture).

5 Interpreting the map: methods of evaluation and analysis

CHAPTER OVERVIEW

5.1 EVALUATION, ANALYSIS AND INTERPRETATION

Evaluating methodology and methods

> Analysis is not about adhering to any one correct approach or set of right techniques; it is imaginative, artful, flexible and reflexive. It should also be methodical, scholarly, and intellectually rigorous. (Coffey and Atkinson, 1996, p. 10)

In any research project, the methodology and methods used need to be evaluated as to their effectiveness in structuring the research and generating/yielding good quality data. This is an essential part of demonstrating the rigour of the research. If the overall methodology turns out to be inappropriate then this throws the validity of the research into question. For instance, much of the early research into creativity adopted a purely scientific approach, trying to 'measure' and 'explain' the 'results', rather than understand the person and the process in relation to the outcomes. This early research is now considered unreliable in many ways.

Similarly, flaws in the choice and application of research methods will produce data that will be limited in providing useful evidence for analysis, for example a poorly structured interview schedule, inaudible audio tapes, sloppy transcription. It is better to revise and re-apply the method rather than attempt what will be an ill-fated analysis! This is why the piloting of all methods is so crucial. However, if revision and reapplication are not possible then at least the limitations of the research must be critically evaluated and discussed as part of the analysis of your research project.

Validity and reliability: towards research quality

Two key terms appeared in the last section – validity and reliability. These concepts (and others, as we shall see later) are concerned with establishing research quality. In scientific methodologies, objectivity, validity, reliability and replicatability are the cornerstones of research quality. Put simply, these are concerned with making sure that the research is understood by other scientists (consensible) and there is general agreement amongst them (consensual). The issue of shared standards is important, but in alternative research paradigms different terms have been developed which are more suitable for human inquiry, and inquiry which is 'real world' and practice-based. Tesch (1990) summarizes well the position of qualitative researchers:

> Qualitative research is to a large degree an art. The question of its validity does not depend on replicable outcomes. It depends on the employment of a data 'reduction' process that leads to a result that others can accept as representing the data. The result of the analysis is, in fact, a representation in the same sense that an artist can, with a few strokes of the pen, create an image of a face that we would recognise if we saw the original in a crowd. The details are lacking, but a good 'reduction' not only selects and emphasises the essential features, it retains the vividness of the personality in the rendition of the face. In the same way a successful qualitative data reduction, while removing us from the freshness of the original, presents us instead with an image that we can grasp as the 'essence', where we otherwise would have been flooded with detail and left with hardly a perception of the phenomena at all. (Tesch, 1990, p. 304)

Instead of using the terms 'validity' and 'reliability' in their scientific sense, 'trustworthiness' has been suggested as being more appropriate for naturalistic inquiry (Lincoln and Guba, 1985). Robson (1993) suggests that by asking yourself key questions a sense of how believable and trustworthy your research has been can begin to be established:

> Have you done a good, thorough and honest job? Have you tried to explore, describe, explain in an open and unbiased way, or are you more concerned with delivering the required answer or selecting the evidence to support a case? If you can't answer these questions with yes, yes and no respectively, then your findings are essentially worthless. . . . (Robson, 1993, p. 66)

Trustworthiness still encompasses the term 'validity' but in a modified sense. Validity is concerned with whether the research findings make sense, and are credible to the research context – its users, our peers, our readers. Trustworthiness also encompasses 'generalizability' – the extent to which the research findings are more generally applicable (transferable) to other contexts. In qualitative research, the development of criteria for evaluating research quality is a discursive task, involving inter-subjectivity and negotiation. We work towards shared approaches and being able to speak the same research language, whilst not necessarily being in complete agreement![1]

Spectacles and sieves: criteria

Most researchers would concur that preliminary evaluation and analysis take place in parallel with data generation/collection and are iterative, reflexive activities. At best they are playful and creative, yet rigorous. There are many parallels between the construction of an art/design work and the construction of a research argument, not least in the way that the form is proposed, critiqued, deconstructed, remodelled, and resolved. Much of this process is evaluative and analytical, reflective and deconstructive, creative and synthetic. As practitioners we engage in these activities constantly and most of the time unconsciously. As reflective researchers we must make these activities explicit and accessible.

To recap from Chapter 4 (Section 4.4) evaluation and analysis are two distinct activities:

- to 'evaluate' is to ascertain the value of something and to judge or assess its worth;
- to 'analyse' is to examine something in detail in order to discover its meaning.

However, nothing can be evaluated or analysed without criteria with which to make judgements/assessments. For example, what makes 'good' design could be articulated in relation to three key criteria: effectiveness, efficiency, economy. These, in turn, could be 'unpacked' to provide more focused criteria, for example effectiveness in relation to context and aesthetics; efficiency in terms of function and use; economy in terms of cost and use of materials. It is essential that the criteria you develop relate to the aim and objectives of the research. For example, if your research aims to develop an understanding of the use of multimedia to practitioners in Art and Design then the criteria for evaluation and analysis should focus on, for instance, the user-friendliness or otherwise of the technologies involved, the problems/challenges that emerge for users, the benefits and limitation of multimedia for practitioners, and the impact of the technologies/media on practitioners' working processes and products.

Criteria are like spectacles and sieves: they are the means by which we focus, capture and distil value and meaning. Different spectacle lenses allow us to see in various ways – to see some things whilst not being distracted by others, for example Polaroid sunglasses can allow us to see below the surface of water by eliminating glare. Different meshes in sieves allow us to capture some things while discarding others, for example in panning for gold. Conversely, paper coffee filters capture the unpalatable grounds leaving us with the essential distilled liquid. These different lenses, meshes, filters are metaphors for the sets of criteria by which we evaluate, analyse and make sense of research outcomes (Figure 5.1).

But how do we know that these tools are appropriate? The best way is to try them out! Never assume that your initial set of criteria is perfect. As soon as you try to apply them they might reveal their inadequacies. It is a good idea to talk through your criteria with a colleague. As soon as you try to explain your criteria and how you have arrived at them, questions can be asked and discussion can reveal strengths and weaknesses. Your criteria for evaluation and analysis should be robust, transparent and related to the research context. You should explain the context in which the criteria have been generated. For the purposes of this discussion let us presume that the methods you have employed have provided usable data for analysis, and that you have an initial set of criteria – different kinds of spectacles and sieves! We can now look at how we might analyse the resulting information.

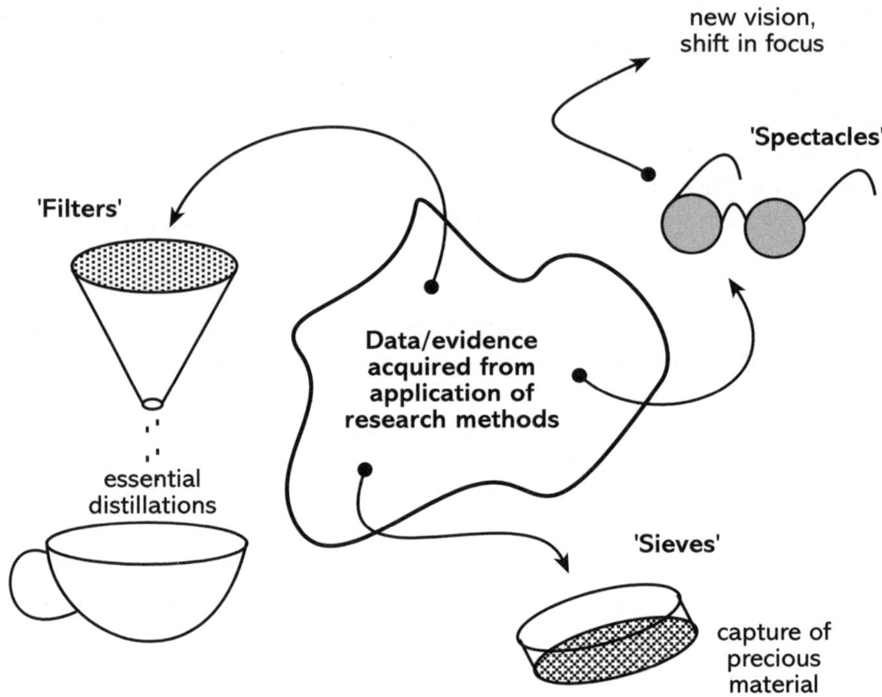

Figure 5.1 Spectacles, sieves and filters provide metaphors for different criteria in analysing data (💻)

Analysis: some considerations

As usual in practice-based research in Art and Design, there is no 'right way' to analyse research findings. Coffey and Atkinson urge us to be 'artful' and 'imaginative' but also 'rigorous'. Qualitative analysis is 'intellectual craftsmanship' – playful but methodical and intellectually competent. The parallels with our own discipline's processes and values are encouraging and inspiring. Imagination, crafted construction and artful persuasion are things to which we can relate. Integrate these with critical thinking and response – essential intellectual elements of the creative process – and we have a sound basis for analysis.

From the key texts available[2] and from our own experiences of practice-based research, there are some considerations that may be helpful in considering the process of analysis:

- Analysis is not the last phase in the research process. It is concurrent with data gathering/generation and is cyclic/iterative, serving to inform and drive each other.
- The broad aim of analysis is to look for meanings and understanding.
- Analysis begins by taking into account all the data to achieve a sense of the whole.

The data can then divided up into meaningful units (segmented and categorized), but a connection to the whole must be maintained.

- Analysis is a systematic process, requiring discipline and perseverance.
- Data analysis encompasses any approach to reduce the complexity in the data material, and to come to a coherent interpretation of what is and what is not the case.
- Analysis is a reflective activity, aiming to move from the data to a conceptual level. It is helpful to track this reflection (using notes/journal). This record of reflection not only helps in shifting from detail to big picture, but also provides accountability of the analytical process.
- Data can be categorized either in relation to some organizing system; for example, criteria related to the research questions and/or a conceptual framework, or 'interrogated' through an inductive process where categories emerge as a result.
- There must be a clear and explicit rationale for the criteria used in analysis and these criteria must be applied with consistency.
- The main intellectual tool of analysis is comparison. The aim is to discover similarities and/or differences by the use of comparison and contrast. This helps to form categories, establish boundaries, find inconsistencies, discover patterns and connections, and paint the larger picture beyond the specific detail.
- There are various visual devices for sorting and structuring data, for example a matrix, mind maps, network diagrams, and so on; for a text – marking, highlighting/colour coding (relating to criteria), adding notes and comments, graphical representations, note cards/'Post its'. (Some of these are described in Section 5.3.) Try out different devices. This process is tentative and preliminary at the beginning and must remain flexible. Be prepared to modify. Do not get locked into conclusions too early.
- Analysis is an eclectic activity. Play with the data and immerse yourself in it. The creative involvement of the researcher is important, but this must be tracked/recorded for accountability. Use the data to think with.
- In many research areas (involving human inquiry) the research outcomes are negotiated between the researcher and the participants in the research so as to create resonance and shared meaning.
- Be sceptical and alert to the limits of evidence. If evidence is inadequate then this must be acknowledged.
- Employ alternative strategies, for example work in two ways: quickly and imaginatively in order to create insights, and slowly and methodically for close reading and reflection.
- An interpretation develops/evolves through both visual and discursive analysis. As this occurs it is important to revisit the raw material to ensure that a 'chain of evidence'/audit trail is clear.
- The result of analysis is some type of higher-level synthesis and interpretation. Although much of analysis is taking apart, the final goal is emergence of a larger consolidated picture, for example a composite summary, a description of patterns/themes, an identification of a fundamental structure, a new concept or theory, new/alternative meanings.
- Analysis is never exhaustive and never really finished. It is complete to a degree when

the specific question or point has been addressed, and therefore it is important to state the scope/confines of the analysis. Analysis ends only after new data no longer generate new insights – the process exhausts the data.

Frameworks for analysis

Depending on your research area, there may already exist useful 'organizing systems' for analysis you might use. Trying to make sense of your data through such conceptual/theoretical frameworks is a useful analytical strategy. These existing frameworks may need to be adapted in some way. It is extremely important that such frameworks be acknowledged and detailed references given. Here are some examples of analytical frameworks from recent formal research.

In *On the Notion of Test* (Douglas, 1997) John Cage's 'conditions for improvisation' in music were used as a framework for Douglas's analysis of understanding the structure of improvization in the development of her own sculpture. Using Cage's 'conditions' as a basis (structure, method, form, frequency and duration, timbre and amplitude) Douglas related these to making sculpture and produced a set of criteria for her own analysis. (This multimedia essay is included in 'Sculpture, Method, Research', 1997, but only in a Mac version.)

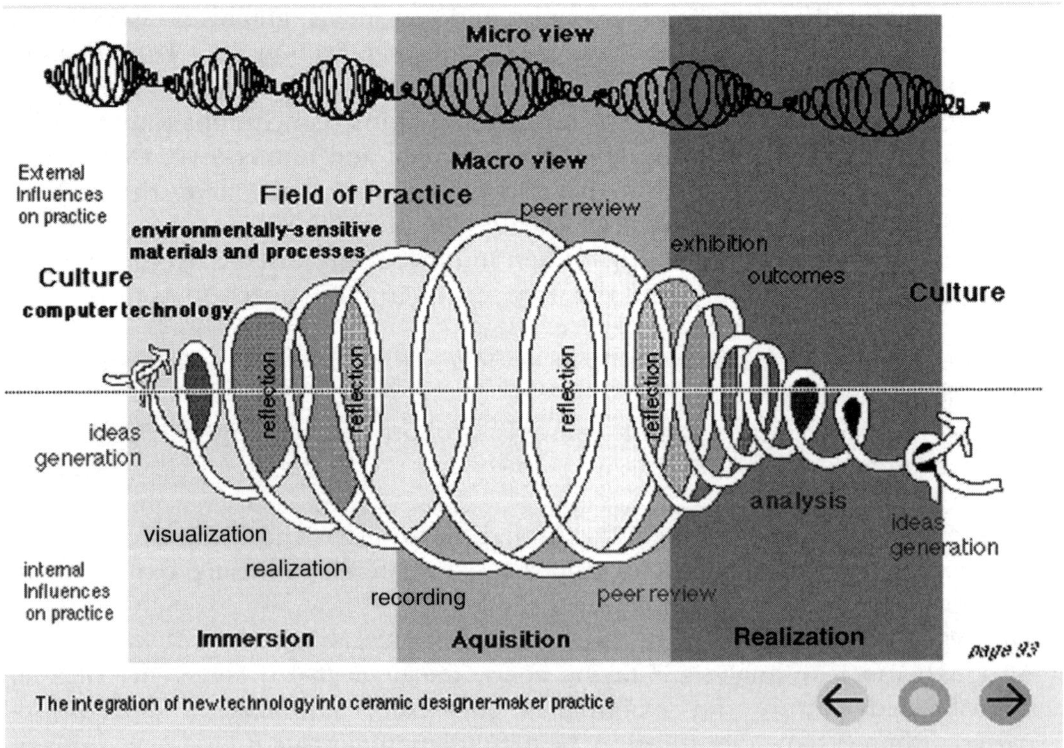

Figure 5.2 A visual model of the researcher's creative process (💻)
(from Bunnell, 1998 – thesis in digital format)

Both Bunnell (1998) and Silver (1999) made use of Getzels and Csikszentmihalyi's model of artists' creativity as an analytical framework. Bunnell used the model in order to extend her understanding of her own creative process and make it more explicit (PhD thesis – described as part of Methodology, Section 3.3.2, and also in Analysis, Section 4.4).

Silver used the model in order to analyse three artists' generative processes in her research on the role of artists in public contexts. Data from a case study project – 'Taming Goliath' – was analysed using a technique of 'code-and-retrieve' to track certain generic strands (criteria) derived from Getzels and Csikszentmihalyi's model. This was probably the first application of the 'sweatbox' method (reflection in and on action captured through video – see Chapter 4, Section 4.3) combined with content analysis techniques in art and design research.

The use of existing frameworks for analysis also help to link your research outcomes to established research. This does not mean that your outcomes simply reinforce or extend the status quo – they might well do – but they may also challenge it, and propose something alternative in its place.

Making sense

The outcome of the analysis is usually some kind of higher level synthesis – a big picture, an interpretation. The process of interpretation necessitates 'going beyond the data' to develop ideas that might be valuable and applicable in wider contexts. This stage of 'generalization' is an important indicator of research quality. An honest evaluation of the scope of the transferability of the research must be made. Most practice-based and qualitative research is case and context specific, transferable in broad principles but usually not in specific detail.

Interpretation is only *one* version, *one* reading of the research outcomes from the perspective of the researcher. Again, Douglas (1997) provides us with a helpful overview of the paradigm of interpretation in relation to practice-based research:

> Contemporary Hermeneutics, unlike Positivism in science and technology and Structuralism within social science (anthropology), acknowledges a diachronic, changing, dynamic view of its subject, as opposed to a synchronic, cross-sectional view. In doing so it allows for multi-meaning as opposed to the functional language of science and technology, where words carry single meanings. (Douglas, 1997, section: *The Paradigm of Hermeneutics*).

A hermeneutic approach seeks to 'elucidate and make explicit our practical understanding of human actions by providing interpretations of them' (Packer, 1985, p. 1088). This idea of making explicit practical understandings and making sense of them in appropriate ways is important in art and design research.

Your interpretation (related to your argument) must be based on the available evidence, and all research evidence must be accessible to others in order that they could make *their own* interpretations if necessary. This is why most primary data should be available as part of the research report or dissertation/thesis. This usually takes the form of appendices. (More information on this in Chapter 6, Section 6.2.) The accessibility of the data allows for multiple meanings to be developed.

However, essential though your interpretation is, in 'naturalistic inquiry' it is sometimes necessary to negotiate research outcomes as part of establishing the trustworthiness of the research. This is a dialogic process – through conversations with others (peers, supervisors) you can propose different interpretations and get some feedback. You may think it appropriate, especially if you have engaged participants or collaborators in your research, to discuss your interpretation with them. In human inquiry this process is called 'communicative validation' where the outcomes of the research are fed back to the respondents/participants who are asked to agree/disagree to ensure their situation/views are not misrepresented. This kind of feedback and negotiation may prompt you to reconsider some issues, to revisit the data, and to revise your interpretation. The analytical process should be flexible and iterative.

Finally, let us return to the metaphor of the research journey. This chapter is about *Interpreting the Map*. You should now be in a new position on the map, probably on higher ground so that you can look back and over the landscape. In reflecting on this view you should be able to see where you have been and what kind of terrain you have crossed. You should be able to say if your 'vehicles' were trustworthy and have enabled you to cross the terrain effectively. You should be able to sense that you are now on new ground and have a view from it that you could not see before – both back and forward. You should be able to make sense of where you are and what possible tracks you could take next. Can you see other researchers in the terrain? What is your relative position to them? Will your paths cross in the next part of the journey?

Reflection and action: suggestions

- Can you answer Robson's questions about the credibility of your research?
- Identify two possible existing analytical frameworks that may be helpful to your research analysis.
- If the concept of 'negotiated outcomes' is relevant for you, how might you conduct this with the participants in your research?

5.2 EXAMPLES OF ANALYSIS FROM COMPLETED FORMAL RESEARCH IN ART AND DESIGN

As there are many different approaches to analysis, it is essential to consider as many examples as possible to get a feel for what approaches are acceptable and what methods have been formally validated. ARIAD (www.ariad.co.uk) provides access to examples of completed formal research in Art and Design. In using the Index look out for examples of particular analytical strategies, frameworks and methods. The Research Training Initiative also provides a selection of case studies of completed research in Art and Design (http://www.biad.uce.ac.uk/research/index.html). Similarly, it may be useful to consider examples from other disciplines, especially the performing arts and humanities. The Index to Theses (www.theses.com) may be helpful in this. Just a few examples of analysis are presented here. All have their limitations and they are neither exhaustive nor comprehensive, but they should give you some leads in your wider search.

Analysis using triangulation

Although essentially a social science thesis on 'Teaching styles in higher art education', Gray (1988) made a conscious attempt to develop methodological procedures that were more qualitative, visual and interactive. Her analysis involved three perspectives – that is, a triangulation (Figure 5.3):

- lecturers' perceptions of their own teaching styles (captured through a 3D 'game' model);
- students' perceptions of lecturers' styles (captured through audio interviews);
- the researcher's perceptions and observations (extended by video documentation of studio teaching).

Preliminary interviews with students and lecturers identified 14 'important factors in teaching'. These factors (criteria, in fact) were used to interrogate the data generated from the various methods. Corroboration between the three perceptions supported the argument that different teaching styles did exist and could be distinctly characterized.

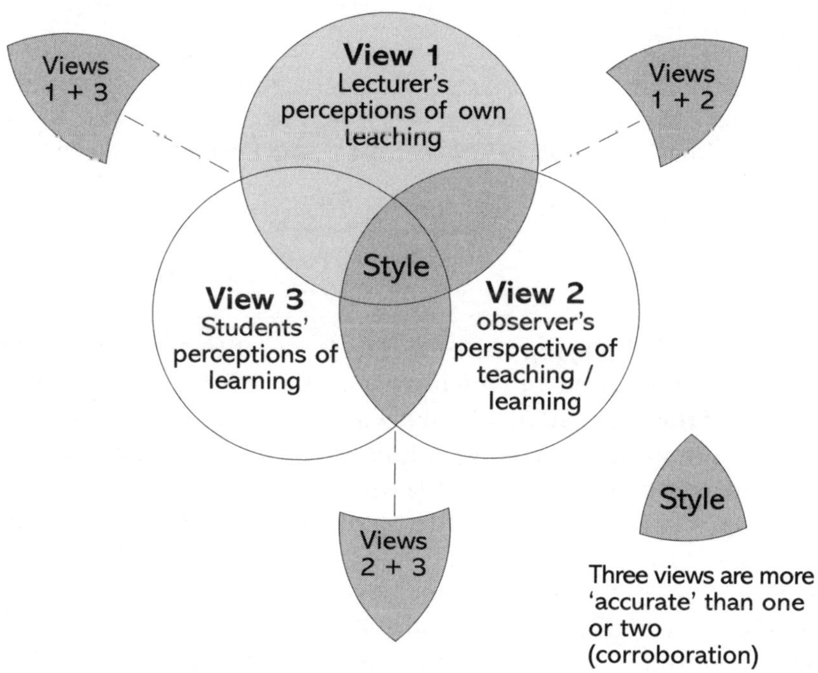

Figure 5.3 Three methods used to provide different perspectives on the central issue – teaching styles (💻)

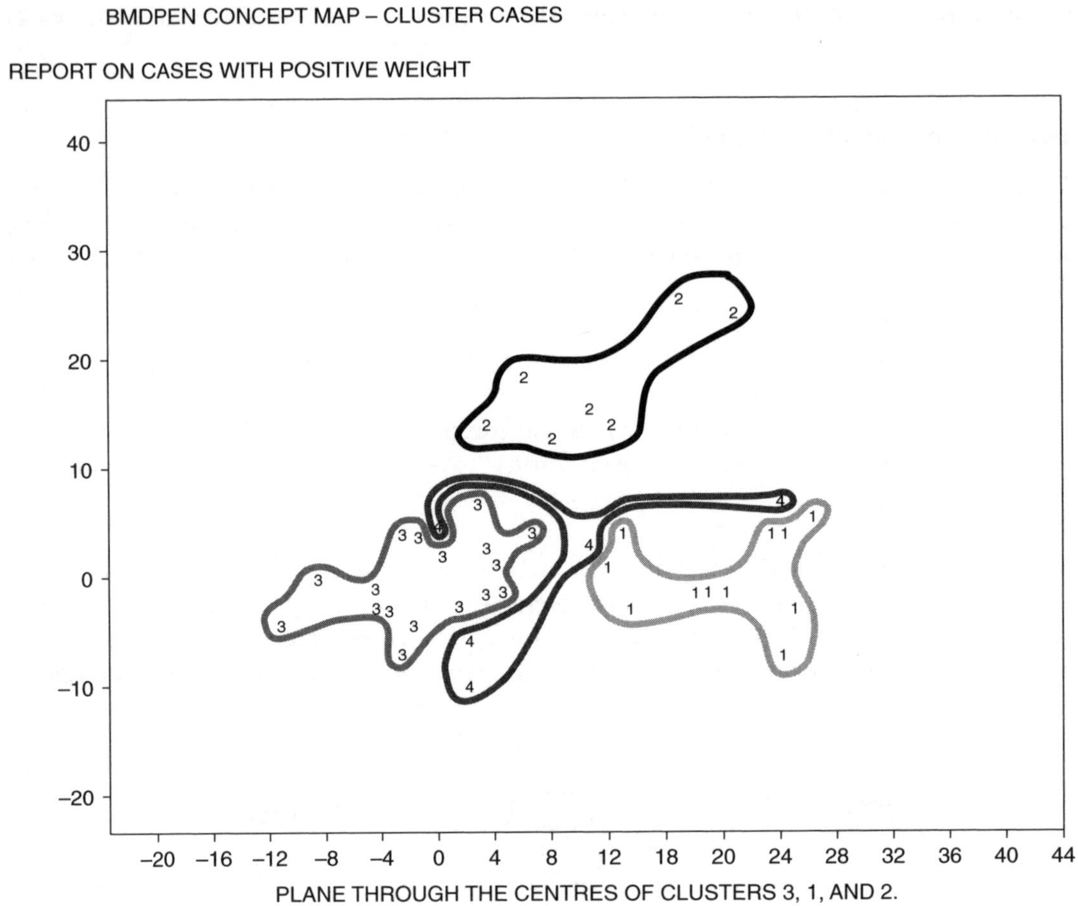

Figure 5.4 Example of a cluster map indicating four different teaching styles

The analysis involved playing with the data in order to see patterns. Many different visualizations were tried, none of which were available 'off the peg', but were invented or adapted. One of the main methods used was *cluster analysis*. Although this technique is basically used for sorting out large volumes of data using a computer program, its principle is useful in that what is sought is the identification of 'groupings'. This analytical process relies on the criteria of likeness/similarities and differences/contrasts in order to generate clusters or typologies. The program usually provides visual maps of clusters, which can help the researcher to describe relationships between clusters, and identify specific characteristics of each cluster.

The analysis proved to be the hardest part of the research, but the most enjoyable. Initially the naïve expectation was that styles existed 'out there' waiting to be discovered. In fact, the eventual set of teaching styles was a 'construction' made from the available evidence.

Visual analysis: two examples

Douglas started using multimedia towards the end of her PhD (1992) as she sought out the most appropriate methods to present her practice-based research. In subsequent post-doctoral research she produced a multimedia essay – *On the Notion of Test* – which makes a visual analysis of her PhD research, and its development from a positivist paradigm to a hermeneutic one. In the essay, Douglas provides a visual and interactive overview of the whole development over time and in relation to the philosophical and working context. The main framework for analysis is Cage's 'conditions for improvisation' that Douglas adopts and adapts in order to analyse and interpret her own sculpture.

The PhD work is analysed in a series of matrices, where each sculpture (information in columns) is interrogated in relation to a number of 'constants', for example structure, form, method, materials (information in rows). The intersecting cells contained the analysis. The matrix structure allows for a comparative analysis of the body of work (Figure 5.5).

As a multimedia document, the essay allows for hyper-linked levels of information within one matrix. This kind of multimedia matrix goes beyond a two-dimensional

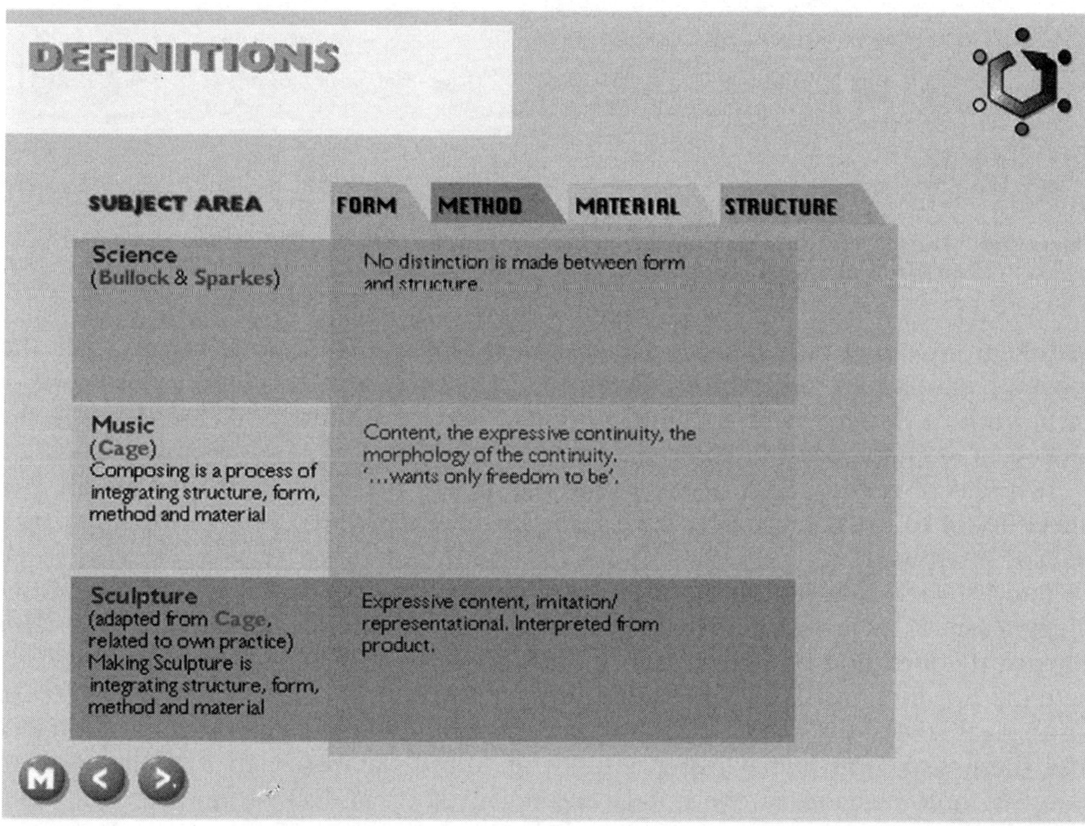

Figure 5.5 Hyper-linked matrix structure for comparative analysis of form, method, material, structure in science, music and sculpture (💻)

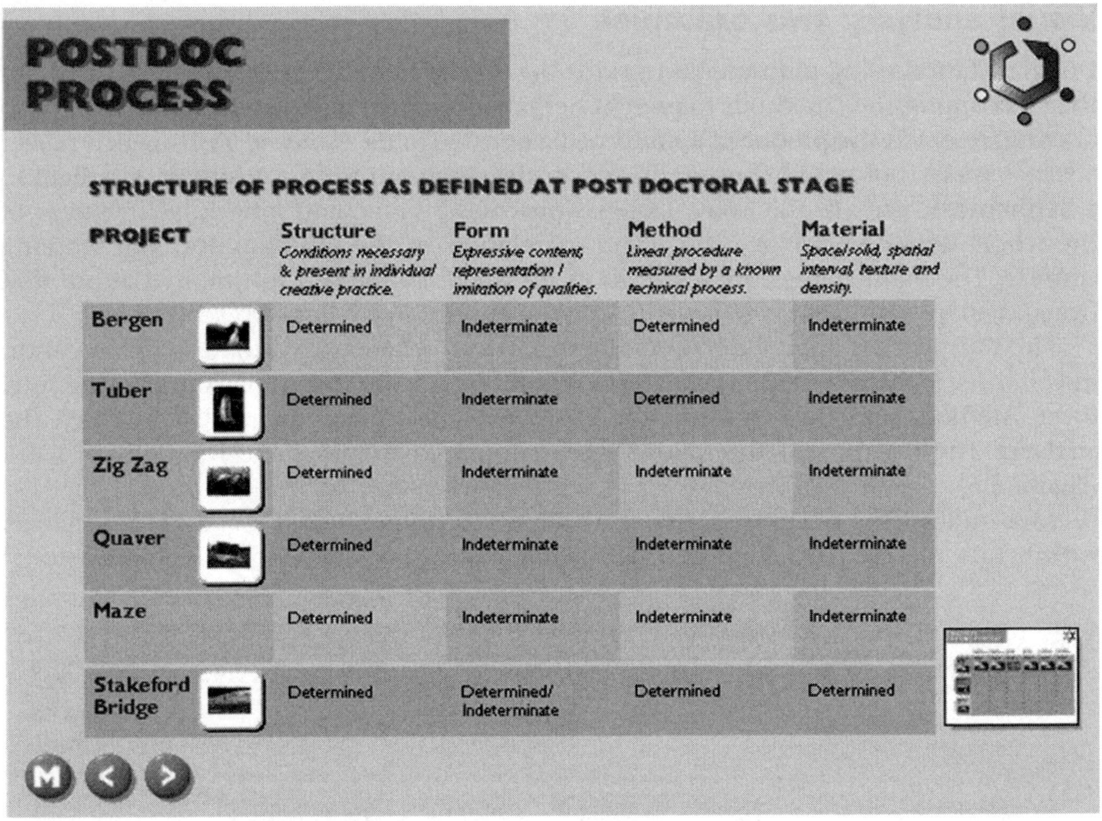

Figure 5.6 Hyper-linked matrix structure for comparative analysis of form, method, material, structure in six different sculptures (💻)

matrix in providing an extensive set of data that can include text, visuals (still and moving), animations, and sound (Figure 5.6). The essay also provides 'slide shows' of each work in development including detailed textual information, for example the process of mould making, texture, site, and so on.

In terms of making an analysis and presenting it, the multimedia matrix can give direct access to the data (located in deep levels of the matrix), as well as presenting a holistic interpretation.

Bunnell's research resulted in a PhD thesis submitted in digital format (as a CD – 'Integration of new technology into designer-maker ceramic practice', 1998). This allowed the inclusion of a great deal of interactive visual material to comprehensively describe her investigation: still images of experimental and resolved work, video of lustre glaze effects, interactive diagrams, 2D visualization and 3D modelling techniques. The thesis was constructed using a series of linked databases. In a similar way to Douglas' multimedia essay, the storage and organization of data within these databases enabled direct access to evidence, which could be used as part of her analysis. The analysis (Section 4 of the PhD) attempted to be as visual as possible. An overview of the analysis is offered appropriately enough on a 'plate' (Figure 5.7).

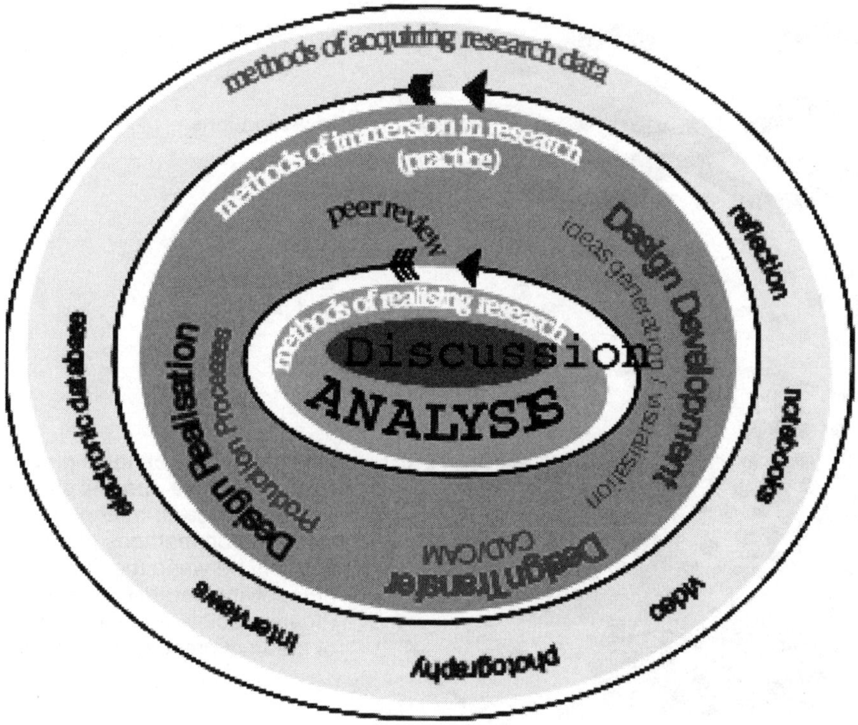

Figure 5.7 Visual overview of analysis using the metaphor of a 'plate'

Bunnell drew on Miles and Huberman's (1994, pp. 10–12) definition of analysis as 'three concurrent flows of activity' – data reduction, data display, and conclusion drawing. She used two 'sieves' or 'filters' – criteria relating to the benefits and limitations of using new technology in designer-maker practice – as a means of reducing the data and bringing some order to it. Concurrent with this she began mapping, grouping and relating the data by means of visual displays. Tentative conclusions as to the effectiveness of integrating new technology into practice were proposed through interrogating the actual body of experimental work. More developed conclusions emerged through concentrating on three different examples of resolved work (Figure 5.8).

Other completed formal research in Art and Design provide examples of different analytical strategies, for example:

- using corroboration between three sets of outcomes – from practice, from student projects, and from 'expert' participation;
- a series of interviews with commissioners/clients, 'expert' designers, users, as well as the designer-researcher's own critical evaluations;
- site-specific artworks as 'cases' involving the feedback of all the participants in the research – architects, users of buildings, commissioners, and the critical analysis of the artist researcher.

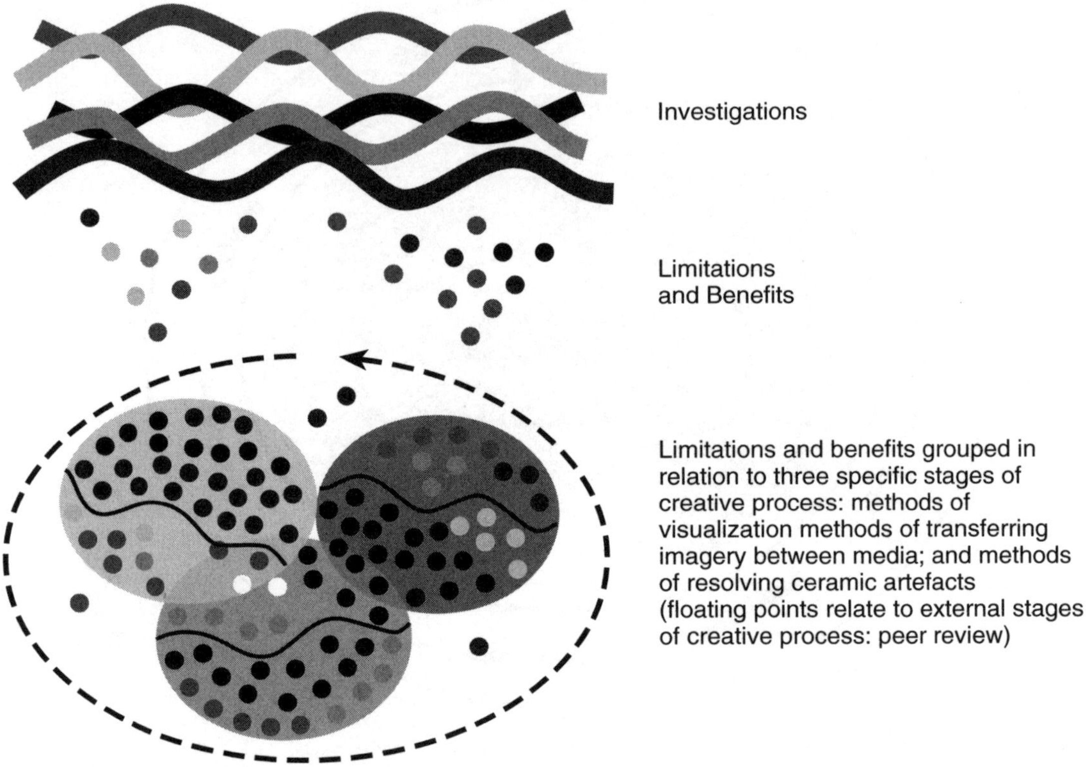

Figure 5.8 Three stages of analysis – filtering, mapping/grouping, and interrogation of the body of work towards conclusions (💻)

Multiple perspectives in analysis

Most of the examples cited demonstrate the use of multiple perspectives in analysis. This is a particularly important methodological consideration. As we saw in Chapters 1 and 3, the use of multiple methods in generating and gathering data offers the opportunity for using triangulation to help get a 'fix' on a complex something in order to understand it more fully by examining it from different perspectives (Figure 5.9).

The different views either come together to support your argument or make you question your original research proposition. Both outcomes are valuable in research terms. Obviously, it is satisfying to have arrived at some kind of consensus or broad agreement; however, it is equally interesting to have a range of different and possibly conflicting views. When dealing with complex, real-world issues, rarely does everything fit neatly and resolve into an elegant whole. Contemporary research practices must be prepared for this and make an interpretation of the research that acknowledges pluralism. An honest appraisal of the strengths and limitations of the analytical approach and methods used is an important part of a research report or dissertation. A rigorous and robust argument can still be made based on the evidence from the research.

Reflection and action: suggestions

- Examine three completed PhDs in order to find out more about different analytical approaches/methods that have been validated. What analytical strategies and specific methods might you adopt/adapt?
- If appropriate, how will you seek the opinions of others in your analysis?
- Look at selected reviews in professional magazines, periodicals, journals, for example *Art Monthly, Design Week, Crafts, Artists Newsletter, Blueprint, Flash Art, Design Journal, Wallpaper, Architectural Review, Digital Creativity, Journal of Visual Arts Practice,* and so on. Can you identify different styles of critical analysis in these publications?
- Read Umberto Eco's small book *Reflections on 'The Name of the Rose'*. This provides a superb example of a concise and clear analysis of a much larger work by 'telling the process'.

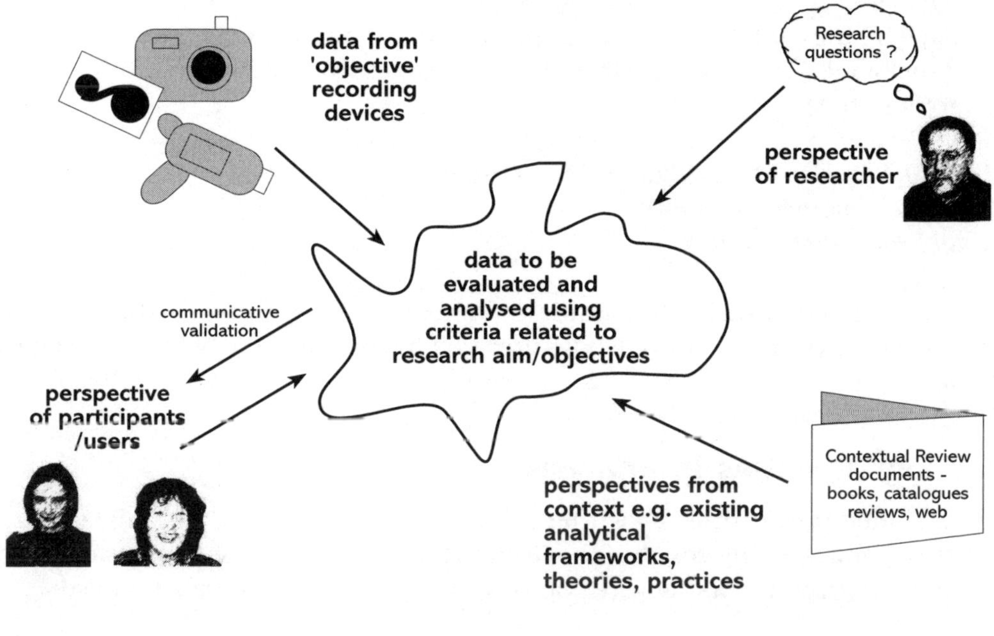

Figure 5.9 'Triangulation' in analysis: the use of multiple and diverse perspectives

5.3 'PLAYING' WITH DATA: TOOLS FOR ANALYSIS

This topic describes a range of visual structures by which to analyse and make sense of data resulting from the use of research methods. As there are many different analytical approaches, presented here are only the *principles* of various structures for analysis and no detailed content examples. We offer these as 'tools' for possible ways of looking at data, 'playing' with them as a creative activity and finally making sense of them.

Again, these are not comprehensive and not exhaustive. You should seek out other structures/tools in your wider search for examples of analysis.

Useful references on analytical tools

There is a reasonable amount of established literature on analytical structures and techniques, mostly in relation to quantitative data, for example Robson (1993, Section 11) – frequency distribution table, histogram, pie chart, scattergram, chi square, and so on. This topic does not describe these. (For further details read Bryman and Cramer, 1990.) There is a developing body of published work on visual research in the social sciences, for example Sage publications such as *Visual Methodologies* (Rose, 2001); *Visual Methods in Social Research* (Banks, 2001). Whilst any information on visual research methods is welcomed, the emphasis in these books is on sociology, ethnography, cultural studies, semiology, and so on. Although we acknowledge the usefulness of this, what is presented here tries to relate as much as possible to Art and Design research. In our view, some of the best examples of visual analysis are contained in Edward Tufte's three books (all Graphics Press):

- *The Visual Display of Quantitative Data* (1983)
- *Envisioning Information* (1990)
- *Visual Explanations* (1997)

Every page contains excellent examples of visual analysis, some of the principles of which are described here, but we would urge you to consult these before you begin your analysis.

Three key activities in analysis

Miles and Huberman's 'three concurrent flows of activity' in analysis – data reduction, data display, and drawing conclusions from these first two – provide a basic framework for analysis. Within this framework, various structures/tools can be employed:

- data *reduction* – any structures/tools that encourage you to sort, select, focus, order, simplify data; for example, applying criteria – 'spectacles', 'sieves' and 'filters'; coding data by colour highlighting (relating to criteria); condensing, grouping/clustering.
- data *display* – any structures/tools that present data in an organized and usually compressed visual format, so that the user can gain an overview and understanding of the whole – literally, 'see what you might mean'; displays can show links and relationships between concepts/variables, and can bring relevant data together to encourage the drawing of conclusions.
- *drawing conclusions* – once the data are in some kind of display they can be interrogated for example:
    - How many times . . . ?
    - What kinds of patterns . . . ?

- Are themes/clusters apparent . . . ?
- What relationships exist . . . ?
- How does this relate to existing concepts . . . ?

Using the principle of the 'whole being greater than the sum of the parts' the display can be used to 'go beyond the data' – to generate new perceptions/meanings towards generalizing and theorizing. This process of conclusion drawing is tentative and preliminary at the beginning and must remain flexible. Be sceptical. Be prepared to revisit the data and to modify. Structure and re-structure in different forms. Do not get locked into conclusions too early.

As with the application of research methods in your project, it is important to keep track of your analytical process for the purposes of transparency and accountability. You could use a set of trigger questions such as 'what?, why?, how?, when?, where?, who?'. Keep an 'analysis log' as part of a reflective journal.

Some tools

Various kinds of techniques/structures are suggested, for example matrices, mind maps, networks, activity records, flow charts, and so on. The only way to evaluate their appropriateness to your research data is to try them out. If they are not useful for you then adapt or reject them and seek other techniques.

Matrices

Probably one of the most useful visual tools is a matrix, which is capable of conveying a great deal of information in a compressed space (Figure 5.10). The matrix is a very versatile tool for both information management and for analysis. A matrix comprises 'columns' and 'rows', which represents two different dimensions, concepts or sets of information; for example, 'criteria' in relation to 'research data'. Where these two dimensions cross, a new 'cell' of information emerges, for example by interrogating your 'research data' in relation to your 'criteria' you will derive aspects of a 'research outcome'. In designing a matrix we are considering how to 'partition' information and there are usually many different ways to do this (see Miles and Huberman, 1994, Chapter 9).

The matrix can also be a useful device for making comparisons across the data set, for example identifying differences and similarities in research data against one criterion (across rows), and how different criteria generate different research outcomes from the original data (down columns). Summary information can be added to each row and to each column. Equally interesting are the 'gaps', the matrix helps to identify. This may indicate a difficulty or anomaly in the analysis, that further analysis is required, or that the research is incomplete. Colours can also been used to provide another way of coding the information. Different colours might represent different research methods, or different criteria. You need to try out several different dimension labels to see what works best.

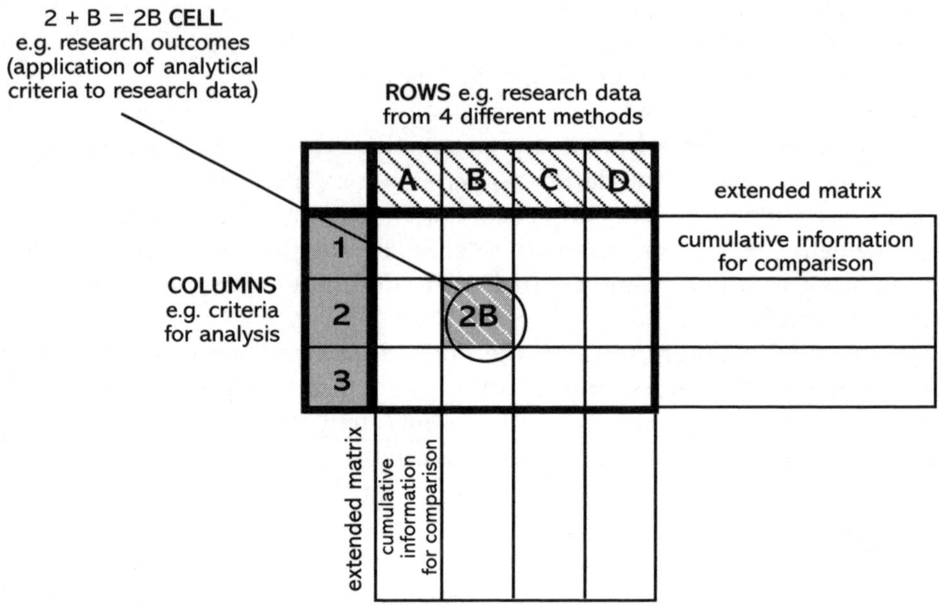

Figure 5.10 A matrix demonstrating some of the features discussed in the text

Mind maps

The ubiquitous mind map is valuable at all stages of the research process, not least in analysis. Whereas usually a matrix can only show the relationship between two variables, a mind map can show a more complex set of relationships. For example, a mind map could be used to interrogate and organize data in relation to the criteria related to your research questions. A map forces you to extract and select from a large amount of data and present your understanding in a single visual. In considering the relationships between keywords on the mind map you may be prompted to rethink how you have dealt with the data. Buzan (1998) provides some good examples of how mind maps can help someone gain an understanding of something and generate meaning from the map, for example the comprehensive visual on organizational structures (Buzan, 1948, p. 262) see also Chapter 4, Section 4.3, Figure 4.3.

Networks

The same kind of concepts used in a matrix can be used in a less rigid structure like a network. A network is a collection of 'nodes' (points) connected by 'links' (lines) and can be visualized as a tree structure with branches or a plant with roots. In analysis network displays are useful for:

- visualizing the relationship between many variables (the extent of the data network),
- visualizing groups and sub-groups (why data 'branches' off, what similarities/ differences there are in the data),

- describing an unfolding narrative (presenting a big picture, from which to draw conclusions).

There are many different kinds of network displays, for example context charts, causal networks, hierarchical networks. A good example – a taxonomy of cars and trucks – can be found in Miles and Huberman (1994, p. 133).

Activity records

Many everyday activities can be analysed visually to gain a holistic understanding of any process. For example, in the visual *Activity Record* (Box 5.5, p. 117, Miles and Huberman, 1994), the first impression is of a kind of beautiful wire frame necklace structure – completely symmetrical and delicately constructed. On closer inspection this turns out to be something much more ordinary – a visual analysis of changing a tyre! This kind of activity record can make actions very explicit, indicate important contextual preconditions, identify important phases and reveal the decision-making process. This visual tool could be used in the analysis of making a piece of work for example, or in demonstrating the structure of a particular process.

Flow charts

A flow chart is the classic method of tracking decision making, and seeing the whole picture of that process. An example of this kind of visual tool can be found in Robson (1993, pp. 396–397, Figure 12.3. A flow chart was used to good effect in research on the influence of chance/choice in making sculpture (Figure 5.11).

The chart tracked both decisions and subsequent actions as well as providing an essential record of activity for later analysis. The integration of data into a single display leads to an overview and understanding of a complex process.

A completely different style of flowchart is a multimedia experiment visualizing this kind of decision-making process through animation. In *Dining Out?* (Burt, 2000) you are offered a tantalizing (and humorous) array of choices and all your decisions can be seen at a glance (Figure 5.12).

'Dimensional' analysis

A useful way of sorting out data and generating clusters/groups is to apply some kind of 'dimensional' analysis. The simplest form of this is when two dimensions, say 'function' and 'scale', are crossed (Figure 5.13).

In this example, the portfolio of a contemporary product design company is analysed in relation to the dimensions of 'function' and 'scale'. The resulting analysis space allows for individual pieces of work to be located in relation to these dimensions and a broad brush mapping of the product range to be seen. More detailed structure could be applied to the analysis, for example actual physical measurements of products, a ranking scale for function, and so on. The use of photographs of the products would add to the visual impact of this kind of analysis. The same portfolio could be analysed again using other dimensions, for example 'cost' and 'sales', 'production method (mass or batch)' and 'quality'. More sophisticated analyses could be achieved by combining three dimensions,

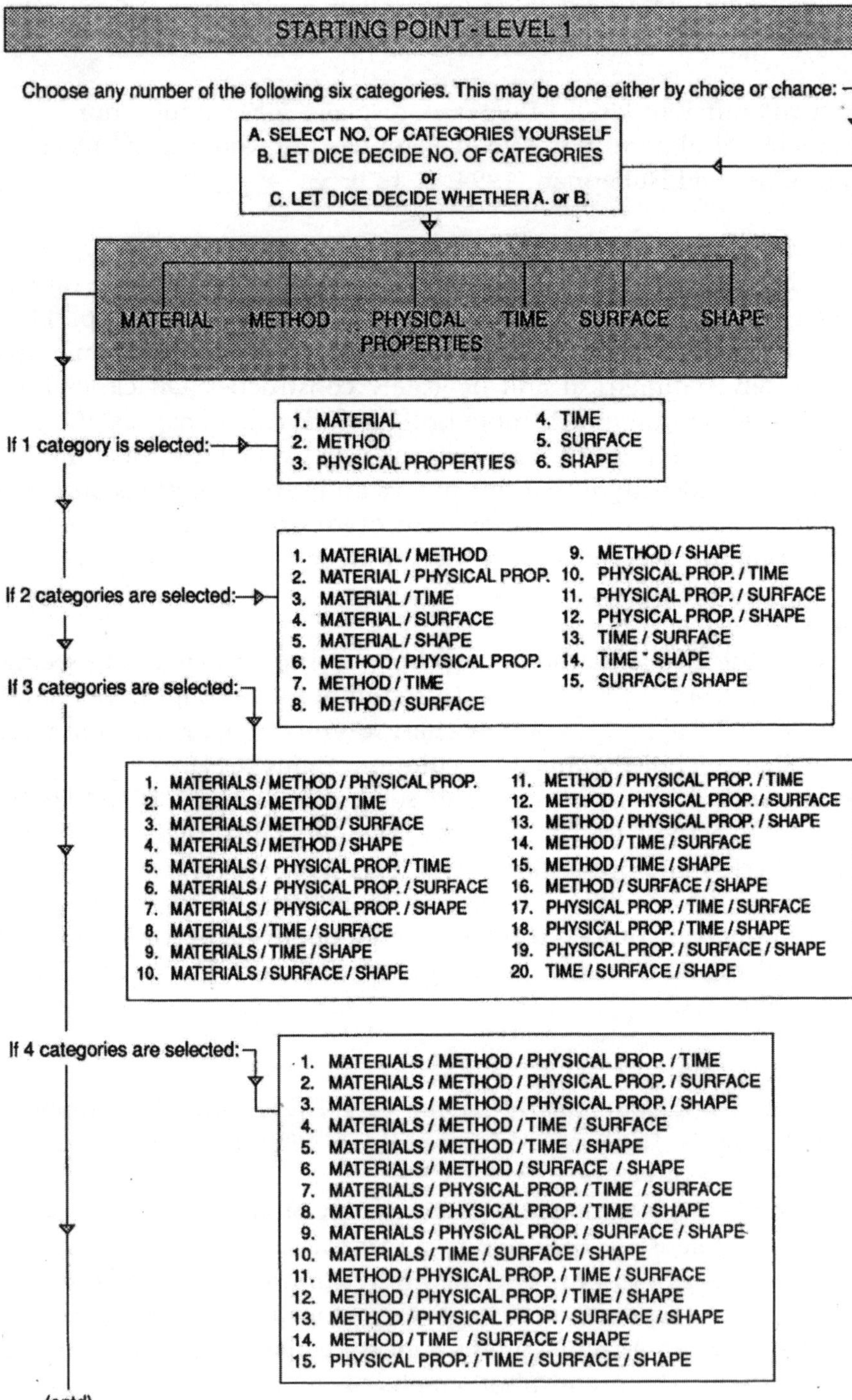

Figure 5.11 Example of a flow chart (Watson, 1992)

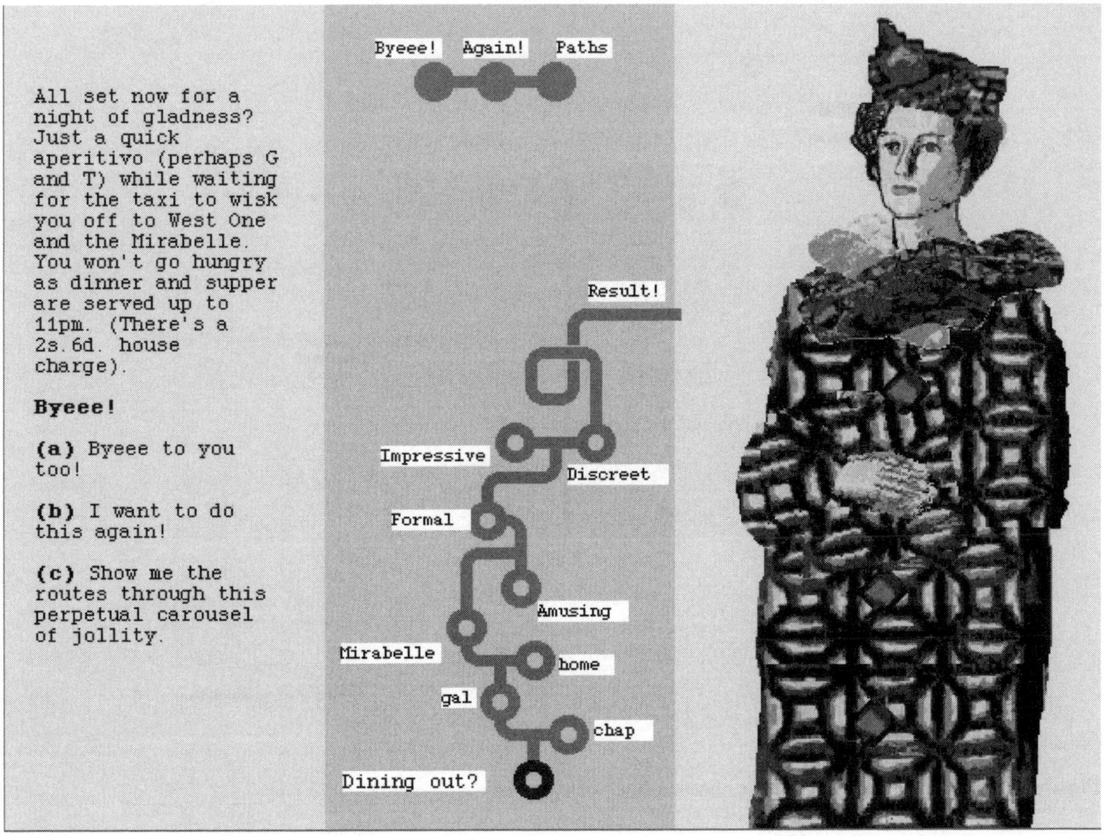

Figure 5.12 A frame from the animated flow chart Dining Out? (💻)

for example function, scale, production method. This technique encourages you to view data from different perspectives, enhancing greater understanding.

Chronological analysis

In the multimedia example, 'Visual analysis of air pollution' the effect of air pollution on humans is analysed and compellingly animated (Burt, 2000 – visit the book's website) see Figure 5.14.

In the main interface, the central large face has descriptions of the variables used in the analysis of air quality, for example the nose shape, scale and orientation represents the level of sulphur dioxide in the air. By moving to any of the 24 outer faces the effect on humans of the whole set of pollutant variables can be seen at any particular hour of the day. The pollution effects are obvious by the expressions on the faces. This animation has been developed from a static visual based on an original data set that was probably completely numeric – a matrix of variables over time (Barnett, 1981, pp. 258–259). The animation is an excellent example of how an interactive visual can bring to life analysis and generate meaning directly related to our own experiences.

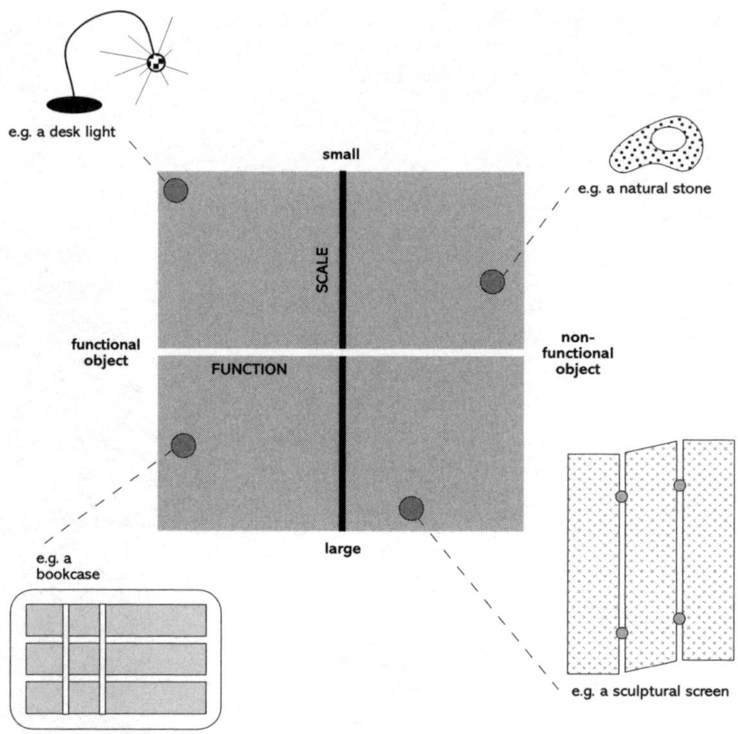

Figure 5.13 Example of a simple dimensional analysis structure

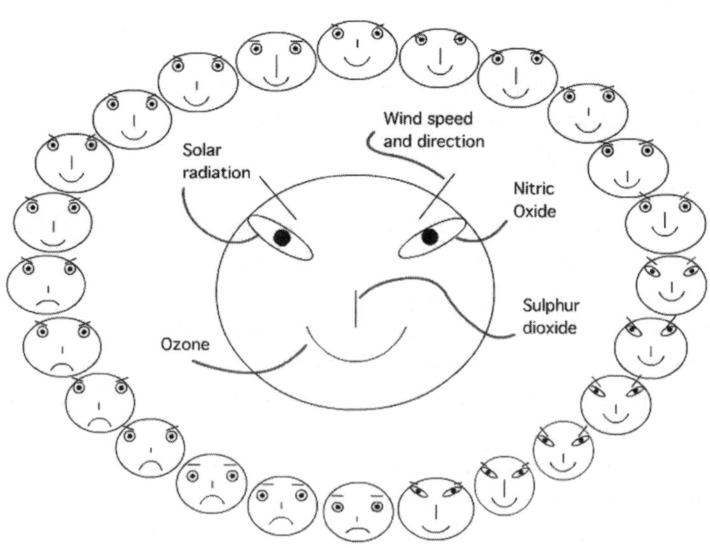

Figure 5.14 Visual analysis of air pollution (💻)

Another interesting visual example can be found in Tufte (1997, pp. 18–19) – an analysis of Giacometti's figurative sculpture in terms of his experimentation with scale and form over time. Actual photographs of the works are displayed as a sequence demonstrating a general shift over time from linear elongated forms to more volumetric ones. This is an interesting way of presenting and analysing a body of work and its developments over time in relation to specific criteria.

Similarly, the development of a designed product can be analysed and visually presented. In Figure 5.15 the process of rapid prototyping is documented and analysed over time and in relation to the 'growth' through layering material in the production of a cup (Burnett, 1999). This analysis helps us to understand the development process involved in using rapid prototyping technology, which turns out to be not so rapid!

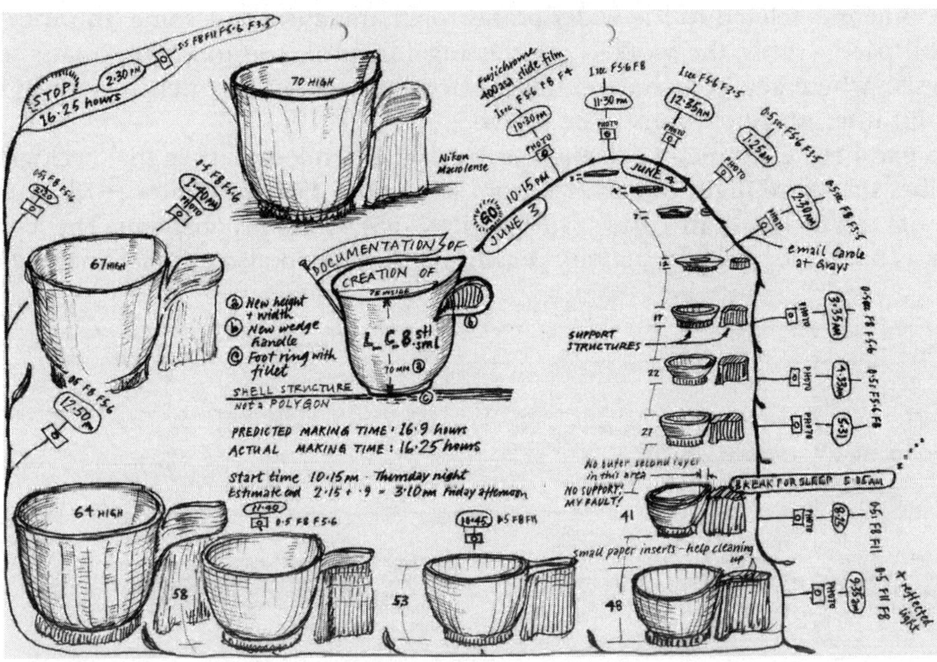

Figure 5.15 Analysis of a digitally crafted object (💻)

Analysis of physical and social environments

Zeisel (1984) provides some good visual examples of the analysis of various environments and how people behave in them. For example, using photographs of a swimming pool and its surroundings (Zeisel, 1984, p. 125) he interrogates the situation by asking:

- what is the physical setting?
- what is the socio-cultural context?
- who are involved?
- what are they doing? with whom?
- what are the relationships between the people in the setting?

The photographs are then annotated with text accordingly, and an understanding of the situation developed. Zeisel (1984, pp. 97, 209) also provides examples of juxtaposed visuals and text in the analysis of architectural space usage. This juxtapositioning allows us to 'see' what we 'mean'. (See also Figure 4.4 for an example of an annotated photograph.)

Analysis of a reflective journal/development log

A reflective journal can become an unwieldy research document! In order to reduce data, display them and make sense of them, an 'elongated' matrix structure can be helpful. In Figure 5.16 the matrix describes 'content of activity' in relation to 'time'. A 'diary' section provides regular extracts in descriptive detail; a 'documentation' section includes visuals of a developing body of work; a 'context' section makes sure that the development is related to the wider professional arena; there is some (intuitive) indication of 'pace' – how the work is progressing (or not!); the most important section is 'analysis', where key points are extracted from the whole experience week by week in order for interim conclusions to be drawn.

An excellent example of yet another kind of extended diary is the 'cyclogram' that describes the space flight of Salyut 6 from December 1977 to March 1978. This beautiful visual can be found in Tufte's (1997, pp. 92–95) *Visual Explanations*. The 'cyclogram' serves as both a log of daily activity during the flight and also a visual analytical record

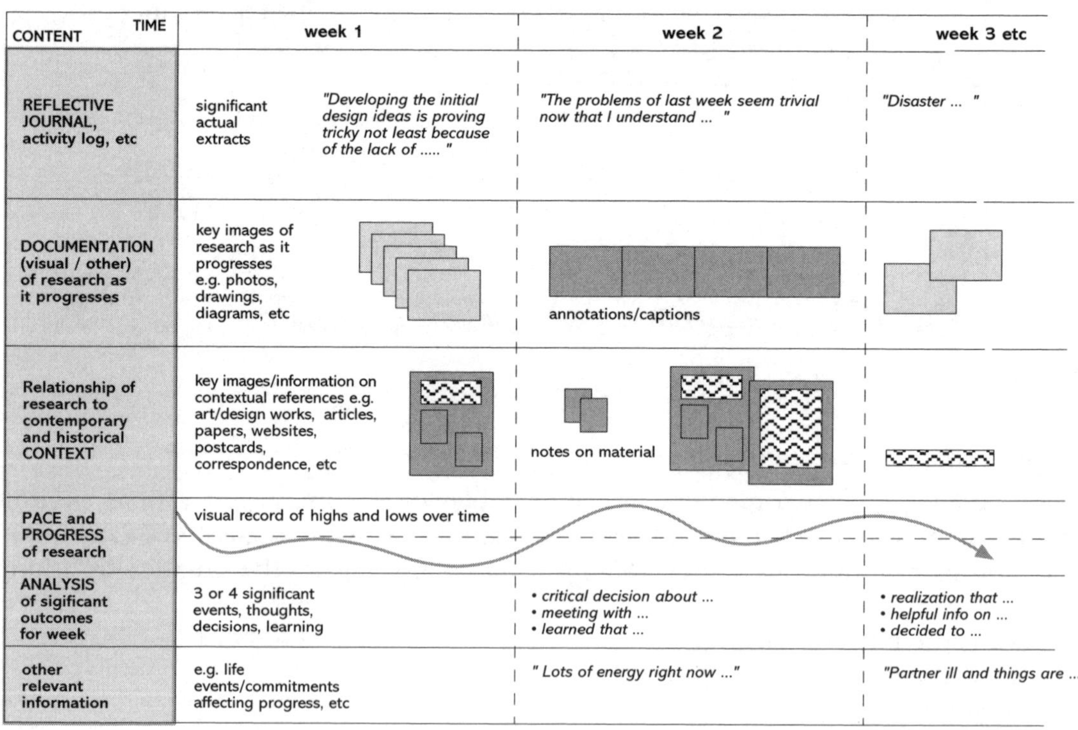

Figure 5.16 Suggested chronological matrix for the analysis of a reflective journal

post flight. The integration of various kinds of data, for example experimental work, dockings with other craft, orbit tracking, nutritional information, and so on, into a single display provides us with an overview and understanding of the whole experience in a way that a textual version might not.

Metaphor and analogy as analytical and interpretative tools

Metaphor

A metaphor is a figure of rhetoric – an implied comparison between two things of unlike nature that yet have something in common. Metaphors convey or create shared meaning. In analysis, the use of metaphor can provide a valuable way of thinking about and interpreting data. Coffey and Atkinson (1996) suggest that:

> Metaphors are a figurative use of language, a ubiquitous feature of a culture's or an individual's thinking and discourse. This is accomplished through comparison or analogy. At its simplest, a metaphor is a device of representation through which new meaning may be learned. At their simplest, metaphors illustrate the likeness (or unlikeness) of two [things]. A metaphorical statement reduces two [things] to their shared characteristics. (Coffey and Atkinson, 1996, Chapter 4, p. 85, text italics in brackets by authors)

In Chapter 3 we described the role of metaphor in problem setting in product development – paintbrush as pump (Schön, 1993). By seeing the paintbrush as a pump – two basically different things – they were using a metaphor as a way of generating new questions and new solutions. This process of 'generative metaphor' is a useful analytical strategy. In being asked to consider the paintbrush as a kind of pump, the product developers were forced into asking the question 'how could that be?' (and finding reasons), 'in what ways are they similar and different?' (thereby making comparisons and contrasts), 'how does this help us to take new approaches to the problem?' (being inventive). They were forced to 're-group' and 're-name' elements of the paintbrush, so that it could be seen as a pump – essentially making a new interpretation.

Schön (1983, p. 78) also gives us another example in describing design as a 'conversation', where design is considered as a dialogue between the designer and her work. By considering this metaphor, we can ask questions related to the process, for example 'what kinds of things happen in a conversation'? Through this we can develop an interpretation and understanding of the design process.

In David Lodge's (1988) novel 'Nice Work' the female protagonist – an English language lecturer – performs a semiotic analysis of a famous cigarette advertisement, providing an excellent example of how the use of metaphor can be used to uncover complex layers of meaning.

Analogy

The use of analogy is also helpful in trying to articulate something that is not fully understood. In the first stages of analysis we usually cannot see the 'whole' only the parts. For instance, in the Hindu story of the blind men and the elephant, analogy was used to describe the various parts of a large complex thing. 'It's like a snake, . . . a fan, .

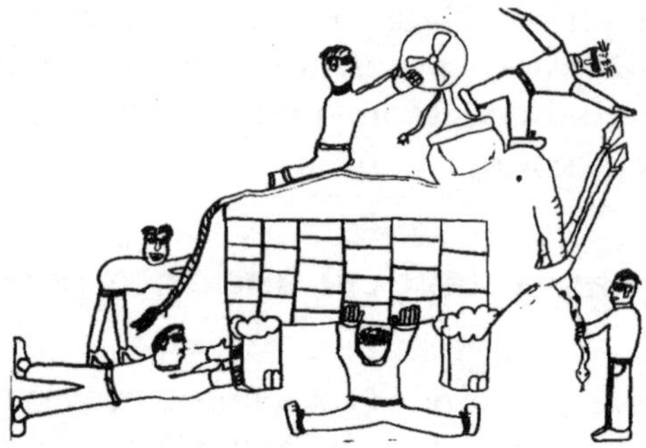

Figure 5.17 Research is . . . like an elephant

. . . a wall, . . . a rope' (Gray, 1998) (Figure 5.17). We are seeking an interpretation of usually a complex thing, difficult to comprehend as a whole, but which may be understandable by analogy in parts.

There are three basic types of analogy:

(1) *Direct analogy*
This is where a situation exists that directly parallels the situation you are investigating. For example, it may be the decline of traditional craft-based businesses. Are there analogies with other industries? Perhaps similar economic pressures or social trends are relevant.

(2) *Biological analogy*
This is where an example drawn from the natural world can be used to provide a model. For example, the branching structure of trees helps describe some hierarchical organizations, whereas others are more like neural networks.

(3) *Personal analogy*
These are somewhat more difficult to picture. In this case, the idea is to imagine yourself as part of the situation under investigation. For example, considering organizational structures again, can you picture yourself as the organization. It may be healthy or ailing. It may require a new set of clothes or a complete make over. Given any situation, how would you deal with it? Can you find a personal analogy that relates to your own area of interest? One way of using analogies is to see them as examples or parallel situations that can be used to suggest new solutions. The use of analogies in the research context is intended both as a method of generating ideas and as new ways of examining your data for analysis and creating an interpretation.

Creative construction: making sense, making meaning

From the previous topics we have seen that analysis is considered as a creative engaging activity – indeed Miles and Huberman (1994, p. 1) go as far as to claim that 'Qualitative data are sexy' leading to 'serendipitous findings and to new integrations'. We have also seen examples of how researchers in Art and Design have tried to use their visual/haptic skills and knowledge to make sense of their research and derive their own interpretations and meaning. Finally, we have encouraged you to 'play' with your data – not in any superficial sense or without serious research intent – but as a way of becoming so familiar with it that you can explore its possibilities and limitations, using various tools, as a way of making sense of it, and ultimately making meaning.

Now we attempt to draw parallels between analysis as a creative construction in the research process and making sense and meaning through the generic creative development of an art/design work. It is offered as a playful observation – one interpretation.

As practitioners in Art and Design, we are at some point involved in 'making', whether in response to a design brief or a more individual means of artistic expression. We usually start with some kind of curiosity. From this stage we might develop an intention (proposition, vision) and imagine the possible ways forward. Depending on our working preferences we might start sketching (testing, shaping) some ideas in two, three or more dimensions. This 'visual thinking' usually involves putting elements together (construction, assemblage, combination) and taking elements apart (deconstruction, separation, isolation). We are concerned with relationships, contrasts, comparisons, patterns – the parts in relation to the whole.

At this stage, we probably don't want to commit to anything too soon – a process of considering various options and alternatives – and things are possibly quite quickly loosely or temporarily connected, so that we can easily take them apart. We are continuously reflecting and evaluating – cross checking against our original intention to see how far we are progressing. It is a process of trial and error – 'let's see if this works . . . ', 'what if . . . '. The strategy is playful – we suspend belief for a moment and just try it. We are continually testing the limits. Things 'fail', things don't fit, things fall apart. Back to the drawing board!

With time, things start to come together – a gradual malleable coherence. We may begin to model this softness into different shapes. This can be both additive and reductive. We may try moulding the material against a given or containing form to see what impressions we get. As ideas cohere they might solidify into a clearly defined form. Yet this might still be open to question and we might carve back into it – paring away to essentials, to essence – to sense.

It's time to commit! Things are never perfect, never totally resolved. We never quite achieve our vision. But there is value in drawing the line, drawing out, drawing conclusions – presenting what we think just now makes sense to us and communicates as much of our original intention to others in a meaningful way.

And so with the process of analysis – it is a creative construction.

Reflection and action: suggestions

- What tools do you think will be useful for your analysis and why?
- Find some examples of different kinds of visual analysis relevant to your research.
- What metaphors and analogies might you use in your analysis and why?
- Think about your own practice – describe your approach to 'creative construction'.

Looking back on Chapter 5: Interpreting the map

In having crossed the terrain, we have now hopefully reached some higher ground – a vantage point from which we can look down on where we have been as well as gain a much closer view of our destination. We need to review and evaluate the quality and trustworthiness of all our evidence. Through the use of various kinds of spectacles and sieves (criteria for analysis) we can begin to select, focus, filter and distil significant material to address our research questions.

To help us in this task we can learn from the analyses and reported outcomes of other explorers. What analytical approaches, frameworks and methods have they used? How have they visualized and made explicit their analyses? Has feedback from multiple perspectives been sought so that different views can be considered? All the while we must acknowledge the strengths and limitations of any analytical strategy that informs ours.

Analysis has been described as 'imaginative, artful, flexible and reflective' – an iterative and cyclical process. The notion of 'playing' with data, being immersed in it, creatively involved with it, using data to think with is especially engaging. A range of 'tools' and techniques for this – some simple and visual, others more complex and discursive – can be used to explore and interrogate the research evidence in different ways.

Eventually, however, the provocative 'so what?' presents itself and challenges us to make sense of our journey of exploration. The creative construction of a convincing argument drawing on robust evidence, must be made. We draw out, shape, model, carve, cast, mould, weld. Make a point, underline. We reach a plane of understanding. We offer a mass of solid argument. We make an interpretation – our own map. We make new meaning.

REFERENCES AND FURTHER READING FOR CHAPTER 5

References

Banks, M. (2001) *Visual Methods in Social Research* (London: Sage).

Barnett, V. (1981) *Interpreting Multivariate Data* (Chichester: Wiley).

Bauer, M.W. and Gaskell, G. (eds) (2000) *Qualitative Researching with Text, Image and Sound: a Practical Handbook* (London: Sage).

Bryman, A. and Cramer, D. (1990) *Quantitative Data Analysis for Social Scientists* (London: Routledge).

Bunnell, K. (1998) *The Integration of New Technology into Designer-maker Ceramic Practice.* PhD thesis, The Robert Gordon University.

Burnett, G. in collaboration with Birch, T. (1999) Australian cultural issues re-defined by digitally crafted domestic objects. *Exhibition Catalogue* (Monash University and The Robert Gordon University).

Burt, I. (2000) *The Use of Multimedia for Practitioners in Art and Design.* PhD thesis (on CD-ROM) The Robert Gordon University.

Buzan, T. (1998) *The Mind Map Book* (London: BBC Books).
Coffey, A. and Atkinson, P. (1996) *Making Sense of Qualitative Data: Complementary Research Strategies*, Chapter 1 (Thousand Oaks, CA: Sage).
Csikszentmihalyi, M., Getzels, J. W. and Kahn, S. P. (1976) *The Creative Vision: A Longitudinal Study of Problem-finding in Art* (Chichester: Wiley).
Douglas, A. (1992) *Structure and Improvisation: The Making Aspect of Sculpture*. PhD thesis, Sunderland University.
Douglas, A. (1997) On the notion of test (multimedia essay on CD ROM) in: S. Evans, J. Greenhill and I. Svenson, *Matrix 3D: Sculpture, Method, Research* (London: Lethaby Press).
Eco, U. (1985) *Reflections on 'The Name of the Rose'* (London: Secker & Warburg) (translated from the Italian by William Weaver).
Gray, C. (1988) *Teaching styles in Higher Art Education*. PhD thesis, Aberdeen University.
Gray, C. (1998) Inquiry through practice: developing appropriate strategies, in: *No Guru, No Method? Discussions on Art and Design Research* (Helsinki: University of Art & Design).
Lincoln, Y. and Guba, E. (1985) Naturalistic Inquiry (Thousand Oaks, CA: Sage).
Lodge, D. (1988) *Nice Work* (London: Secker & Warburg).
Miles, M. B. and Huberman, A. M. (1994) *Qualitative Data Analysis*, Chapter 9, Matrix displays: some rules of thumb (Thousand Oaks, CA: Sage).
Packer, M. J. (1985) Hermeneutic inquiry in the study of human conduct, *American Psychologist*, 40(10), pp. 1081–1093.
Robson, C. (1993) *Real World Research: a Resource for Social Scientists and Practitioner-Researchers*, Section 12, pp. 370–407 (Oxford: Blackwell).
Rose, G. (2001) *Visual Methodologies* (London: Sage).
Schön, D. (1993) Generative metaphor: a perspective on problem-setting in social policy, in: A. Ortony, *Metaphor and Thought*, Chapter 9 (Cambridge University Press).
Silver, S. (1999) *The Roles of Artists in the Public Realm: an Investigation into Artists' Generative Processes in Context*. PhD thesis, The Robert Gordon University.
Tesch, R. (1990) *Qualitative Research: Analysis Types and Software Tools*, pp. 77–111 (Basingstoke: Falmer).
Tufte, E. (1987) *The Visual Display of Quantitative Data* (Cheshire, Connecticut: Graphics Press).
Tufte, E. (1990) *Envisioning Information* (Cheshire, Connecticut: Graphics Press).
Tufte, E. (1997) *Visual Explanations* (Cheshire, Connecticut: Graphics Press).
Watson, A. (1992) *An Exploration of the Principle of Chance as a Stimulus to the Creative Activity known as Sculpture*. PhD thesis, The Robert Gordon University.
Zeisel, J. (1984) *Inquiry by Design* (Cambridge, UK: Cambridge University Press).

Suggested further reading

Booth, W. C., Colomb, G. G. and Williams, J. M. (1995) *The Craft of Research* (Chicago: University of Chicago Press).
Cage, J. (1961) *Composition as Process* (Massachusetts Institute of Technology).

Cohen, L. and Manion, L. (1994) *Research Methods in Education* (London: Routledge).

Research Training Initiative (1996) *Research Perspectives in Art & Design: Case Studies* (Birmingham Institute of Art & Design, University of Central England) http://www.biad.uce.ac.uk/research/index.html.

Van Leeuwen, T. and Jewitt, C. (2000) *Handbook of Visual Analysis* (London: Sage).

NOTES

1. For further details see Robson, (1993, pp. 66–75, 402–407); see also Miles and Huberman (1994, pp. 277–280) for a useful set of questions you can ask of your research in order to describe and confirm its quality.
2. Published sources include:
   Tesch, R. (1990) *Qualitative Research: Analysis Types and Software Tools*, section: 'Types of Qualitative Analysis' pp. 77–11 (Falmer).
   Bauer, M. W. and Gaskell, G. (eds) (2000) *Qualitative Researching with Text, Image and Sound: A Practical Handbook* (Sage).

6 Recounting the journey: recognizing new knowledge and communicating research findings

CHAPTER OVERVIEW

6.1 RECOGNITION OF NEW KNOWLEDGE: JUST ANOTHER BRICK IN THE WALL!

'. . . original and independent contribution to knowledge'

In this topic we concentrate on PhD level research and discuss what is meant by the terms 'independent' and 'original' contribution to 'knowledge'. At this stage the assumption is that from your research evidence a credible argument has been developed through which the creative construction of a new or alternative perspective is offered. But how do we know that this is 'knowledge' and how do we know that it is 'original' and 'independent'?

In Chapter 1 we suggested that knowledge is contingent and dynamic and has a 'sell by' date. The implications of this are that, in order to know where the frontiers of knowledge are in your particular subject, you must be constantly aware of any relevant new developments. It is only in relation to this that your contribution can be evaluated.

In the UK's QAA's criteria for assessing PhD work (2001) in terms of 'knowledge' a student would be expected to:

> demonstrate a critical, detailed leading edge knowledge and understanding at the forefront of one or more specialisms and/or contribute to scholarship and the development of the subject/discipline
> OR
> demonstrate originality and creativity in the application of new knowledge, skills and practices, as well as design and execute inquiry/research projects to deal with new problems and issues.

These two types of contributions to knowledge could simplistically be categorized as 'theoretical' (the first) and 'applied' (the latter). In our view, however, the distinction is not helpful, as it suggests the separation of theory and practice, reflection and action that we would not endorse. The design and execution of an inquiry, critical understanding, and contribution to the development of a discipline are all requirements in good research. We would encourage any contribution to knowledge to demonstrate the following.

- The research has identified new challenges/issues at the leading edge/forefront of what already exists.
- An appropriate inquiry has been designed and implemented, involving in-depth/specialist critical thinking and action.
- The new knowledge, skills and practices developed through the research have been creatively applied, and this has contributed to the development of the subject/discipline/sector.

Independence

Given the necessity of the supervisory system in most higher degree frameworks, 'independence' is acknowledged to be relative in that the student and supervisor(s) must have an agreed balance between the degree of advice and support available and the freedom and responsibility of the research student. The balance is likely to shift during the development of the research programme – reasonably high contact and support early in the process (probably in line with the MPhil stage or equivalent) reducing in frequency but increasing in depth towards the finalization of the programme. At some point in this process, the student is likely to become more specifically expert in the particular research area than the supervisor, and the student takes responsibility for his/her research. The relationship shift is from student and supervisor to peer and peer. If you consider a higher degree (and especially a PhD) to be training for independent research – which we do – then the gradual development of confidence and capacity for autonomous working is an essential part of the learning process (QAA, 2001).

However, as collaborative research becomes a more accepted model in Art and Design (major research projects funded by AHRB, for example), the ability to work as part of a research team is also a desirable postgraduate skill (Green and Shaw, 1996). Research studentships attached to these kinds of collaborative projects present interesting challenges – how to ensure that the student is working self-critically and independently whilst at the same time benefiting from the relationship to, and support from, the bigger project; how to ensure that an original contribution to knowledge can be developed which is distinct from the objectives of the bigger project. Obviously, specifically focused student research plans help to identify potential contributions to knowledge but it is essential that independent thinking and action be tracked and acknowledged.

Originality

'Original' presents a more complicated picture! We need always to ask – original in relation to what? Originality is dependent on context, hence the absolutely essential activity of making a serious survey of your research area and a critical review of it. Your understanding of the research context, especially in terms of what exists at PhD level, enables you to demonstrate a clear space for your potential contribution. This understanding also enables you to gauge the significance of your contribution to the existing research area.

It is a common misperception that your research will in some way be earth shattering! In reality, although the research experience will probably be life-changing for you in some respect, your contribution to the broad scheme of things is likely to be modest but valuable. The analogy of 'a brick in the wall' is apt – the research process is usually constructive, additive, incremental – and just very occasionally revolutionary (Kuhn, 1970), probably as a result of a life's work rather than a higher degree programme.

A dictionary definition of 'original' suggests 'fresh and unusual; novel' (*New Collins Concise Dictionary*, 1982). Wakeford (2002) has proposed no less than 18 'fairly distinct' definitions of 'original' (see Appendix 3 for full list). This is very helpful as it indicates many different ways of bringing to our attention something previously not obvious. For example through:

- re-interpretation (making new sense of, re-visioning),
- making new connections (putting ideas/things together in different ways),
- re-contextualizing (placing ideas in alternative contexts/frameworks),
- extending existing research (building a new level, expansion sideways),
- capturing new and/or additional evidence (perhaps using new techniques/tools),
- working in under-researched areas (on the 'edge' of a subject domain or at a greater depth),
- alternative methodological approaches (developing an alternative research strategy and invention/adaptation of robust methods).

(These are not exhaustive – you might identify others from Wakeford's list.)

Types of original contributions in PhD research in Art and Design

Example 1

Research area: architectural ceramics.

Research proposition: the use of ceramic materials in contemporary architecture is underused and could, if revived in a contemporary way, offer a new approach to the decoration of the built environment.

Methodology/methods: inquiry through practice, case study (implementation of commissioned projects).

Output: four site-specific commissions involving the use of sculpted and glazed ceramic brick, exposition of documentation and material samples, written text.

Type of contribution to knowledge:

- re-interpretation by making new sense of ancient material,
- making new connections between architecture and ceramics, integration,
- re-contextualizing by reviving an ancient decorative form,
- extending existing research by developing ceramics on an architectural scale.

Example 2

Research area: interactive computer-based artworks.

Research proposition: a better understanding of artwork/audience relationship in gallery settings can inform how curators develop interactive exhibitions.

Methodology/methods: production of an interactive artwork, observational case studies of exhibited works, curation of an exhibition of interactive artworks, use of 'conversation/host' metaphor, questionnaires.

Output: a series of curated new media exhibitions (book and video), written text.

Type of contribution to knowledge:

- re-interpretation by making new sense of how people interact with artworks,
- extending existing research by building a new level of understanding,
- capturing new and/or additional evidence by using new media techniques/tools, for example video,
- working in under-researched areas, for example interactive new media,
- alternative methodological approaches, for example curating thematic exhibitions as a way of experiencing and exploring a range of new practices.

Example 3

Research area: sculpture

Research proposition: the methodology of chance can extend the practice of sculpture.

Methodology/methods: inquiry through practice, projects involving different groups, decision flow charts, 'Art as Random Process' (ARP) database as a stimulus to creative thinking and action.

Output: exposition, written text, ARP database.

Type of contribution to knowledge:

- re-interpretation by making new sense of how artists use chance,
- making new connections between diverse ideas as a creative stimulus,
- capturing new and/or additional evidence on the decision-making process in developing an artwork,
- alternative methodological approaches, for example group projects.

For more examples please visit the Research Training Initiative website that has case studies of completed PhD research in Art and Design – http://www.biad.uce.ac.uk/research/rti/case_studies/ (accessed 12 June 2003).

Checking your progress towards making a contribution to knowledge: putting together a portfolio of evidence

All too often, criteria for achieving academic standards for postgraduate degrees are not seen by the student as remotely interesting or valuable as a learning framework. If we look again at Green and Shaw's 'Taxonomy of Assessment Domains' (admittedly not the most engaging title!) we can see that it does indeed provide some helpful information about levels and standards of postgraduate performance and learning outcomes (albeit generic and requiring customization and interpretation). Believing this to be a potentially valuable learning tool, we have adapted this matrix to include a space for indicating evidence from your research project and learning experience (see Appendix 4). For example, in the 'creativity' domain can you provide some evidence from your research that 'displays originality in . . . developing and/or extending existing knowledge and theoretical perspectives'? This evidence might be incomplete or very modest, but in revisiting the matrix throughout your research programme you will begin to build up a set of different kinds of evidence that demonstrates you are achieving the required standard. The gradual population and update of this matrix could prove invaluable when you come to reflect back on your journey and stake your claim on new territory.

This kind of accumulation of evidence to demonstrate learning achievements is called 'portfolio assessment' (Baume, 2001). The concept of 'portfolio' is one which we as practitioners in Art and Design are familiar. A portfolio usually consists of a selection of our best work in a range of media, which can most effectively demonstrate our expertise and experience. Increasingly, the concept has been taken up by education as a means of allowing students in any discipline to present selected evidence of their achievements outside examination-based assessments. Portfolios provide a valuable method of assessing achievements, particularly in situations beyond the formal learning situation. Portfolios enable students to provide evidence of achievement of specified competencies, sometimes as a result of learning derived from a variety of informal and formal contexts including work, leisure, home and from independent study, as well as obviously higher education courses themselves. Portfolios are particularly useful for presenting evidence of achievement from work-based or practice-based projects.

Types of assessment portfolios and the key elements

Portfolios come in all shapes and sizes according to the type of work being assessed. For example, an architecture student may need to include responses to client briefs, proposed plans, 3D models, site photographs, material samples, and so on. Medical students may need to include examples of their patient notes, analyses of X-rays, diagnoses, rationale for prescription, and so on. There are three main elements of an assessment portfolio – learning outcomes, evidence of achievement, and reflective statements.

Learning Outcome, for example the ability competently to visualize and communicate concepts.

Evidence of Achievement, for example

- a mind map,
- a network display,
- a set of photographs.

Reflective Statement, for example

> This evidence demonstrates that I have really understood the importance of visual communication methods. The *mind map* in particular shows that I can organize my ideas effectively and can understand relationships between them. However, I am not altogether happy with the quality of the map – perhaps more colour and shapes could have been used to make better distinctions between things. The *network display* demonstrates that I am able to classify information effectively. This display has been incorporated in one of my student projects, and they have found the visual helpful. In retrospect my *photographs* (although others have commented positively on them) are not as effective in communicating my ideas. They do not hold together as a coherent set. I think that more annotation would have helped. However, taken together these examples are adequate evidence for my claim of achieving this particular learning outcome.

In this example, in relation to the learning outcome the student has provided three pieces of evidence, which each display different characteristics and qualities of visualization and communication. These differences are elaborated upon in his reflective statement and their strengths and weaknesses described. The language is self-critical, but in the end we are persuaded that through the set of evidence (physically available for inspection) the student has achieved a competency in respect of that particular learning outcome.

A PhD evidence portfolio

The aim of Chapter 6 is to help you identify and articulate your research contributions and to examine methods for bringing together research findings and experience in a coherent way so that they can be communicated effectively. One method of doing this is by collating a portfolio of evidence. Portfolios can be very extensive documents; however, a good portfolio should not comprise a vast volume of work. Selection is critical, and in itself demonstrates a key professional capability. Your portfolio should comprise evidence drawn from work you have previously completed. It does not require you to produce new work but rather review the work you have completed and reflect on how this shows you have achieved key learning outcomes. The items of evidence that you might cite could be text, visuals, video, models or just about anything that provides clear evidence that you have achieved the learning outcomes, for example.

- a mind map describing the relationship between your research project and the wider professional context,
- a selected set of bibliographic references,

- a set of keywords,
- selected critical review of key references that have focused your research area,
- an external and personal rationale for your research,
- a plan of work, for example Gantt chart,
- videotape extracts and commentary,
- interview schedules,
- a set of annotated photographs,
- extracts from your reflective journal,
- a matrix showing criteria used for analysis,
- a diagram summarizing research outcomes.

The reflective statements should be honest and use critical language, and provide some insight into how you feel.

The ability to make a coherent set of evidence is important as a basis for a viva examination in which practice provides research evidence.

Reflection and action: suggestions

- Analyse three completed PhDs in terms of their types of contributions to knowledge.
- Consider the idea of developing a 'portfolio' of research evidence. Discuss this with your supervisor(s).
- In what ways might your research be 'original' and make a new contribution to knowledge? Identify evidence for any claims made.

6.2 RECOUNTING THE JOURNEY: COMMUNICATING RESEARCH FINDINGS

'Thesis' as argument

As we saw in Chapter 1, the term 'thesis' means argument and not simply the end product of the research process manifested in a classic bound tome. Your convincing argument rests upon claims substantiated by evidence derived from the rigorous use of appropriate research methods. Research involving practice will usually have developed different kinds of evidence in different media, which relate to a range of senses – visual, textual, aural, tactile, for example still and moving images, sound, objects, material samples, site specific work, performance, etc. It is important then that these different kinds of evidence are allowed to 'live on' in their original form within the thesis, so that we avoid 'language doing the work of eyes' (Tyler, 1986). The logical consequence of this is that the thesis could comprise a number of components such as a body of practice (for example art/design works, performance), an illustrated written text, other supporting/complementary evidence, for example video, material samples, website, database, and so on. Taken as a whole, this provides the basis for a convincing argument – at this stage, still only a part of your submission for a higher degree – which is then explored and questioned through a viva voce (see Section 6.3) completing the submission.

Of course, it may be entirely appropriate that because of the research topic the most appropriate way of presenting your argument is in a textual format. Indeed, you may feel that there is no better means of communicating your research findings than a written text. Whichever format you choose, it is clearly important to consult your own institution's regulations to find out what may or may not be permitted.

Possible structure and key sections of a written component

Most institutions require a PhD submission to include some kind of written component. The purpose of this component is to help you critically reflect on, and distil, your research experience by:

- introducing and contextualizing the research topic,
- describing and evaluating the research methodology,
- analysing and discussing the research outcomes.

Different subject areas will have their own ways of structuring this component, and of course the structure will respond to the nature of the research topic, for example some topics will be of a more philosophic and discursive nature, others more pragmatic and experimental. However, we suggest that the following basic structure and generic content might be helpful (and should be adapted as necessary).

1 Abstract (usually 300 words)

2 Introduction
   Including: background and key concepts; aim, objectives; research proposition (argument); rationale for the research; role of practice; definition of key terms.

3 Contextual/Literature review
   Including: structure and scope of the review; critical review of key references in relation to the argument (existing completed PhD research, key published research and other professional references); demonstration of 'gap' in knowledge; position of your research.

4 Methodology
   Including: rationale for methodological approach (including the role of practice if relevant); description of appropriate methods; description of use of methods for generating/gathering and analysing data/information.

5 Outcomes and analysis
   Including: outcomes from the application of methods; critical evaluation of methods (robustness of evidence); analysis and interpretation of outcomes (creative construction of meaning based on evidence).

6 Discussion and conclusions
Including: extent to which aim/objectives have been fulfilled; contribution to knowledge; discussion and conclusions; strengths and limitations of the research; relationship of new knowledge to existing research; recommendations for future research; summary of thesis.

7 References/Bibliography
(Ref. Chapter 2, Section 2.3)

8 Appendices
Including: key evidence (derived from the use of various methods) on which you have based your claims, for example project descriptions and related visuals, evaluations/feedback from others, interview transcripts, sets of visual data, and so on – making this accessible ensures that your claims can be open to scrutiny and others can derive their own interpretations if appropriate.

The written component also demonstrates that the student has acquired a 'language for research' and writing skills with which to express that language. We would argue that this is especially important for Art and Design researchers, who may find writing difficult and who struggle with the accepted languages of research (social science, science). 'Alternative research paradigms' (Guba, 1990) have encouraged researchers to use writing styles that reflect their research concerns and that acknowledge the researcher as involved 'first person', for example the use of 'I' instead of 'the researcher/author'; the abandonment of capital letters in some feminist research – bell hooks for example (hooks, 1989); different kinds of narrative writing in 'queer' research – what Tierney calls 'developing voice' (Gitlin, 1994, p. 109). We are advocating the use of simple, clear language that represents your research argument in your true 'voice' – whatever that is.

'It's a thesis Jim . . . ' (adapted from Press, 1995)

There are some research topics that cannot be easily or adequately presented in anything other than a digital format because the majority of the research evidence is dynamic data (video, sound, animation, performance, and so on). In such instances, a case may be made for the submission of a thesis in digital format. For example, if the research topic is an exploration of multimedia in art and design practice then it is absolutely right that the thesis format should enable the key content to be properly experienced and the argument supported with the appropriate kinds of evidence. The consideration of an appropriate thesis format should take place at the research project planning stage, as it is essential to capture and manage key dynamic evidence throughout the research process.

The Visual Arts Data Service (VADS) offers some advice on digital formats for research degrees (Graham, 1999, http://vads.ahds.ac.uk/guides/using_guide/sect35.html accessed 10 April 2003). This is an area that is likely to expand as technology becomes more user friendly. However, it is important to anticipate the extra workload in developing a truly interactive thesis (Malins and Gray, 1999). In terms of responding to the need for research to be made as accessible as possible the use of PDF (Portable Document Format) offers a way of widely publishing any research document as a download from the internet or circulation by e-mail. Higher degree submissions are increasingly accessible via the internet (for example, http://scholar.lib.vt.edu/theses/ accessed 4 June 2003) also allowing for a range of media to be included. As with any formal research the issue of proper archiving and future proofing should be considered.

Exhibition to exposition

When research involves practice, it is likely that some new work (art work, design, performance, and so on) has been developed to explore the research questions. These may be resolved pieces embodying some of the research concepts or they may be experimental 'sketches' or prototypes revealing methodology. Whatever the status, the work itself may well form part of the submission for the award of a higher degree. This particular research framework requires that the work be considered in quite a different way than one would usually view art/design works.

The concept of 'exhibition' carries with it much baggage! Historically, the model has involved the artist/designer (usually an artist, as single author) displaying a body of work for public appreciation and consumption (by an audience and market), and for professional evaluation (by critics). Although the work may be obviously thematic and have accompanying catalogues with critical writings, usually we are not fully aware of the artist/designer's intentions for the work, and we are not obliged to evaluate it against their specific criteria. We will make of the work whatever we like and apply, usually in a very unconscious way, our own implicit criteria for judging the quality of what we see. For most of us, the experience of viewing the work might be a purely visual and aesthetic one, possibly even mystical. Surely the work 'speaks for itself'? We may go home edified but not necessarily any the wiser!

The word 'exposition' seems much more appropriate for research purposes, as its suggestion of exposure and explication matches very well the key characteristics of good research – accessibility, transparency, transferability. Douglas (1997) suggests that an exposition should reveal 'stages of research thinking, diagrammatic mapping of the evolving research process and its evidence "in product", evidence of failure and changes of direction'. Explicitness about criteria for evaluating research findings – especially art/design work produced as part of a research argument – is an essential feature.

Criteria for evaluating research outputs involving practice

There are commonly agreed generic criteria for assessing the quality of research. Cooper (1996) identifies four 'basic requirements for research, and certain levels of acceptability of performance':

- rigour, for example thoroughness, depth, critical approach, use of method,
- revelation, for example new contribution, dissemination, public output,

- relevance, for example value of contribution to the discipline, society, industry, education, and so on.
- return, for example feedback – economic, physical, psychological.

Although these are general criteria, these four 'Rs' can be turned into useful questions for you when considering the quality of your own research findings, both in a specific project sense and in your research's contribution to the wider professional context. Any research undertaken for a higher degree will have both generic and specific criteria for assessing the quality of research (see Appendices 1 and 2). Nesting within these larger frameworks are specific research projects, which themselves have quality criteria related to project objectives.

For any research involving practice, it is essential that the role of the art/design work in the argument and the criteria for its assessment be made clear. In a research exposition one would expect to see articulated:

- the research questions which were posed,
- the project objectives,
- the methodology including how practice has been involved, and
- some positioning of the project in relation to other key research in the field (research context).

One would expect to know precisely:

- what the criteria were (derived from project objectives) for evaluating the artefacts in relation to the research evidence they demonstrate, and
- what were the 'failures' as well as the successes, the experiments as well as the resolved pieces.

One might also expect to discuss with the practitioner-researcher some of the issues raised by the research. In this sense, the research exposition is didactic/heuristic in that it encourages interaction, critical exchange, understanding and learning for all concerned. In a classic exhibition, probably these features would remain tacit and implicit. In the case of higher degrees, the viva voce examination offers an essential opportunity for the researcher to discuss the work produced and its role in the research (See Section 6.3).

Resolved pieces may visualize or embody some of the research concepts and findings. For instance, in Pengelly's (1996) research on environmentally sensitive printmaking the series of large scale prints shown in his PhD examination deliberately set out to test the parameters of what could be achieved using alternative materials and methods. They visualize some of the research questions: 'what happens if I use safer *X* instead of more hazardous *Y*?' In the context of the PhD examination, the artwork was compelling evidence of an active pursuit of the research questions and the researcher's response to those questions. The work was subsequently open to the public accompanied by a fold-out colour pamphlet that set the work in the research framework.

Similarly, but in a different way, the ceramic pieces and other artefacts Bunnell (1998) produced as part of her PhD submission were largely experiments with new technologies and new forms – prototypes that acknowledged 'failure' as an essential part of the investigation. In research terms these 'failures', as Feyerabend (1988, p. 164) says, are 'preconditions of progress'. They can tell us much more about the research question and research process than pieces that seemingly appear successful (resolved) as ceramic objects. She also included in her examination exposition examples of extrusion templates and jigs that helped to reveal exactly how some of the ceramic forms were developed. These would not in classic exhibition contexts be considered appropriate, but in a research exposition they function very well in revealing methodology.

A research exposition: possible elements of a research display and presentation

Different research contexts and study levels will have different requirements for display and presentation, directly related to the criteria for the degree. Similarly, there may be other more public occasions for the presentation of your research, for example conferences, seminars, symposia.

What is described here is a possible set of elements that could make up a research presentation as part of the examination for your specific degree award or for other academic/professional situations. It is up to the researcher to select and adapt elements for the specific occasion/situation and level.

The following are suggestions for possible research presentations/displays.

An overview of the research: elements visualizing the process and products

In most research events, such as conferences, seminars, symposia, and so on, you may only have a limited time to report on your research. Something like 15 to 20 minutes is usual. It is therefore essential that you give your audience a quick but effective overview of your research. For instance, for describing the structure and content of this book we have used a visual overview (see Figure 1) enabling a rapid understanding of key content. The visual shows the introduction and six chapters of this book with associated subsections arranged as a 'web' diagram.

In a different and more detailed way, the map of a craft research project in Australia clearly shows the researcher's concerns and activities (Figure 6.1).

In addition to describing the process, it may be pertinent quickly to give an overview of outcomes from the research. Many kinds of visual documentation can be used for this – perhaps the simplest and most effective is a set of photographs with captions in a two-dimensional display.

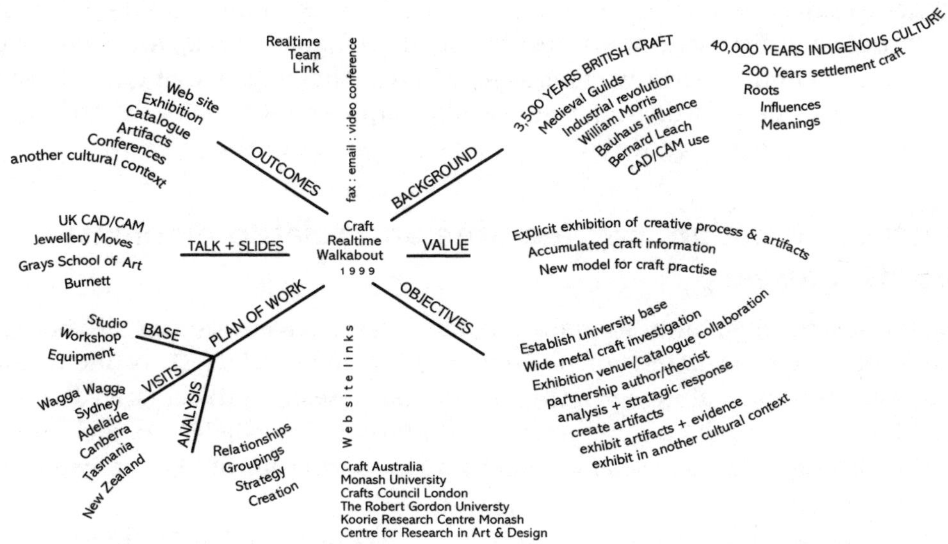

Figure 6.1 Project map for 'Craft Realtime Walkabout' research project (Burnett, 1999)

A body of work

For some occasions it may be possible to display/present an actual body of work or selected key examples from it. This gives an opportunity for peers and public actually to experience first-hand evidence of the research inquiry, demonstrating in various ways and through different media the exploration of the research questions and methodology. Research conferences in Art and Design usually try to give access to examples of relevant practice and give the opportunity for researchers to answer questions and receive feedback in relation to explicit evaluation criteria. Within the higher degree framework there should be stages in the process where this opportunity can be given, for example MPhil/PhD transfer, annual progress review points, preparation for public presentation. Of course the actual viva itself is a key opportunity (more details in Section 6.3).

A concise critical evaluation: key features

Some research occasions may call for a concise critical evaluation of your research. The key features of this evaluation should be:

- a statement of the aim and objectives of the research project,
- a statement about the extent to which the objectives have been met and outcomes achieved,
- strengths and limitations of the research methodology and outcomes,
- implications for future research.

A concise critical evaluation, although aiming for succinctness similar to an abstract (see next section), differs from an abstract in the language used. An abstract usually employs fairly neutral descriptive language, whereas the language of critical evaluation focuses on the value or worth of the research, and would usually, as an aspect of a regular reviewing process, contribute to the development of the research.

An abstract: function, key features and related elements – keywords, glossary

In formal research, the ability to make a concise descriptive summary of your research is a core skill. To encapsulate your research in a few hundred words is one of the most difficult tasks. However, along with the title of your research project (see Chapter 3) the abstract is the first introduction to your contribution to knowledge. As such, it needs to be clear, accessible and concise and present a true reflection of your research without being simplistic. A tall order!

There are no right or wrong ways to write an abstract – different disciplines require different approaches. For instance, in science the structure and language of the abstract would reflect the explanatory nature of discipline; whereas, in the humanities, a much more discursive approach might be taken. However, there are generic features:

(1) state research issue/question,
(2) describe briefly the context and rationale,
(3) describe briefly procedures/methods,
(4) end with a statement of the main point/outcome/contributions to knowledge.

PhD abstracts usually have a 300 word limit, therefore economic choice and use of words and preciseness of phrasing is important. A good abstract will probably need several revisions before the final version is achieved. (Examples of PhD abstracts can be found at www.theses.com)

Abstracts are also used to describe projects not necessarily within educational frameworks. Let us examine an example of a public art project abstract from the ARIAD database (Tebby, 1995) for structure.

> Concept, design and building of an environmentally integrated water feature within a public place: Chatham High Street, Kent
>
> The aim of the project was to evolve designs and ultimately build an environmentally integrated water feature, for a specific site, as a focal point within the general refurbishment of a pedestrianised High Street. The site is on a pronounced slope at a meeting point of two inclined axes, running approximately west and south east. The size of the water feature was limited to about 8 × 4 metres.
>
> To identify appropriate concepts, themes and sculptural design features, a number of surveys were carried out. These included the geomorphology of the site (walking, observation, photography, ordnance surveys, library search); architectural studies (drawing, photography, library search); local history (Kent Archaeological Society publications); maritime history (Chatham Historic Dockyard site and museum, archives, etc.); observations of the way people used the space.

The second investigative process involved potential designs for the water feature with respect to the qualities and characteristics of various materials, and how its formation might best accommodate both the slope and 'bent' axis of the High Street to maximum physical and aesthetic advantage. Consideration also had to be given to various bye-laws and health and safety regulations. The eventual solution consisted of three descending and one ascending terraces with perimeter channels. The height of the pool surrounds was determined by the decision to use them as integral seating; the end bench units were designed to house the pumps and other technical devices. (232 words)

In these three paragraphs we can identify the following structure:

- 'aim of the project' (key issues),
- 'the site' (social and physical context),
- 'to identify appropriate concepts, themes and sculptural design features, a number of surveys were carried out' (purpose, general methodology/specific methods),
- 'second investigative process involved potential designs' (practice-based methods, considerations, evaluations),
- 'the eventual solution' (main outcome).

In some instances it may be appropriate to make a visual overview of your abstract, for example (see Figure 6.2).

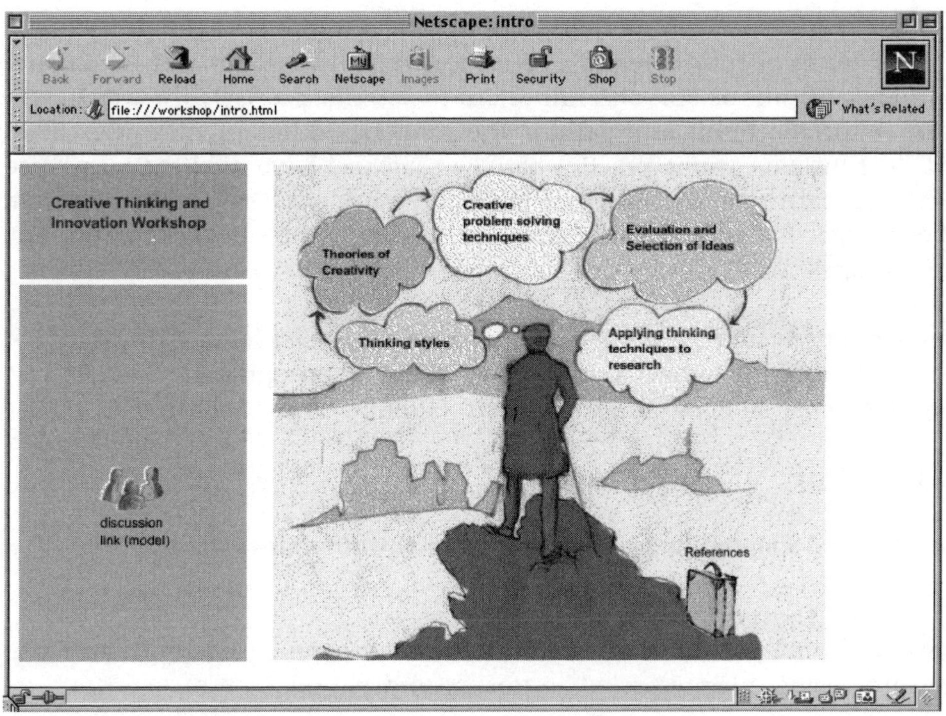

Figure 6.2 Example of an on-line document (💻)

Again, this kind of visual may be helpful in giving your audience quick access to the key content and structure of your research.

Keywords

From your title and abstract, keywords should be identified. Keywords are essential in allowing other researchers to find your research (ref. Chapter 2; see also Orna and Stevens, 1995, Chapter 3, p. 41). Try to keep your selection tight – say six words if possible. Too many keywords can weaken the focus and description of the research. Taking the previous example we can identify possible keywords:

> DESIGN, PUBLIC ART, REFURBISHMENT, ENVIRONMENTALLY INTEGRATED, WATER FEATURE, SITE-SPECIFIC

This of course is just one interpretation – you might like to see if there are other keywords more appropriate.

The Allison Research Index of Art and Design (www.ariad.co.uk) and the British Library Index to Theses (www.theses.com) are prime sources of abstract examples and keywords. Visit these sites and analyse a few different examples.

Glossary

A glossary is a set of special terms pertinent to your research area and project. These may be technical terms or subject specific terms for which the reader/viewer may need definitions and clarifications. It is also important to describe precisely the way in which you are using a specific term, especially if the term has different meanings in different contexts. For instance, some practice-based researchers have used the term 'case study' to describe a particular method, for example Wheeler's (1996) use of this term to describe site-specific commissions. With such usage it is particularly important in the glossary to state:

- the original derivation of the term, for example in social science research,
- the definition of the term (dictionary definition if appropriate),
- references to key sources, for example Yin (1986); Robson (1993),

and to say exactly

- how you have adapted or are using the term within your research.

(See this book's Glossary.)

This is all in the pursuit of accessibility and transparency, and to reduce the risk of your research being misinterpreted and/or misunderstood.

Mapping the terrain: elements that help to contextualize your research project

In any research presentation your audience will want to know how your research connects with the wider context and possibly to their own research (if at all). This is where a selected bibliography and a concise review of context are required. (Please revisit Chapter 2 when considering the following two elements.)

Selected Bibliography

The presentation of a selected bibliography is a good way of quickly indicating where your research is located in relation to the wider context. In Chapter 2, we discussed the importance of accurate detailing of public output for traceability reasons, so any references you select should be carefully checked. The display of these might be simply a classic alphabetical listing or you might consider that a relational map or other visual might more easily convey the thematic areas of research.

Concise Contextual Review

Although the Selected Bibliography is a useful positioning device for your research project, more sense can be made of this if those key references are described (however briefly) and related. Your Contextual Review and related visuals may serve as the basis for a more concise version, which helps quickly and effectively position your research in presentation situations. Again, a text version might be absolutely appropriate, but consider the visualization of the key contextual issues so that your audience may quickly gain an overview to which you can speak. In Figure 2.3, three areas of literature/contextual information are shown as having relevance to, and impinging on, the research topic.

What has been suggested here is not exhaustive – there may be other ways of recounting your journey that are more interactive and informal. It is important to try out your own ideas and adapt/extend what we have proposed here.

Reflection and action: suggestions

- What are your own thoughts on the notion of 'exposition'? Use them to make a table comparing features of 'exhibition' with 'exposition'.
- Find two different examples of an abstract and associated keywords, that is a PhD abstract (www.theses.com), a project abstract (www.ariad.co.uk). What kind of structure and content do the abstracts have? What kinds of writing styles do they have?
- What might your own display/presentation consist of for your postgraduate degree?

6.3 DESTINATION ACHIEVED! DEFENDING YOUR TERRITORY, DISSEMINATING YOUR RESEARCH, AND FUTURE EXPEDITIONS

Defending your territory: viva the viva!

The term 'viva voce' in Latin means 'by or with the living voice' and refers to the final part of a formal examination for an academic award in which the student answers questions about his/her research. An excellent generic description of the entire viva process is given in 'The Viva Voce' (Swift, 1997, Research Training Initiative – http://www.biad.uce.ac.uk/research/rti/rtrc/pdfArchive/V01.PDF accessed April 2003). This includes issues such as selection of examiners, preparation strategies, and the viva experience and advice. Also included is an essay on particular considerations for the viva in practice-based research (Douglas). It is this latter issue we concentrate on here, but first a few summary statements about the purpose of the viva.

The viva helps to ensure that degree award standards have been met and that there is external accountability in the examining process, hence the importance of external and independent examiners. The viva provides the opportunity for the 'defence' of your argument – a somewhat unfortunate term! The viva situation should definitely not be antagonistic as this is completely counter-productive. The best viva situations are those that result in a lively debate with peers, because with research – especially at PhD level – the student may well be in the position of 'expert' on many of the more specific research issues. So the viva should be approached with confidence but not arrogance. The event allows you to clarify and expand on various issues in your argument, and take questions (usually difficult!) from examiners. It is an opportunity for your examiners to ascertain 'authorship' (an important consideration in collaborative research) and for you to demonstrate ownership and mastery of your research area. Finally, the viva is a good means of evaluating studentship and learning – the PhD especially is seen as a 'rite of passage' to becoming an independent researcher.

The importance of the viva in Art and Design research

Douglas (1997) provides some important thinking and valuable considerations (towards guidelines) on the role of the viva in PhD submissions involving practice. The viva is crucial in providing a context within which the different and partial elements of the PhD submission – body of work/other artefacts and written text – can be brought together and sensibly interrelated by the researcher to form a complete and comprehensive argument, demonstrating fully 'the connections between practice and research, the effect of research on practice, and the embodiment of research within practice' (Douglas, 1997, p. 21). This situation offers everyone concerned – examiners included – a unique opportunity to learn.

The structure of this particular kind of viva needs careful consideration and planning. Everyone involved needs to be aware of what is expected.

The PhD candidate (advised by supervisors) needs to 'choreograph' how the different elements of the argument relate:

> The role of written to practical work within practice-led research does not fall neatly into two categories . . . the two represent different aspects of a complex evolving process which is reflexive: the critical element of the work can be contained as much within a piece of work as in a written text and certainly the other way round (Douglas, 1997, p. 20).

This interrelating and critical reflection might be done through a structured presentation that is considered an essential and documented part of the final thesis. The criteria for the evaluation of practice elements need to be explicit (even visibly displayed) and derived from the research objectives. If the exposition is subsequently open to the public then the different character of the research exposition must be conveyed, ideally through some imaginative visual means and maybe through the active participation of the researcher.

The examiners need to be informed in advance of the viva that the thesis comprises a number of elements and how these interrelate. Some elements may be accessible in advance, for example through a written and illustrated text or a multimedia document. The partialness of this must be acknowledged. Some elements may need to be experienced as part of the viva itself, for example a performance, site visits, interactive artworks, and so on. This may necessitate a much longer examination than the orthodox viva (and could have cost implications). The examiners need to know what the criteria are for evaluating practice elements.

If all these issues are taken into consideration then the viva should provide a fitting end to the process of learning through research and inquiry through practice, enabling the doctoral graduate to engage confidently with new research territory.

Disseminating your research findings in the public domain

Any kind of formal research is worthless if aspects of it are not disseminated in the public domain in some way. The transition from private to public is essential in order that the contribution (however humble) be recognized and debated, and crucially built upon. This is essential validation for your research. All formal research contributions constitute 'a brick in the wall' of the knowledge base of the discipline. There may be many different kinds of opportunities for dissemination of your research, from informal presentations to peers and collaborators within a course or project to a refereed international research event. In each case, your presentation must be responsive to the particular audience and the focus of the event/opportunity. For instance, a presentation/publication for an international interdisciplinary audience/readership will necessarily be more general and accommodating than that for a small, specialist one, say on non-toxic ceramic glazes. However, whatever presentation/publication you produce should aim for maximum clarity with minimum materials and should use the generic language of research in order to communicate widely.

Aside from the general principles of dissemination, there are quite pragmatic things to consider. Let us examine a typical process of research dissemination and the outputs involved in this. What do the outputs of each stage look like?

Imagine this. An international conference is advertised and a call for research papers/output is made. You and your research colleague agree that it is a good opportunity to report on your recent research. You would like some feedback on your ideas too. The requirement is usually for:

- *an abstract* – a brief summary of the research of not more than 300 words – to be sent to the organizers and vetted for quality and fit with conference themes. This process may be extended to include external referees – a good thing as this level of selectivity is likely to increase the quality of the conference. Your abstract is accepted, and you are invited to develop your conference contribution. Let us imagine that this is in the form of:
- *an illustrated paper,* which must be no longer than 3000 words. This will be published in the conference proceedings – a book sometimes available at the beginning of the event, but usually a post-event publication.

For the actual event you have been given a slot of 20 minutes to present the gist of your paper and highlight some issues for discussion. You decide to make:

- *a PowerPoint presentation,* sections of which each of you present in turn. This requires some 'orchestration' – like a duet! The presentation uses a combination of key words/phrases and visuals to provide prompts around which you will extemporize, avoiding the need to read verbatim from your original paper. A period for questions from the audience follows. The discussion (although not a viva!) requires that you convincingly defend the argument proposed in your presentation. You receive some interesting observations and some difficult questions!

After the conference the organizers invite you to develop your paper into:

- *a chapter for a book* based on one of the conference themes. The chapter, although having your paper as a basis, needs to take into consideration what you have learnt from the conference debate. The book will be published by an international publisher and disseminated globally.

If this model is followed you can see that the dissemination of the research output requires first of all:

- an extreme conciseness (abstract),
- then an expansion through more text and visuals but still within fairly tight parameters (proceedings paper),
- then a contraction through keywords and visuals (for example, PowerPoint),
- another expansion through discussion,
- and finally a greater expansion of both text and visuals (book chapter).

The requirements involved in this 'muscle flexing' exercise all your research skills and experience, and often the task cannot be accomplished alone. Dissemination is often a collaborative venture.

Increasingly, international conferences on Art and Design issues are acknowledging that practice-based formal research requires particular spaces and facilities for dissemination. This consideration has been evident in events organized by the European Academy of Design (for example, www. mailbase.ac.uk/lists/ead.html) and CADE (Computers in Art & Design Education – www.gsa.ac.uk/cade/640.html). In addition, the increasing use of web-based conference materials allows practitioners to disseminate their research findings through a variety of media – audio, video, animations, web-cam, as well as text. Obviously the possibilities afforded by developing web technologies will enable researchers to disseminate their findings to a global audience.

Envisioning the future: making an impact with your research

The idea of action and change reflects the essential philosophy of this book – that research should make some kind of contribution, have some impact on real situations – namely the situations that you find yourself in as practitioner-researchers. Our assumption is that having completed your postgraduate study you will continue to do research in some capacity – applying research skills and thinking into real working contexts on a day-to-day basis, or developing a new research project, perhaps within a higher degree framework if you haven't done so already. Most research usually ends up generating more questions than it has answered, providing new routes for exploration.

Making use of your research findings may be relatively straightforward; for example, in situations where you have some control and responsibility you may be able to introduce some of your ideas directly. Some aspects of your research findings may have longer-term implications, which require a more strategic approach.

A strategic plan

Developing some kind of strategic plan that runs over three to five years can help to frame the implementation of your research findings. You have already developed a plan of work related to your postgraduate project and many of the principles within that structure (aim, objectives, tasks within a specific time scale) are the basic features of a longer-term plan. (You may want to revisit Section 3.3, in Chapter 3.)

An example of a strategic plan

The Corporate Plan of the Arts and Humanities Research Board (AHRB) provides an example of a long-term strategic plan (www.ahrb.ac.uk/strategy – accessed July 2003). Any strategic plan should have a vision – something that is ambitious and possibly dramatic so that it is memorable – but which is achievable through purposeful objectives and actions. The vision is usually articulated through a 'mission statement'. In the case of the AHRB this statement comprises four key bullets using action verbs, such as promote, support, improve, enhance, enable. The rest of the plan's structure (without content) is now analysed. The plan contains:

- identification of priorities (eight headings each defining a strategic aim),
- each aim then has an 'introduction' (a paragraph providing background/rationale for the aim),
- for each strategic aim a number of objectives are identified (again using action verbs which are more specific, for example pursue, redesign, establish, employ, put in place, acquire, consult),
- a series of numbered actions (very specific tasks) all with a specific time scale are detailed (which ultimately adds up to a considerable number of actions!),
- a summary of strategic aims closes the plan.

Strategies – macro structures – are only valuable when they translate directly into real achievements – at micro levels. The best way to make this happen is to develop an implementation plan. This involves breaking down the actions into tasks for which very specific information is agreed, for example identification of:

- *who* will take responsibility for carrying out the task? (human resource),
- *when* does the task need to be completed? (specific deadline),
- *where* will the work take place? (implications for facilities/travel),
- *how* will the task be carried out? (methods).

Clearly the AHRB example relates to a large organizational/corporate plan to be achieved over five years, but the principles of it can be adopted and adapted for a smaller scale venture.

A portfolio for future expeditions

The collation of a portfolio of evidence is a valuable 'portable document' that could be used (in various amended and extended forms) to provide evidence of your research capabilities in the future. A portfolio can also include your 'personal development profile' – evidence of how your professional and transferable skills have developed and been successfully used over time. Finally, good practice-based research materials are uncommon, and your portfolio may provide valuable examples to other researchers.

Reflection and action: suggestions

- Consider how you might approach your viva voce. What kinds of questions can you anticipate?
- Find three different examples of conference contributions. Analyse their structure and content.
- Find two different examples of a strategic plan. What kind of structure and content do they have?

Looking back on Chapter 6: recounting the journey

You are now on what you sense is new ground – a space previously unclaimed. It may be modest in scale but affords you the opportunity for making an original contribution to knowledge. Throughout the journey you have developed a portfolio of evidence through which you can make your claim for new knowledge. You have also carried with you a growing understanding of what makes good research (quality standards and criteria, examples of other projects) to help you recognize the significance and value your own contribution. Time to stake that claim!

Making sure that your new territory is recognized by other explorers is critical – otherwise your efforts will have been in vain and your contribution invisible. You need to make explicit both your journey and its outcomes through the making of a clear and concise thesis – whatever format that might take – and/or through various other convincing and persuasive ways of describing and visualizing your new territory.

Other explorers will be curious and want to check out this new space. Some might observe and comment from a distance but others will want to have a very close view, scrutinizing and questioning all aspects of your journey, evidence and claim. You will need to defend your territory as well as learn from the experience of expert explorers. Once satisfied that the contribution is of quality and significance, your new territory will be 'on the map'. From your established base you can venture out to share and test your ideas with other explorers. Some may invite you on new expeditions, and so your horizons are widened.

Postscript: journey's end?

In the book *Sophie's World* by Jostein Gaarder, a mysterious old philosopher, Albert Knox, poses some fundamental questions that propel Sophie into her own 'wonderland'. *Who* are you? *Where* does the world come from? *What* is philosophy? 'What annoying questions!' Sophie declares exasperated and confused. Much like Alice in Wonderland, 'burning with curiosity' and entering the rabbit hole, Sophie is compelled to think about the possible responses.

> Wasn't it extraordinary to be in the world right now, wandering around in a wonderful adventure! . . . For the first time in her life she felt it wasn't right to live in the world without at least *inquiring* where it came from. *Sophie's World* (Gaarder, 1996, pp. 6 and 7)

As well as asking annoying questions, Albert tells stories and paints word pictures about philosophy, bringing it to life for Sophie. Socrates asked questions to begin a conversation – a discussion, a discourse – so Albert engages Sophie in a dialogue – questions, stories, conversations, emerging meaning. He guides her through the seemingly impenetrable jungle of philosophical thought to a clearing of understanding and self-confidence.

The intention of *this* book has been to provide guidance – a route map – for postgraduate students and their supervisors on how they might negotiate the uncharted terrain of research for postgraduate degrees. Most guidebooks are consulted before you set off and you dip into them in anticipation of the then unknown, abstract experience.

But once on the journey you consult them more thoroughly to avoid ending up where you don't want to be, and not missing those 'must see' attractions. Of course, there comes a point where your own experience takes over and you will make your own interpretation of your journey – enabling you to guide others through it.

Art and Design research is a rapidly evolving activity. With each successful completion of a research degree along with a new contribution to knowledge it is likely that new or alternative research methodologies are proposed and validated. All Art and Design researchers should regard themselves, to some extent, as 'methodological trailblazers' (Lincoln and Guba, 1985). We hope that this book has gone some way to illuminating that trail, establishing possible way markers for you to follow.

We encourage you to make both 'pictures' and 'conversations'. Visual thinking and actually visualizing ideas allows for ideas to be communicated and discussed. We can have conversations both with ourselves as reflective practitioners and with our peers as critical and credible persuaders; we can have dialogues with our research material – interrogating, deconstructing and re-constructing to make sense and meaning. We hope that this book is useful in helping you to do just that – for indeed as Alice asks herself 'what is the use of a book without . . . pictures or conversation?'

REFERENCES AND FURTHER READING FOR CHAPTER 6

References

Baume, D. (2001) A briefing on assessment of portfolios. Assessment Series No. 6, Learning and Teaching Support Network Generic Centre.

Bunnell, K. (1998) *The Integration of New Technology into Designer-maker Ceramic Practice*. PhD thesis, The Robert Gordon University.

Burnett, G. in collaboration with Birch, T. (1999) Australian cultural issues re-defined by digitally crafted domestic objects. *Exhibition Catalogue* (Monash University and The Robert Gordon University).

Cooper, R. (1996) Assessment issues in design research. In: *RADical International Research Conference* proceedings (on CD ROM), The Robert Gordon University, Aberdeen.

Douglas, A. (1997) Observations and comments on 'The Viva Voce'. In: J. Swift *The Viva Voce*, pp. 20–25, Research Training Initiative, Birmingham Institute of Art and Design, University of Central England (http://www.biad.uce.ac.uk/research/rti/rtrc/pdfArchive/V01.PDF).

Feyerabend, P. (1988) *Against Method*, revised edition (London: Verso).

Gaarder, J. (1996) *Sophie's World* (London: Phoenix).

Gitlin, A. (ed) (1994) *Power and Method: Political Activism and Educational Research* (New York: Routledge).

Graham, B. (1999) Using new formats for PhDs and research degrees. In: *Using Digital Resources in Teaching, Learning and Research in the Visual Arts*, Section 3.5. Visual Arts Data Service (VADS), http://vads.ahds.ac.uk/guides/using_guide/sect35.html (accessed April 2003).

Green, H. and Shaw, M. (1996) Standards in research awards: length, weight or quality? Developing an approach for resolving the dilemma. *Innovation & Learning in Education: The International Journal for the Reflective Practitioner*, 2(3), 4–10.

Guba, E. G. (ed) (1990) *The Paradigm Dialog* (Thousand Oaks, CA: Sage).

hooks, b. (1989) *Talking Back: Thinking Feminist, Thinking Black* (Boston: South End).

Kuhn, T. S. (1970) *The Structure of Scientific Revolutions*, 2nd edn (Chicago: University of Chicago Press).

Lincoln, Y. and Guba, E. (1985) *Naturalistic Inquiry* (Newbury Park, CA: Sage).

Malins, J. and Gray, C. (1999) The digital thesis: recent developments in practice-based Art & Design research for PhD. *Digital Creativity*, 10(1), 18–28.

New Collins Concise Dictionary of the English Language (1986) Managing editor W. T. McLeod (London & Glasgow: Collins).

Orna, E. and Stevens, G. (1995) *Managing Information to Support Research* (Maidenhead, Berkshire: Open University Press).

Pengelly, J. (1996) *Environmentally Sensitive Printmaking: A Framework of Safe Practice*. PhD thesis, The Robert Gordon University.

Press, M. (1995) It's Research Jim . . . *Co-design: the Interdisciplinary Journal of Design and Contextual Studies*, 34–41.

Quality Assurance Agency, Codes of Practice – quality and standards in Higher Education, Postgraduate Research Programmes – www.qaa.ac.uk/public/COP/cop/contents.htm (accessed 21 July 2003).

Robson, C. (1993) *Real World Research*, Section 5; Chapter 13, p. 420; Chapter 14, esp. p. 438; table on p. 443 (Oxford: Blackwell).

Swift, J. (1997) *The Viva Voce*, Research Training Initiative, Birmingham Institute of Art and Design, University of Central England.

Tebby, S. (1995) Concept, design and building of an environmentally integrated water feature within a public place: Chatham High Street, Kent. Project abstract in: Allison Research Index of Art and Design (1996) (On CD-ROM and web www.ariad.co.uk).

Tyler, S. A. (1986) Postmodern ethnography: from document of the occult to occult document. In J. Clifford, J and G. F. Marcus (eds) *Writing Culture: the Poetics and Politics of Ethnography*, pp. 122–140 (Berkley: University of California Press).

Wakeford, J. (2002) What does it mean to be original? Document used in various workshops on PhD developments.

Wheeler, E. (1996) *The Role of Architectural Ceramics in Contemporary Site-specific Art*. PhD thesis, University of Northumbria, Newcastle.

Suggested further reading

Day, A. (1999) *How to Get Research Published in Journals* (London: Gower).

Drew, S. and Gibson, R. (1999) *The Student Guide to Making an Oral Presentation* (Gower) (available as a CD Rom, ISBN: 0 566 08246 2).

Race, P. (1999) *2000 Tips for Lecturers* (London: Kogan Page) (includes information on portfolio assessment).

Appendix 1
Taxonomy of assessment domains (Green and Shaw, 1996)

Domains	*Masters*	*MPhil*	*PhD*
Organization and Planning	Ability to set, negotiate and meet own objectives and deadlines to identified standards and involving the sensitive organization and management of others.	Ability to set negotiate and meet own objectives and deadlines in a wide variety of contexts over extended periods of time with a high level of autonomy and involving sensitive and ethical organization and management of others from a wide range of cultural/social/political backgrounds and contexts.	
Communication	Ability to select appropriate styles and modes of communication for complex tasks and purposes.	Able to communicate effectively in the full range of formal styles appropriate to and consistent with research in the chosen cognate area, for the production and defense of extended academic theses, and for a wide range of presentation and publishing goals and targets.	
Group/ Interpersonal	Ability to interact sympathetically and ethically with individuals and groups in varied settings to achieve a major research task.	Ability to interact sympathetically and ethically with individuals and groups in varied settings to achieve a major research task.	
		Able to interact sympathetically and ethically with individuals and groups from a wide range of cultural/social/political backgrounds in varied settings over extended and intensive periods of time with accurate notions of the precise impact of themselves on the settings in which they are operating.	
		Able to clearly delineate, negotiate and subscribe to agreed parameters and limits of responsibility in group/team settings and ventures.	Ability to develop ways of coping/operating in novel settings with novel group/groupings.
Information/ Data Collection	Ability to devise valid and reliable methods and instruments for data and information collection in relation to an extended piece of research.	Ability to carry out a full literature search and identify sources relevant to the field of research.	Ability to carry out a complete literature search, critical review and appraisal of all literature and primary sources of relevance to the research study.

Domains	*Masters*	*MPhil*	*PhD*
Information/ Data Collection (continued)		Ability to make reasoned judgements regarding the appropriateness of a range of typologies of methods and instruments for data/ information collection.	Ability to make reasoned judgements regarding the appropriateness of a range of typologies of methods and instruments for data/information collection.
		Able to adapt and apply methods and instruments appropriately to novel situations/contexts with due concern for matters of reliability and validity.	Able to devise and design novel methods and instruments for application in novel situations and/or contexts with a clear and critical perspective on the levels of reliability and validity achieved.
Theory and Principles	Knowledge and understanding of a range of subject-specific advanced and contemporary theory, and of strategies and methodologies for investigation/solution of professionally oriented research problems.	Knowledge and understanding of the range of subject-specific contemporary theory and of appropriate methods and strategies for investigation and solution of identified issues/ problems.	Knowledge and understanding of theory, methods and strategies in the specific and related fields of study, with a clearly articulated contextualization of this study with its wider subject environment.
Analysis and Reflection	Analyses problems objectively using the main theoretical perspectives of the cognate area and the appropriate research methods and strategies with appropriate and rational sensitivity to the opinions and views of others.	Analyses problems objectively using the main theoretical perspectives of the field of study and appropriate methods and strategies for investigation and solution of identified issues/problems.	Analyses problems objectively using critically evaluated novel (or extended) theoretical perspectives from this (or related) fields of study, with rational sensitivity to, awareness of and allowance for, effects on the opinions/ views/feelings of all others involved.
Application and Reflection	Applies theories, methodologies and strategies in rational and valid ways, demonstrating empirical/experimental rigour in identifying solutions to complex and significant problems.	Applies knowledge, theory, methodology and strategies in rational and valid ways, demonstrating experimental/research rigour in identifying solutions to complex and significant problems.	Applies knowledge, theory, methodology and strategies in rational and valid ways, demonstrating experimental/research rigour in identifying solutions to complex and significant problems.

Domains	*Masters*	*MPhil*	*PhD*
Application and Reflection (continued)	Reflects both extensively/objectively on methods, process, outcomes.	Reflects objectively, particularly on the methods, the process and the outcomes of the study.	Reflects extensively and critically on all aspects – knowledge, theory, methods, process, and outcomes of the study and on the implications for the wider context within which the study is located.
Synthesis and Evaluation	Critically evaluates outcomes and relates them to existing knowledge structures and methodologies. Reviews validity of theoretical perspectives, methods and strategies applied.	Critically evaluates outcomes and relates them to existing knowledge structures, theoretical perspectives and methodologies suggesting further topics for research.	
			Reviews and reappraises knowledge and the validity of theoretical perspectives and methodology in the wider context and proposes areas for research that will further explore these and other related fundamental issues.
Creativity	Identifies modifications to, and impact on, existing knowledge structures/ theoretical frameworks. Proposes new areas for investigation/new problems/ new methodological approaches.	Displays originality and/or novelty in some (MPhil)/ most (PhD) of the following: • application of different existing methods/ instruments to known areas of study • transfer of existing methods/instruments to a different/related context • development and/or extension of existing knowledge and theoretical perspectives • application of existing research approaches to new populations • new attempts to corroborate earlier work • identifies implications for existing theory and knowledge structures • identifies new areas for investigation, topic/focus of study • development and application of new methods/instruments for investigation • application of existing instrumentation/methods to new/original contexts • development of new knowledge and/or theoretical insights • new attempts to critically question and re-examine earlier research work	

Domains	Masters	MPhil	PhD
Creativity (continued)			• critically examines the implications of the outcomes and proposes new theoretical perspectives and knowledge structures • opens up new areas for fundamental and significant research.

Green, H. and Shaw, M. (1996) Standards in research awards: length, weight or quality? Developing an approach for resolving the dilemma, *Innovation & Learning in Education*, 2(3), 4–10.

Green, H. and Shaw, M. (1999) Quality standards in postgraduate education, *Newsletter of the UK Council for Graduate Education*, Issue 11, February.

Appendix 2
Criteria for assessing PhD work

Note. This framework is based on the Scottish Credit and Qualifications Framework (SCQF).

It should be used only as a Guide.

Domain	*Description*
Knowledge	Demonstrate a critical, detailed leading edge knowledge and understanding at the forefront of one or more specialisms and/or contribute to scholarship and the development of the subject/discipline; OR demonstrate originality* and creativity in the application of new knowledge, skills and practices, as well as design and execute inquiry/research projects to deal with new problems and issues.
Application	Use a range of standard and specialized instruments, tools, methods and techniques of enquiry.
Critical thinking	Autonomously uses available theories and evidence to formulate logical reasoning and argument to create, validate and appropriate new knowledge to practice; and applies new knowledge in appropriate situations to: solve problems, improve and enhance performance and practice, and contribute to scholarship.
Argument and Discourse	Develop a highly effective, coherent and lucid argument to support and/or substantiate the hypothesis, theoretical underpinning; and results/findings of the study.
Analysis, Evaluation and Synthesis	Demonstrate critical analysis, evaluation and synthesis of new and complex ideas, information and issues, and make informed judgements in the absence of complete or consistent data/information.
Communication	Communicate at an appropriate level to a range of audiences and adapt communication to the context and purpose, as well as at the standard of published academic work and/or critical dialogue and review with peers and experts in other specialisms.
Information Technology	Communicate information and evaluate numerical and graphical data using a range of appropriate software.

Domain	Description
Reflection	Enhance performance through critical self-evaluation and reflection on own and evidence-based practice; Work autonomously, clarify goals, manage and evaluate own learning and identify new learning needs; Use given feedback or evidence-based practice to effectively improve own performance and practice.
Accountability and Ethics	Deal with complex ethical and professional issues, as well as make informed judgements on new and emerging issues not addressed by current professional and/or ethical codes or practices.
Referencing and Bibliography	Referencing is up to date/current, relevant to the given context, accurate, sufficient, consistent and compliant with an approved standard (for example Harvard Method or APA Style) including the first and last pages of the referenced item.

* To be read in conjunction with the definition of originality.

Source: Quality Assurance Agency (QAA), Universities Scotland and Scottish Qualifications Authority (SQA) (2001). An Introduction to the Scottish Credit and Qualifications Framework [SCQF], p. 37.

Appendix 3
What does it mean to be 'original'?

At a conference in 1992, E. M. Phillips presented a compilation of 21 definitions of 'originality' in a thesis. She had compiled these definitions from her own studies of supervisors and students and from the work of Francis. Removing three cases of equivalent definitions in these three sources, there remain 18 fairly distinct definitions which are listed here.

1. Saying something nobody has said before.
2. Carrying out empirical work that has not been done before.
3. Making a synthesis of things that have not been put together before.
4. Making a new interpretation of someone else's material or ideas.
5. Trying out something in this country that has previously been done only elsewhere.
6. Taking a new technique and applying it to a new area.
7. Being cross-disciplinary and using different methodologies.
8. Looking at topics that people in my discipline have not looked at before.
9. Adding to knowledge in a way that has not been done before.
10. Testing existing knowledge in an original way.
11. Writing down a new piece of information for the first time.
12. Giving a good exposition of another's idea.
13. Continuing a previously original piece of work.
14. Carrying out original work designed by the supervisor.
15. Providing a single original technique, observation or result in an otherwise unoriginal but competent piece of research.
16. Having followed instructions and understood the original concepts.
17. Having many original ideas, methods and interpretations all performed by others under the direction of the postgraduate.
18. Bringing new evidence to bear on an old issue.

Phillips, E. E. and Pugh, D. S, (2000) *How to get a PhD*, 3rd edn (Milton Keynes: Open University Press).

Copy from John Wakeford's original (2002)

Appendix 4
Postgraduate portfolio of evidence (using taxonomy of assessment domains, see Green & Shaw, 1996)

Domains/Levels	***Masters***	***MPhil***	***PhD***	***Evidence from research project to demonstrate that the criteria have been met***	***Reflective statement***
Organization and planning	Ability to set, negotiate and meet own objectives and deadlines to identified standards and involving the sensitive organization and management of others.	Ability to set negotiate and meet own objectives and deadlines in a wide variety of contexts over extended periods of time with a high level of autonomy and involving sensitive and ethical organization and management of others from a wide range of cultural/social/political backgrounds and contexts.			
Communication	Ability to select appropriate styles and modes of communication for complex tasks and purposes.	Able to communicate effectively in the full range of formal styles appropriate to and consistent with research in the chosen cognate area, for the production and defence of extended academic theses, and for a wide range of presentation and publishing goals and targets.			
Group/ Interpersonal	Ability to interact sympathetically and ethically with individuals and groups in varied settings to achieve a major research task.	Ability to interact sympathetically and ethically with individuals and groups in varied settings to achieve a major research task.			
		Able to interact sympathetically and ethically with individuals and groups from a wide range of cultural/social/political backgrounds in varied settings over extended and intensive periods of time with accurate notions of the precise impact of themselves on the settings in which they are operating.			
		Able clearly to delineate, negotiate and subscribe to agreed parameters and limits of responsibility in group/ team settings and ventures.	Ability to develop ways of coping/operating in novel settings with novel group/groupings.		

Domains/Levels	*Masters*	*MPhil*	*PhD*	*Evidence from research project to demonstrate that the criteria have been met*	*Reflective statement*
Information/Data Collection	Ability to devise valid and reliable methods and instruments for data and information collection in relation to an extended piece of research.	Ability to carry out a full literature search and identify sources relevant to the field of research. Ability to make reasoned judgements regarding the appropriateness of a range of typologies of methods and instruments for data/information collection. Able to adapt and apply methods and instruments appropriately to novel situations/contexts with due concern for matters of reliability and validity.	Ability to carry out a complete literature search, critical review and appraisal of all literature and primary sources of relevance to the research study. Ability to make reasoned judgements regarding the appropriateness of a range of typologies of methods and instruments for data/information collection. Able to devise and design novel methods and instruments for application in novel situations and/or contexts with a clear and critical perspective on the levels of reliability and validity achieved.		

Domains/Levels	*Masters*	*MPhil*	*PhD*	*Evidence from research project to demonstrate that the criteria have been met*	*Reflective statement*
Theory and Principles	Knowledge and understanding of a range of subject-specific advanced and contemporary theory, and of strategies and methodologies for investigation/solution of professionally oriented research problems.	Knowledge and understanding of the range of subject-specific contemporary theory and of appropriate methods and strategies for investigation and solution of identified issues/problems.	Knowledge and understanding of theory, methods and strategies in the specific and related fields of study, with a clearly articulated contextualization of this study with its wider subject environment.		
Analysis and Reflection	Analyses problems objectively using the main theoretical perspectives of the cognate area and the appropriate research methods and strategies with appropriate and rational sensitivity to the opinions and views of others.	Analyses problems objectively using the main theoretical perspectives of the field of study and appropriate methods and strategies for investigation and solution of identified issues/problems.	Analyses problems objectively using critically evaluated novel (or extended) theoretical perspectives from this (or related) fields of study, with rational sensitivity to, awareness of and allowance for effects on the opinions/views/feelings of all others involved.		
Application and Reflection	Applies theories, methodologies and strategies in rational and valid ways, demonstrating empirical/experimental rigour in identifying solutions to complex and significant problems.	Applies knowledge, theory, methodology and strategies in rational and valid ways, demonstrating experimental/research rigour in identifying solutions to complex and significant problems.	Applies knowledge, theory, methodology and strategies in rational and valid ways, demonstrating experimental/ research rigour in identifying solutions to complex and significant problems.		

Domains/Levels	*Masters*	*MPhil*	*PhD*	*Evidence from research project to demonstrate that the criteria have been met*	*Reflective statement*
	Reflects both extensively/ objectively on methods, process, outcomes.	Reflects objectively, particularly on the methods, the process and the outcomes of the study.	Reflects extensively and critically on all aspects – knowledge, theory, methods, process, and outcomes – of the study and on the implications for the wider context within which the study is located.		
Synthesis and Evaluation	Critically evaluates outcomes and relates them to existing knowledge structures and methodologies. Reviews validity of theoretical perspectives, methods and strategies applied.	Critically evaluates outcomes and relates them to existing knowledge structures, theoretical perspectives and methodologies suggesting further topics for research.			
			Reviews and reappraises knowledge and the validity of theoretical perspectives and methodology in the wider context and proposes areas for research that will further explore these and other related fundamental issues.		

Domains/Levels	***Masters***	***MPhil***	***PhD***	***Evidence from research project to demonstrate that the criteria have been met***	***Reflective statement***
Creativity	Identifies modifications to and impact on existing knowledge structures/ theoretical frameworks. Proposes new areas for investigation/new problems/new methodological approaches.	Displays originality and/or novelty in some (MPhil)/ most (PhD) of the following: • application of different existing methods/ instruments to known areas of study • transfer of existing methods/instruments to a different/related context • development and/or extension of existing knowledge and theoretical perspectives • application of existing research approaches to new populations • new attempts to corroborate earlier work • identifies implications for existing theory and knowledge structures • identifies new areas for investigation, topic/focus of study • development and application of new methods/ instruments for investigation • application of existing instrumentation/methods to new/original contexts • development of new knowledge and/or theoretical insights • new attempts to critically question and re-examine earlier research work • critically examines the implications of the outcomes and proposes new theoretical perspectives and knowledge structures • opens up new areas for fundamental and significant research.			

Green, H. and Shaw, M. (1997) Quality Standards in Postgraduate Education. Newsletter of the UK Council for Graduate Education, Issue 11, February.
Green, H. and Shaw, M. (1996) Standards in research awards: length, weight or quality? Developing an approach for resolving the dilemma. *Innovation & Learning in Education*, 2(3), 4–10.

Glossary
Research terms relevant to the Art and Design context

Alternative research paradigms (see also 'paradigm')
Frameworks for inquiry that offer alternative approaches to research from the scientific, positivist research paradigm. For example, post-positivistic frameworks, such as constructivism and critical theory, including feminist methodologies, decolonizing methodologies, appreciative inquiry, and 'artistic' or 'designerly' methodologies.

Further references:
Guba, E. (1990) *The Paradigm Dialog* (Thousand Oaks, CA: Sage).
Tuhiwai Smith, L. (1999) *Decolonizing Methodologies: Research and Indigenous Peoples* (Dunedin, New Zealand: University of Otago Press).
Cooperrider, D. L. and Whitney, D. (1999) *Collaborating for Change: Appreciative Inquiry* (San Francisco, CA: Berret-Koehler).

Argument (see also 'thesis')
Argument is a process of reasoning in which you attempt: '. . . to influence someone's belief that what you are proposing is the case. . . . Whichever way someone makes an argument they are attempting to convince others of the validity . . . of how they see the world and convince us that we should see it the way they do.' (Hart, 1998, pp. 79–108).

Further references:
Hart, C. (1998) *Doing a Literature Review* (London: Sage).
Kuhn, D. (1992) Thinking as argument. *Harvard Educational Review*, 62(2), 155–178.
Phelan, P. and Reynolds, P. (1996) *Argument and Evidence* (London: Routledge).
Toulmin, S. (1958) *The Uses of Argument* (Cambridge, UK: Cambridge University Press).

Case study
A qualitative research method characterized by the in-depth study of a particular example, usually a person, for example an artist or designer, or a project; rich in detail and context bound, the case study attempts to present a complete picture, usually by the use of multiple research methods.

Further reference:
Yin, R. K. (1984) *Case Study Research* (Thousand Oaks, CA: Sage).

Concept mapping
'A technique for externalising concepts and propositions' through visual means of a concept map – 'a schematic device for representing a set of concept meanings embedded in a framework of propositions' (Novak and Gowan, 1984).

Further reference:
Novak, J. D. and Gowan, D. B. (1984) *Learning How To Learn* (Cambridge University Press).

Constructivist (see also 'alternative research paradigms')
An alternative research paradigm (to positivism, for example), which is characterized by a relativist ontology (realities exist as personal constructs), a subjectivist epistemology (contextual and relative), and a hermeneutic (interpretative) and dialectic methodology. Where positivist inquiry aims to explain, constructivist inquiry aims to understand.

Further reference:
Guba, E. (1990) *The Paradigm Dialog* (Thousand Oaks, CA: Sage).
Schwandt, T. A. (1998) Constructivist, interpretivist approaches to human inquiry, in: N. Denzin and Y. Lincoln (eds) *The Landscape of Qualitative Research* (Thousand Oaks, CA: Sage).

Contextual review (see also 'literature review')
An expansion of the term 'literature review' to acknowledge a range of contextual materials in the public domain, which are not simply text based or 'published' in the orthodox sense, for example images, art/design objects, websites, video/film, performance, documented conversations/events, etc. These types of 'public output' must be referenced in some way, in order for them to be traceable and usable by others.

Further reference:
http://www.unn.ac.uk/central/isd/cite/ – a useful resource on a range of citation protocols

Epistemology
The subject concerned with the origins, nature and forms of knowledge, how it can be acquired and communicated. In Art and Design research, personal and tacit knowledge are often the starting points for inquiry.

Further references:
Polanyi, M. (1958) *Personal Knowledge: Toward a Post-critical Philosophy* (University of Chicago Press).
Polanyi, M. (1958) *The Tacit Dimension* (University of Chicago Press).

Hermeneutics
'The art or science of interpretation' (OED, 2002). Hermeneutics is a research method that allows for multiple interpretations and meanings giving 'each speaker his or her own voice' (Friedman, 2002).

Further references:

OED (2002) *Oxford English Dictionary* (Oxford: Oxford University Press).

Friedman, K. (2002) Hermeneutics and hermeneutical research methods: a brief overview (post to phd-design@jiscmail.ac.uk, 3 April 2002).

Douglas, A. (1997) On the notion of test. Section: *The Paradigm of Hermeneutics* (Multimedia essay on CD ROM). In: S. Evans, J. Greenhill and I. Svenson (eds) *Matrix 3D: Sculpture, Method, Research* (London: Lethaby Press).

Inductive process

'A process of reasoning by which a general conclusion is drawn from a set of premises, based mainly on experience or experimental evidence' (*Collins Dictionary*, 1982). In Art and Design we learn by doing – inductive learning through the particular experience of practice – and make broader sense of this through reflection and discussion.

Inter-subjective

If complete individual objectivity is impossible then the most reliable method of understanding and evaluating an issue must involve others. The negotiated consensus of two or more subjective views on an issue could be called inter-subjective.

Further reference:

Reason, P. and Rowan, J. (1981) On making sense. In: P. Reason and J. Rowan, *Human Inquiry: a Sourcebook of New Paradigm Research* (Chichester: Wiley).

Literature review (see also 'contextual review')

'The selection of available documents (both published and unpublished) on the topic, which contain information, ideas, data and evidence written from a particular standpoint to fulfil certain aims or express certain views on the nature of the topic and how it is to be investigated, and the effective evaluation of these documents in relation to the research being proposed', Hart (1998, p. 12).

Further references:

Hart, C. (1998) *Doing a Literature Review* (London: Sage).

Orna, E. and Stevens, G. (1995) *Managing Information for Research*, chapter 2, pp. 21–33 (Maidenhead, Berkshire: Open University Press).

Method and **Methodology**

See Chapter 1, Section 1.3 and Chapter 3, Section 3.2.

Mind mapping

A method of generating, organizing and communicating ideas and concepts using text and visual techniques (shape, colour, line, scale, symbol, and so on), which relate concepts in a 'map'.

Further reference:

Buzan, T. (1998) *The Mind Map Book: Radiant Thinking – a Major Evolution in Human Thought* (London: BBC Books).

Morphological matrix
Separating out the form/structure of a system or object from its function and setting it out in a matrix, in order to organize, analyse and present ideas and derive new solutions.

Further references:
Jones, J. C. (1981) *Design Methods: Seeds of Human Futures* (Chichester: Wiley).
Miles, M. B. and Huberman, A. M. (1994) *Qualitative Data Analysis* (Thousand Oaks, CA: Sage). Chapter 9.

Multi-method
See Chapter 1, Section 1.5 and Chapter 4, Section 4.3.

Multiple Sort
A method of categorizing objects (possibly art/design works). For example, photographs of a range of objects may be shown to individuals who may be asked to arrange the photographs according to categories of their own devising. The categorization of objects can provide important insights into how they are perceived.

Further reference:
Canter, D., Branner, M. and Brown, J. (1985) *The Research Interview, Use and Approaches* (London: Academic Press, London).

Naturalistic inquiry
Located within the constructivist research paradigm, naturalistic inquiry acknowledges the importance of a 'natural' setting or context, for example a studio/workshop setting, a project framework, a site. Some key characteristics are: the researcher as primary generator/gatherer of data, the use of tacit knowledge, emergent research design and qualitative methods.

Further references:
Lincoln, Y. and Guba, E. (1985) *Naturalistic Inquiry* (Sage).
Robson, C. (1993) *Real World Research*, Characteristics of Naturalistic Inquiry, p. 61 (Oxford: Blackwell).

Ontology (see also 'epistemology' and 'methodology')
In relation to paradigms of inquiry, ontological assumptions and questions relate to the nature of the 'knowable', the nature of reality – what one believes can be known. 'The answers that are given to these questions . . . are the starting points or givens that determine what inquiry is and how it is to be practiced' (Guba, 1990, p. 18).

Further references:
Guba, E. (1990) *The Paradigm Dialog* (pp. 18–19) (Thousand Oaks, CA: Sage).
Denzin, N. and Lincoln, Y. (1998) *The Landscape of Qualitative Research* (Sage).

Paradigm (see also 'alternative research paradigms)
Research paradigm/paradigm of inquiry – ' . . . a set of overarching and interconnected

assumptions about the nature of reality . . . A paradigm provides the largest framework within which research takes place. It is the world view within which researchers work' (Maykut and Morehouse, 1994).

Further references:
Guba, E. (1990) *The Paradigm Dialog* (Thousand Oaks, CA: Sage).
Maykut, P. and Morehouse, R. (1994) *Beginning Qualitative Research* (London: Falmer).

Paradigm shift
A turning point, a reappraisal and move from one set of beliefs or world view to another, for example from Newtonian science to quantum science, from modernism to post-modernism; from rationalism to anarchy (Feyerabend, 1988).

Further references:
Capra, F. (1983) *The Turning Point: Science, Society and the Rising Culture* (London: Flamingo).
Feyerabend, P. (1988) *Against Method* (London: Verso).
Kuhn, T. (1970) *The Structure of Scientific Revolutions*, chapter 10 (University of Chicago Press).

Participant-observation
A qualitative research method that involves the researcher both engaging in the research (usually with other people), as well as observing that process and others' involvement in it.

Further references:
Cohen, L. and Manion, L. (1994) *Research Methods in Education*, Chapter 5 (London: Routledge).
Spradley, J. (1980) *Participant Observation* (Holt, Reinhard, Wilson).

Personal constructs
The ways in which individuals (for example practitioners, project participants, clients, and so on) construe their 'world' (environment, situations, relationships, and so on) usually using bi-polar constructs, for example friendly – hostile, distant – close, etc). It has been developed in clinical psychology into visualizations like 'personal sphere models' (Schmiedeck, 1978).

Further references:
Kelly, G. (1955) *The Psychology of Personal Constructs* (New York: Norton).
Schmiedeck, R. A. (1978) *The Personal Sphere Model* (New York: Grune & Stratton).

Positivist (see also 'alternative research paradigms')
A paradigm of inquiry characterized by a realist ontology (reality exists 'out there'), an objectivist epistemology (the researcher maintains distance), and a methodology that is experimental and manipulative (control and prediction). Positivist inquiry aims to explain.

Further reference:
Guba, E. (1990) *The Paradigm Dialog* (Thousand Oaks, CA: Sage).

Post-positivist
A paradigm of inquiry that is a modified version of positivist inquiry, in which prediction and control are still important, but which acknowledges the imperfection of human perception and objectivity.

Further references:
Guba, E. (1990) *The Paradigm Dialog* (Thousand Oaks, CA: Sage).
Denzin, N. and Lincoln, Y. (1998) *The Landscape of Qualitative Research* (Thousand Oaks, CA: Sage).

Practice-based research (within the doctoral framework)
'A doctorate where the PRIMARY research is done through producing artefacts, designs, performances, films etc. It implies that the practice is an intelligent discourse in the 'language' of the medium or art form and that this is a dialogue already with the history and other contemporary work in the field. The practice or its adequate documentation will form a significant part of the submitted "thesis"' (LeGrice, M. in: Friedman, 2001).

Further references:
Friedman, E. (2001) Symposium on Doctorates in Design and the Creative and Performing Arts (moderated by Friedman, K. PhD Design list, July 2001) www.jiscmail.ac.uk
UK Council for Graduate Education (2001) *Research Training in the Creative and Performing Arts and Design.*

Professional
' . . . a professional must have a large store of knowledge and the competence to practice his or her art . . . He, or she, would also possess considerable research skill and expertise . . . Inquiry is a form of professional knowledge-getting, and is developed through experience of inquiry. The skills of the . . . artists, dancer, composer are gained through the practice of their art or craft. . . . To behave professionally one must reveal some essence of oneself or character – what Polyani (1973) calls "personal knowledge"' (McKernan, 1998).

Further references:
McKernan, J. (1998) *Curriculum Action Research: A Handbook of Methods and Resources for the Reflective Practitioner* (London: Kogan Page).
Schön, D. (1983) *The Reflective Practitioner* (New York: Basic Books).

Qualitative
'Qualitative research is multi-method in focus, involving an interpretive, naturalistic approach to its subject matter. This means that qualitative researchers study things in

their natural settings, attempting to make sense of, or interpret, phenomena in terms of the meanings people bring to them' (Denzin and Lincoln, 1998).

Further references:

Denzin, N. and Lincoln, Y. (1998) *The Landscape of Qualitative Research* (Thousand Oaks, CA: Sage).

Maykut, P. and Morehouse, R. (1994) *Beginning Qualitative Research* (London: Falmer).

Reflection-in-action

'If common sense recognises knowing-in-action, it also recognises that we sometimes think about what we are doing. Phrases like "thinking on your feet", "keeping your wits about you", and "learning by doing" suggest that we not only can think about doing but that we can think about doing something while doing it' (Schön, 1983).

Further references:

Schön, D. (1983) *The Reflective Practitioner* (New York: Basic Books).

Schön, D. (1987) *Educating The Reflective Practitioner* (San Francisco: Jossey-Bass).

Reflective journal/research diary

A journal/diary that the researcher keeps regularly in order to reflect on self-development, research methodology, and also on progress and change, for example in the development of an art/design work or process.

Further reference:

Newbury, D. (2001) Diaries and field notes in the research process. *Research Issues in Art, Design and Media,* Issue 1 Autumn.

Reflexivity

' . . . a turning back of one's experience upon oneself . . . a circular process . . . This looping back may . . . unfold as a spiralling, if we allow for multiple perspectives, and acknowledge that "the same self" may be different as a result of its own self-pointing. Thus included within this focus are issues of self-reference, and how issues of self-reference can inform methodologies and the research process in general' (Steier, 1991).

Further reference:

Steier, F. (1991) *Research and Reflexivity* (London: Sage).

Semantic differential analysis

A technique often used to compare similar artefacts in which a personal opinion may be expressed by giving each a rating on a scale between two extremes, for example exciting–boring. The results of such a survey can then be subject to statistical analysis to determine whether perceived differences are significant.

Further reference:

Osgood, C. E., Suci, G. J. and Tannenbaum, P. H. (1957) *The Measurement of Meaning* (Urbana: University of Illinois Press).

Thesis (see also 'argument')
Thesis as 'argument' – rather than the commonly held perception of a substantial text as the PhD submission itself. In Art and Design research, a thesis may comprise several elements: a body of creative work, other related/supporting/complementary artefacts, a written text contextualizing and describing the argument.

Index